A PRIEST'S HANDBOOK

The Ceremonies of the Church

A Priest's Handbook

The Ceremonies of the Church

THIRD EDITION
Revisions for Third Edition by Christopher Webber

Dennis G. Michno

Illustrations by Richard E. Mayberry

MOREHOUSE PUBLISHING

An imprint of Church Publishing Incorporated
Harrisburg—New York

Third edition copyright © 1983, 1986, 1998 Dennis G. Michno

Morehouse Publishing
4775 Linglestown Road
Harrisburg, PA 17112

Morehouse Publishing is an imprint of Church Publishing Incorporated.

Library of Congress Cataloging-in-Publication Data

Michno, Dennis
   A priest's handbook : the ceremonies of the church / Dennis G. Michno. —3rd ed.
      p.   cm.
   Includes bibliographical references and index.
   ISBN 10 : 0-8192-1768-9 (hc)
   ISBN 13 : 978-0-8192-1768-4 (hc)
      1. Episcopl Church—Book of common prayer (1979) 2. Episcopal Church—Liturgy—Texts—History and criticism. 3. Anglican Communion—United States—Liturgy—Texts—History and criticism. I. Title.
BX5945.M53   1998
264'.03—dc21   98-17918
                                                                    CIP

Printed in the United States of America

12   13   14   15   14   13   12

To the Glory of God
with grateful affection for
Edward Nason West
Priest, Teacher, and Friend
Qui in Dei gloria ministrans,
Dei ad gloriam servat.

Contents

Alphabetical List of Illustrations 11
Preface to the Second Edition 13
Foreword. 15
Introduction. 17
Liturgical Books. 19
Ceremonial Acts. 21
Manual Acts. 23
Vestments. 25
Concerning Candles 27
Concerning Silence. 27

THE HOLY EUCHARIST. 29
Introduction 30
Preparations for the Eucharist 31
The Entrance Rite. 32
The Collect of the Day. 35
The Word of God. 36
The Lessons 36
The Sermon 38
The Nicene Creed 38
The Prayers of the People 39
Confession of Sin 45
The Peace. 46
The Holy Communion 47
Manual Acts during the Great Thanksgiving. 52-53
The Great Thanksgiving 54
Concerning Proper Prefaces 55
The Eucharistic Prayers 57-70
Eucharistic Prayer I and Eucharistic Prayer II 57-60
Eucharistic Prayer A and Eucharistic Prayer B 61-63
Eucharistic Prayer C 64-66
Eucharistic Prayer D. 67-70
The Lord's Prayer 71
The Breaking of the Bread 71
Administration of Communion. 72

Ablutions 73
Postcommunion Prayer. 73
Blessing and Dismissal. 74
   Concerning Hymns at the Conclusion of the Eucharist. 74
   Concerning Intinction 74
   Concerning the Consecration of additional Elements 74
   Concerning Announcements 75
   Concerning Reservation of the Sacrament. 75
Communion under Special Circumstances 76
An Order for Celebrating the Holy Eucharist 77
   Concerning Concelebration 78
   Concerning the Use of Incense at the Eucharist. 80
   The Censing of the Altar 82
   The Censing of the Gifts at the Offertory. 84
Solemn Eucharist 86
Morning or Evening Prayer as the Liturgy of the Word
at the Eucharist. 91

THE CALENDAR. 93

Introduction 94
Sundays and Principal Feasts. 95-98
Holy Days and National Days. 99-100
Other Feasts and Fasts in the Calendar 101-105
Commemorations not listed in the Calendar 106-108

THE LECTIONARY. 109

Introduction. 110
Eucharistic Lectionary. 111
   Concerning Weekday Eucharists. 113
   Concerning Ember Days 116
   Concerning Rogation Days 117
Daily Office Lectionary 118
Lesser Feasts and Fasts at the Daily Office. 121
Feast Days with Eves and Vigils 122

THE DAILY OFFICE 125

Introduction. 126
Morning Prayer. 126
An Order of Service for Noonday. 130
An Order of Worship for the Evening 132
Evening Prayer. 136
Compline. 140

Solemn Evensong 142
Solemn Te Deum 145

PROPER LITURGIES FOR SPECIAL DAYS
AND OTHER OCCASIONS 147

Introduction 148
The Lighting Of the Advent Wreath 149
Concerning Advent 149
The Presentation of Our Lord Jesus Christ
in the Temple *(Candlemas)* 150
Shrove Tuesday 152
The Preparation of Ashes for Ash Wednesday 153
Ash Wednesday 154
Concerning Lent 155
The Way of the Cross 156
Concerning the Fifty Days of Easter 158
Concerning the Alleluia 159
Commemoration of All Faithful Departed *(All Souls' Day)* . . . 160
A Eucharist for the Departed *(Requiem Eucharist)* 162
Concerning the Alleluia at a Requiem Eucharist 162
The Great Litany and The Supplication 163
The Rogation Procession 166
Solemn Processions 168

HOLY WEEK 171

Introduction 172
The Sunday of the Passion: Palm Sunday 173
The Weekdays of Holy Week 181
Maundy Thursday 184
Good Friday 190
Good Friday Evening 199
Holy Saturday 200
The Great Vigil of Easter 201

HOLY BAPTISM, OTHER SACRAMENTS
AND PASTORAL OFFICES 211

Holy Baptism 212
Emergency Baptism 217
For an Infant Baptized under Emergency Circumstances . . . 217
A Thanksgiving for the Birth or Adoption of a Child 218
Confirmation 219
A Form of Commitment to Christian Service 223

Setting Apart for a Special Vocation 224
The Celebration and Blessing of a Marriage 225
 The Blessing of a Civil Marriage 229
 Anniversary of a Marriage 230
The Exhortation 231
The Reconciliation of a Penitent 232
Ministration to the Sick 233
 Private Ministration to the Sick 233
 Public Ministration to the Sick (A Public Service of Healing) . . 237
Ministration at the Time of Death 240
The Burial of the Dead 241

APPENDIX 247

A Public Service of Penitence 248
Hymns, Versicles, Responses and Collects
 for use in Solemn Processions 250
Hymn at the Conclusion of the Maundy 255
Anthem at the Veneration of the Cross 256
Additional Propers for Various Occasions 258
Propers for Commemorations not in the Calendar 260
Devotions Before the Blessed Sacrament 261
Dedication (and Blessing) of Church Furnishings and Ornaments . . 263
 Blessing of the Creche at Christmas 265
 Forms for the Blessing of Incense during the Liturgy 266
 A Form for Blessing Holy Water 266
Parts of the Eucharistic Liturgy traditionally sung:
 By the Celebrant and Assisting Minister 267
 By the People, Choir, and/or Cantor 268
Private Prayers for the Priest 269
Prayers for use at the Offertory 270
The First Eucharist of a newly Ordained Priest 271
The Burial of a Priest 272
The Vigil of Pentecost 273

Epilogue 275
About the Author and Illustrator 277
Index 279

Alphabetical List of Illustrations

Anointing 238
Blessing of Incense. 81
Burial of the Dead: At the Commendation. 244
Burial of the Dead: Censing of the Altar and Coffin or Urn. . . . 243
Burial of the Dead: Position of Paschal Candle at Coffin. 241
Burial of the Dead: Position of Paschal Candle at an Urn. 242
Censing a Freestanding Altar 82
Censing an Altar Affixed to the Wall. 83
Censing of the Altar and Coffin or Urn. 243
Censing of the Gifts at the Offertory: Circles 84
Censing of the Gifts at the Offertory: Sign of the Cross 84
Commendation: Censing of Coffin or Urn. 244
Concelebration: At the Words of Institution
    and the Epiclesis. 79
Easter Vigil: Lowering the Paschal Candle
    during the Blessing of the Water 208
Easter Vigil: Preparation of the Paschal Candle. 204
Elevation of the Bread and Wine at the Great Doxology
    concluding the Eucharistic Prayer 53
Filling the Thurible. 81
Genuflecting. 22
Genuflecting at the Altar. 22
Gesture of Thanksgiving
    during the Eucharistic Prayer: Bread 52
Gesture of Thanksgiving   .
    during the Eucharistic Prayer: Wine 52
Good Friday: Bringing in of the Cross. 194
Good Friday: Holding the Cross for Veneration: Form B. 196
Hands Clasped 23
Hands Folded 23
Hands on Corporal during the Eucharistic Prayer. 53
Hand over objects. 24
Hands over the Gifts at the Epiclesis. 53
Imposition of Ashes. 153
Kissing the Altar 21
Kissing the Gospel Book. 21
Kneeling 22

Laying on of Hands 24
Ministration to the Sick: Anointing. 238
Ministration to the Sick: Laying on of Hands. 238
Offering the Bread. 47
Offering the Chalice 48
Offering the Money 48
Orans Position. 23, 52
Pointing to Objects 24
Pointing to the Gifts during the Eucharistic Prayer 53
Replacing the Chalice on the Altar
    after Offering or Elevation 48
Showing of the Gifts during the Eucharistic Prayer: Bread. 52
Showing of the Gifts during the Eucharistic Prayer: Wine. 52
Signing the Gospel Book. 37
Sign of the Cross over Elements at the Epiclesis 24
Sign of the Cross over Objects or People at a Distance. 24
Sign of the Cross over Objects or People at a Level Lower
    than the Celebrant 24
Simple Bow. 21
Solemn Bow. 21
Solemn Bow at the Altar. 53
Solemn Procession, Route of. 169

Cover symbol—

Jesus Christ Victor, drawing by Sr. Eleanor Fox, RSCJ.

Frontispiece—

The Holy Trinity, after a brass found in Tedeswell Church, Buxton, England.

On the Epilogue Page—

St. Mary of the Harbor by E. B. Warren, after a drawing in the Church of St. Mary of the Harbor, Provincetown, Massachusetts.

Preface to the Second Edition

Among the major additions to be found in this edition, the following should be noted: an Introduction stating the theological premise for this *Handbook* (page 17); references throughout to both service music and hymns in *The Hymnal 1982;* propers for the eight Commemorations added to the Calendar of the Church Year by General Convention 1985 (page 258); and, three new sets of propers for Various Occasions prepared by the Standing Liturgical Commission (page 262). Also, notice should be given to the Vigil of Pentecost (page 277), concerning Advent (page 149), and a blessing of the Creche at Christmas (page 269). It is hoped that all of these will add to the usefulness of this book.

This handbook seeks to present a way to celebrate the liturgy that promotes dignity and decency, without rigidity or fussiness, yet reclaiming a balance between a sense of mystery and unity of action. The "way" here presented is not the only way; it is not necessarily the only right way; but it is a way of celebrating and officiating that is based on the liturgical scholarship of the present and past decades. Historical arguments for usage are generally not presented. The interested student of liturgy has many sources to turn to for this type of information: some classic and hallowed by years of use, others more recent and arguing for a different way. This book is directive, but at the same time it allows for individual choice and variety while always pursuing simplicity and dignity imbued with a sense of true mystery.

If one asks "Why do we need ceremonial or ritual?" the answer is simply to ensure order so that the liturgy may speak to the hearts of people directly and not confuse them in the name of relevance or freedom. It is the role and obligation of the celebrant at liturgical rites to ensure that the atmosphere in which the liturgy is celebrated is one that will not impede an awareness of the presence of God, an atmosphere that will allow the Word of God to be heard with understanding, and, most importantly, an atmosphere that will allow the sacramental action to work clearly and directly while at the same time acknowledging mystery, the presence of "the Other" in our worship. Thanksgiving for our community in Christ as the people of God, proclamation of the Gospel, and celebration of the Gospel sacraments: these define the function of liturgy.

The Book of Common Prayer (1979), containing many rubrical directions and options, acknowledges the jealously guarded elements of Anglican comprehensiveness and freedom. It is not a rigid book and this handbook for use with the *BCP* does not attempt to be rigid either. Again, it offers a "way" of celebrating, and in intent and content offers not hard and fast rules, but suggests simplicity and order.

Orderly movement, orderly patterns of worship, and orderly "common prayer" are the goals of liturgical worship. In this order we find the freedom to allow our worship of God and the celebration of the Church's sacraments to become truly visible and understandable to God's people. Order in this sense does eliminate surprise, but if anything has been learned over the past decade or more of experimentation, it is that surprise is not a legitimate element of liturgy. Careful planning, teaching and consistency enable the people to worship without the distracting question, "What will the priest do differently today?" This does not mean that all of the options of the *BCP* cannot be used. Indeed, they are meant to be used in their fullness, and this handbook attempts to give ways in which they can be, but as part of decent and orderly worship, the worship set forth and preserved in all Anglican Prayer Books from 1549 to 1979.

As to ceremonial and manual acts, these are meant to heighten an awareness of the mystery that is taking place. Basic ceremonial and manual actions are described and are based on catholic tradition and common sense. After that they are neither argued for nor dictated but only suggested.

If you are looking for a theological definition of every movement, word, or gesture, this is not the book in which to find it. If you are looking for a way that promotes simplicity and recognizes the necessity of care and humility, then read on, and use what is offered here, not slavishly, but to augment your own perception of "the way."

Many persons helped with reading the manuscript, offering valuable suggestions, and assisting tirelessly in editing. My thanks especially to the Rev. Canon Charles W. Scott, Evelyn P. Mallary, the Rev. R. DeWitt Mallary, Jr., the Rev. Raymond L. Harbort, the Rev. H. Gaylord Hitchcock, Jr., the Rev. Chester A. LaRue, Jr., the Rev. H. Boone Porter, the Rev. Holley B. Slauson II, the Rev. Bonnell Spencer, OHC, the Rev. S. Mortimer Ward IV, the Rev. Theodore McConnell, the Rev. J. Robert Wright, the Rev. Thomas J. Talley, and the Rev. James A. Carpenter. Thanks are also due to Raymond F. Glover and Frank E. Hemlin for making available the necessary material for *The Hymnal 1982* references. As the clergy and people of All Saints Church in the City of New York provided the setting in which to write and experience this book in its First Edition, so now I express my thanks to my new parish family at St. Mary of the Harbor in Provincetown, Massachusetts for their loving support.

January 6, 1986   D.G.M.
The Epiphany

Foreword

As I visit Episcopal Churches in the Diocese of New York as well as throughout the entire United States, I find *A Priest's Handbook* in the libraries of numerous priests and deacons. Many tell me how useful this book is or has been to them. Indeed, many can recall the first edition as this third edition arrives in bookstores. In this edition, a number of changes have been made in accordance with the new resolutions passed by General Convention and to conform to changes in agencies of the Church. A handbook such as this one is a monumental accomplishment as it brings together in a concise, useful format the information found in the *Book of Common Prayer, Lesser Feasts and Fasts, The Book of Occasional Services,* the *Constitution and Canons,* and other liturgical resources. Cross-references to other pages within this book and to other sources have been made for the reader's convenience. I commend its wide use to all for greater decency and order in liturgical practices, as this wonderful new edition will certainly be on my bookshelf as the comprehensive guide to liturgy in the Episcopal Church.

The Rt. Rev. Walter D. Dennis
Bishop Suffragan
The Diocese of New York

Introduction

Liturgy celebrates the mystery that is God. This is the fundamental truth on which the celebration of all the Church's rites depends. It is on this conviction that *A Priest's Handbook* is based: to assist the People of God in working to worship and praise God and in working to be reconciled and sanctified in Christ through the Holy Spirit. Other forms of prayer exist as devotional aids, but only in common liturgical worship can the People of God respond to the command, "Do this in remembrance of me."

By its nature liturgy is ordered worship. As creation is ordered in the perfection that is God, so also the response must be ordered. But creation does not realize the perfection for which it is created, for we do not say "yes" to the purpose of God. We deface the image of God through sin. Thus one element of liturgy is to acknowledge imperfection and seek reconciliation; the gathered community confesses its faults and is renewed. Liturgy promises and proclaims the final perfection of all creation.

In Word and Sacrament liturgy proclaims the Incarnation and promises Resurrection. These both point to the Kingdom, in which perfection will be realized in the universal affirmation of the Creator.

In the Word of God the liturgy recalls and makes present the saving work of God. Through the Daily Office, the Liturgy of Hours, the Church offers ceaseless praise. In the Eucharist, the Word teaches, remembers, and prepares the People of God for the Banquet in which the Kingdom is made present and the promise of everlasting glory is given. Liturgical celebration begins with the Word and points to the Kingdom. The ultimate sign is the Eucharistic Banquet in which Word and Sacrament are joined to proclaim the unity of creation with Creator, a unity that tells of the Kingdom of God and celebrates salvation for the People of God. In liturgy we celebrate the mystery that is God.

Celebration is joyfully recalling, reenacting, and sharing in the liturgy which seeks the perfection that is God and the glory that is the Kingdom of God. Liturgy is the Body of Christ saying "yes" to the purpose of creation.

Liturgical celebration implies order if it is to be faithful in proclaiming the unity of celebration. Chaos does not celebrate. Chaos says "no" to God. Likewise, spontaneity that is not grounded in the Incarnate Word is meaningless, for it is through the Word that ordered creation came into being and is redeemed in the fullness of time. Liturgy which does not seek to celebrate the glory and perfection of God is not true celebration.

In the pursuit of this theological ideal, a *Handbook* such as this one is useful, not to inhibit the People of God in their joyful celebration but rather to order that celebration so that it may be true liturgy. If liturgy means the People of God working to praise the Creator, then liturgical celebration must be as nearly perfect as humanly possible. This is not an attempt to equal the perfection of God but to celebrate that divine perfection. Orderly movement, expressive gestures, beautiful art, sensitive poetry, soaring music—these assist in offering our sacrifice. All of these require true and faithful work which is to the Glory of God.

As priests we must take seriously our responsibility to preside at the liturgy with care and humility: with care that all is in order, with humility in recognizing that it is not we who make God's presence real, but that it is our role to allow that presence to be made manifest and not to obstruct God's working. Simplicity bids and binds us to keep "out of the way." Work towards cohesive celebration is implied in liturgy. For it is in liturgy that creation comes face to face with the mystery that is God.

Liturgy that attempts to avoid or abolish mystery is not faithful. Celebration for its own sake abuses the work of God's holy People. True liturgy approaches mystery with a resounding "yes" to the Creator's Gift of Love.

This mystery cannot be made totally relevant, for it is by nature beyond human comprehension. In approaching mystery faithfully, the Church acknowledges her humanity, while seeking perfection through divine grace. Each action, word, or gesture need not be explained as long as it points to the ultimate Mystery. For the People of God to share in liturgical celebration the truth of mystery must be conveyed, not ignored. In the same sense liturgical mystery always points to God, not just to "something out there." Valid liturgical mystery cannot comprehend all that is God, and therefore we approach with humility and awe. In liturgy the mystery is celebrated faithfully when all elements point to God and proclaim the unity that is God. All become one as we offer our imperfect sacrifice of self to the Glory of God. If liturgy is a celebration, then it celebrates the mystery, the Glory, that is God.

Liturgy that is not God-centered is a sham. Liturgy is not a political rally; it is not a sterile dramatic production; it is not done for the enjoyment of those participating. Liturgy centered in God rests in the Word of God, celebrates the presence of God, and points to the Kingdom of God. Attempts to demythologize liturgy often leave God unknown and unapproachable. In the Word Incarnate, God is made known to creation. In the Sacraments of salvation, God's presence is communicated to creation. The function of liturgy is to celebrate this knowledge and presence in the sacrifice of praise and thanksgiving. St. Benedict recalls us to the purpose of liturgy: "That in all things God may be glorified."

Liturgy manifests the relationship of creation to Creator. Liturgy celebrates the self-giving love of the Incarnate Word. Liturgy proclaims the Kingdom of God in the final perfection of the image of God. In all things God is the source, the object, the purpose, and the end.

Liturgical Books

Throughout this book, reference is made to the various liturgical publications of the Church which are used in the ordering and conduct of public worship. These are listed below with the abbreviations as used in this book. *It is desirable that the Lessons and Gospel be read from a book or books of appropriate size and dignity (BCP, 406).*

(AB)   *The Altar Book.* Copyright 1980, The Church Pension Fund. The Church Hymnal Corporation, New York (CPF/CHC).

(BCP)   *The Book of Common Prayer,* 1979.

(BOG)   *The Book of Gospels* (Revised Standard Version, Ecumenical Edition, edited for liturgical use, containing the Gospels appointed for the Sundays and Principal Feasts for Years A, B, and C; Major Holy Days; and Special Occasions [see page 112]). CPF/CHC 1980.

(BOS)   *The Book of Occasional Services.* Church Publishing Incorporated 1995

(ER)   Eucharist Readings. Church Publishing Incorporated 1995

(GR)   Gospel Readings. Church Publishing Incorporated 1992

(Hymnal)   *The Hymnal 1982.* CPF/CHC 1985. Numbers for *The Hymnal 1982* are given first throughout this book. Subsequent numbers in brackets refer to corresponding material in *The Hymnal 1940.*

(HymAccEd)   *The Hymnal 1982, Accompaniment Edition.* CPF/CHC 1986. Various settings for service music are found only in this volume and not in the singer's edition of *The Hymnal 1982.*

(LFF)   *Lesser Feasts and Fasts 1997.* Church Publishing Incorporated 1997

(LTLFF)   *Lectionary Texts for Lesser Feasts and Fasts* (including the weekdays of Lent and Eastertide and the Common of the Saints). CPF/CHC 1981.

(LTVOOS)   *Lectionary Texts for Various Occasions and Occasional Services.* CPF/CHC 1982.

(LTYA)   *Lectionary Texts for Year A.* CPF/CHC 1980.

(LTYB)   *Lectionary Texts for Year B.* CPF/CHC 1978.

(LTYC)   *Lectionary Texts for Year C.* CPF/CHC 1979.

     Note: Each of the above *(Years A, B, and C)* includes the Lectionary texts for Principal Feasts and fixed Holy Days.

(PBO)   *The Prayer Book Office,* compiled and edited by Howard Galley. Copyright 1980, The Seabury Press, New York.

Note: Scriptural citations in this handbook, except for the Psalms, follow the numeration of the Revised Standard Version of the Bible. Citations for the Psalms follow the numeration of *The Book of Common Prayer (1979).*

Ceremonial Acts

Solemn Bow

Solemn Bow: The solemn bow is used in reverencing the altar, the Blessed Sacrament, and at other times of solemnity. The solemn bow is made from the waist, inclining the head and shoulders so that if your hands were out in front of you, they would almost touch your knees.

Simple Bow

Simple Bow: At the name of Jesus and on other occasions of reverence, a simple bow is made with the head, inclining the shoulders slightly.

Kissing the Altar: This ancient and venerable custom as a sign of reverence to our Lord, whose presence is symbolized in our midst by the altar, is appropriate at various points in the liturgy. With hands extended, the celebrant rests hands on the altar and in the same action as a solemn bow kisses the center of the altar. This action is appropriate upon approaching the altar (either at the entrance or at the Offertory) and after the dismissal.

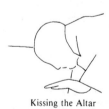

Kissing the Altar

Kissing the Gospel Book

Kissing the Gospel Book: The kissing of the Gospel Book, symbolizing our devotion to the Word, is done in the simplest way possible, taking the book into the hands and raising it to the lips.

Genuflecting

Genuflecting: This sign of reverence is made to the Reserved Sacrament or at certain times during the Eucharist. Standing up straight, bend the right knee until it touches the floor—the left knee will naturally bend a bit—and keep the back straight. When genuflecting at the altar, the celebrant may place hands upon it. This helps keep one's balance and also looks more graceful.

Genuflecting at Altar

Sitting: When sitting the celebrant is still presiding. Therefore, one should sit up straight in the chair. Hands should be either on the knees or folded on the lap. Legs should be kept together and feet flat on the floor. Legs should not be crossed! Eyes should either be on the liturgical action or lowered—not gazing around the church or at the congregation!

Eyes: Especially when facing the people, staring or trying to make "meaningful" contact is only a distraction. Eyes should be kept on the service book, on the altar, or on the liturgical action in progress. If looking at the people is called for, direct your eyes at the whole assembly and not at individuals. It is equally distracting for the celebrant to close the eyes when celebrating or presiding.

Censing: (See pages 80-85)

Walking: Keep hands either folded, holding a book or carrying an object. Do not let them swing at your sides.

Standing: Stand up straight. You are presiding and the focus of attention is on you. Your posture should not be a distraction.

Kneeling: Kneel upright with your weight on your knees and your back straight. If kneeling at the altar or a kneeling bench, hands may be placed on it. If kneeling otherwise, hands should be folded or holding a book, not down at your sides.

Kneeling

Manual Acts

The positions of hands for prayer and other manual actions by the celebrant, officiant and others are important and appropriate only as they point up and underscore the action taking place. The multiplication of signs of the cross, pointings and other gestures only confuse the people, especially if the celebrant is facing the congregation. Here follows a brief description of the basic manual acts. In the rest of this handbook they will be referred to by title only.

Orans Position

Orans position: This is the appropriate placement of the celebrant's hands when singing or saying a collect or prayer on behalf of the congregation, and the basic position of hands during the Eucharistic Prayer.

The arms are extended to a comfortable position (elbows in). Remember to keep in mind the size of the space you are celebrating in as well as your own size! Exaggeration of the orans position can look quite silly in a small space, whereas in a large space, a stronger motion is necessary.

The palms of the hands are traditionally held facing inward toward each other, or the hands may be held with palms slightly upwards.

Hands Folded

Folded Hands: Hands are folded at the chest at various times. They may be held together with the palms and fingers touching and the fingers raised upward, or the hands may be clasped.

Hands Clasped

At no time should the celebrant or any other person officiating or assisting allow hands to swing at the sides or dangle. This looks unseemly and does not enhance reverence.

The Sign of the Cross:

1. The celebrant makes the sign of the cross at various times during the liturgy. With the right hand, fingers together, touch your forehead first, then your chest, then your left shoulder, and finally your right shoulder. Hands are then brought back to a folded position and then to the orans position or kept folded.

Sign of the Cross
at Distance

2. When the sign of the cross is being made over people or objects:
   a. The cross is traced with the right hand, fingers together, palm inward. This motion should be in proportion to the celebrant's body and not exaggerated. The celebrant should look directly at the person or object being blessed.

Sign of the Cross
over Objects

   b. When the sign of the cross is made over an object or person at a level lower than the celebrant, the right hand is held as indicated above and the cross traced over the person or object.

In both cases, the left hand is on the chest, palm against the right breast. The left hand should not dangle or be held in midair. (See *Note* below.)

Pointing

Pointing: At various times during the liturgy, a discreet pointing with the right hand to an object on the altar is appropriate. This motion should be unobtrusive and convey the idea of showing.

Note: During the Great Thanksgiving, when the sign of the cross is made, it is customary to place the left hand on the corporal (see also page 55).

Hands over Objects

Hands over Objects: At certain points (see pages 57-70) it is appropriate for the celebrant to extend hands over an object. The thumbs may be crossed with the index fingers touching.

Laying on of Hands

Laying on of Hand(s): The laying on of hands in the Ministration to the Sick, and at other times, such as Reconciliation of a Penitent, is done in the same manner as above with one or both hands on the person's head. A cross may be traced (with oil if appropriate) on the person's forehead with the thumb of the right hand while hands are placed on the head.

Vestments

1. Eucharistic Vestments

   a. Celebrant

      cassock ⎫
      amice ⎬   *or* cassock-alb
      alb   ⎭
      cincture
      stole (uncrossed or crossed at the waist)
      (maniple, worn on left arm)
      chasuble (the stole uncrossed may be worn over the chasuble)

   b. Deacon

      cassock ⎫
      amice ⎬   *or* cassock-alb
      alb   ⎭
      cincture
      stole, worn over left shoulder and tied or crossed under the right
         arm at the waist
      dalmatic (the stole may be worn over the dalmatic)

   c. Assisting or Concelebrating Priests

      cassock ⎫
      amice ⎬   *or* cassock-alb
      alb   ⎭
      cincture
      stole (uncrossed or crossed at the waist)
      or
      cassock
      surplice
      stole

2. For Processions and other non-Eucharistic Liturgies

   a. Celebrant

      as above, but with a cope worn instead of chasuble (and maniple)
      or
      cassock, surplice, stole and a cope

   b. Deacon

      as above
      or
      cassock, surplice and stole worn over the left shoulder (and a cope)

   c. Assisting Priests

      as above
      or
      cassock, surplice, stole and a cope

3. For the Daily Offices

  a. Officiant

    cassock, surplice, (a scarf may be worn over the surplice and an academic hood may be worn—note: the hood is worn over the surplice and then the scarf is put on)

  b. Other assisting ministers

    same as for officiant

4. For special liturgies and other occasions directions are given in the body of the text of this book.

Some things to remember:

  1. A cassock-alb is not usually worn over a cassock.
  2. A cope is not worn over a chasuble.
  3. A stole is not worn with an academic hood.
  4. A stole is not worn over a scarf.
  5. A stole is proper for preaching, but not for the Daily Offices unless the Eucharist is to follow immediately or if the Office is used as the Liturgy of the Word at the Eucharist.

Note on Copes: According to long tradition, copes may be of any suitable color or combination of colors. (Colors of festive appearance are not suitable in Lent.)

Concerning Candles

Although it would sometimes appear to the contrary, candles are not decorative in liturgical celebrations. They have a purpose, either to give light for reading, or to signify a special action or a place of devotion.

Multiplication of candles can make the best architectural setting look cluttered. On the main altar, only two candles are necessary for the celebration of the Eucharist. If there are six office lights on the altar, these may be lighted for the Eucharist as well as for other liturgies.

Candles in processions were originally used to light the way. They are seldom needed for this purpose now (however, see An Order of Worship for the Evening, pages 132ff.). When carried in a Gospel procession, they emphasize the special honor accorded to the Word of God. Candles may also be burned at a shrine as a sign of devotion.

If the Liturgy of the Word takes place in a part of the church away from the altar, it is fitting that candles call attention to this area. Two "pavement" lights work quite well for this purpose. It is traditional at the principal celebration of the Eucharist on Sundays and Holy Days to light the candles on altars that are used for Eucharists at other times.

Candles for the congregation are appropriate at the Great Vigil of Easter, on Candlemas, and at other times when their purpose is clear, but the significance is lost if they are overused.

"Candlelight services" at Christmas or other times are fine, if indeed the purpose of the candles is to provide light. Discretion must be employed.

A white candle or oil lamp is always kept burning before a tabernacle or aumbry to signify that the Blessed Sacrament is reserved.

Concerning Silence

Silence is an integral part of liturgical worship, for it affords us the opportunity to reflect, to think, to pray, to offer personal petition and praise, and above all, to be in the presence of God. Silence should never be seen as a waste of time or a needless addition to the service. Silence marks different stages in the liturgy as well as providing time for the above.

Generally silence is desirable:

1. before a collect, after the words "Let us pray."
2. after a reading of Scripture (before the musical or other response).
3. after the invitation, before the Confession of Sin begins.
4. either after the initial bidding in the Prayers of the People or in those prayers which provide for silence.
5. after the final petition in the Prayers of the People, before the celebrant sings or says the concluding collect.
6. at the postcommunion prayer, after the words "Let us pray" and before the prayer is begun.

At certain other times liturgical silence is suitable and suggested in this book.

The Holy Eucharist

The Holy Eucharist

Introduction

Anglican tradition has never explicitly spelled out ceremonial action except where such movement is part of the "sign" to the people of the sacramental experience. The rubrics surrounding the words of institution in the *BCP* are a case in point, as is the signing with the cross at Baptism, or the laying on of hands in Ordination. However, order is necessary both to increase an understanding of the liturgical action and to provide for decency of movement. When the new rites first began to emerge in the late sixties, many priests and congregations felt that they not only gave license to informality but also allowed and even encouraged sloppiness, and yet did little to heighten the level of participation in worship. This confused and alienated more people than it attracted.

These perceptions were mistaken, for if there is anything the new Eucharistic rites seek to emphasize it is the encounter with the living presence of our Risen Lord through Word and Sacrament. It is the celebrant who presides, and therefore it is the obligation of the celebrant to ensure that this presence is realized and shown forth to its fullest extent—with simplicity, order and devotion.

Thus, in the Holy Eucharist, the principal act of worship in the Christian community, the elements of mystery, order, continuity, artistic taste and clarity must be joined together carefully so that expressiveness, simplicity, and beauty may reach out and touch the hearts of the people of God gathered together to proclaim the Lord in their midst.

Preparations for the Eucharist

On the credence:

a. chalice, purificator, paten, bread or host on the paten, pall, and corporal. Whether the chalice is covered with a veil or not, the purificator is normally placed on top of the chalice and the pall on top of the purificator. The burse is normally placed on top of the pall (and veil) and it contains the corporal and an extra purificator.
b. lavabo bowl and towel
c. (a cruet of water)
d. a second chalice and purificator, if needed
e. an extra cruet or flagon with wine, if necessary

On a table in the midst of the congregation or at the door of the church:

a. bread box with wafers or bread
b. a cruet of wine
c. (a cruet of water)

Note: If the gifts are not presented from the congregation the bread box and wine are placed on the credence.

The Altar Book and stand should not be on the altar until the Offertory. If there is room it may be on the credence or on some other shelf or table.

Note: The chalice should not be on the altar, nor the corporal laid, until the Offertory.

The Holy Table is spread with a clean white cloth during the celebration (BCP, 406).

The Entrance Rite

Prayers in the Sacristy

A short prayer or moment of silent prayer before the entrance is desirable. Too often the atmosphere before the service is hectic, and a prayer before beginning helps to focus the thoughts of the clergy and servers on what is about to happen. These prayers should not be prayers involving the congregation. For prayers before the Eucharist, see page 273.

The Entrance

The entrance rites (from the entrance itself to the Collect of the Day) can easily become cluttered and hence confusing. The purpose here is simply to begin the liturgy. The goal is to gather the people through hymns, psalms and prayers of preparation. If too much goes on during this period, the idea of gathering is lost and the rite becomes overburdened with nonessentials.

Form A.

1. The celebrant and assisting ministers enter during a hymn, psalm or anthem (or in silence). All reverence the altar and the celebrant may approach it and kiss it. (The deacon stands at the celebrant's right.)
2. The appropriate acclamation *(BCP, 323 or 355; AB, 9 or 147;* music, *AB, 372 or Hymnal, S 76-83)* is sung or said by the celebrant, the people responding (see page 34).
3. In Rite I the Collect for Purity follows; in Rite II the Collect for Purity *may* be said.
4. In Rite I the Decalogue *(BCP, 317)* or the Summary of the Law *(BCP, 324) may* be said after the Collect for Purity. (The deacon or assisting minister may read the Decalogue and/or the Summary.)
5. In Rite I the Kyrie (in English or Greek, said or sung) may follow, and when appointed* the Gloria in excelsis or other song of praise may be said or sung. Note: The Trisagion ("Holy God . . .") is not appropriate if the Gloria is to follow, since the Trisagion is a song of praise. In Rite II the Gloria or other song of praise is used when appointed,* and at other times the Kyrie or the Trisagion is used.
6. The opening hymn, psalm, or anthem may be omitted at the entrance. The celebrant may sing or say the acclamation immediately, process to the altar during the song of praise (cense the altar, see pages 86-87), and continue with the salutation and the Collect of the Day.

---

* *The Gloria in excelsis is sung or said from Christmas Day through the Feast of the Epiphany; on Sundays from Easter Day through the Day of Pentecost, on all the days of Easter Week, and on Ascension Day; and at other times as desired; but it is not used on the Sundays or ordinary weekdays of Advent or Lent (BCP, 406).* Traditionally, the Gloria in excelsis is used on all Principal Feasts, Major Holy Days and Sundays (except during Advent, Lent and the Sunday of the Passion).

Form B. (A Penitential Order)

1. The celebrant and assisting ministers enter during a hymn, psalm or anthem (or in silence). All reverence the altar and the celebrant may approach it and kiss it. (The deacon stands at the celebrant's right.)
2. The appropriate acclamation *(BCP, 319 or 351;* music, *AB, 372 or Hymnal, S 76-83)* is sung or said by the celebrant, the people responding (see page 34).
3. The Decalogue *(BCP, 317 or 350;* for music see *HymAccEd; S 353-354)* may be said, the people kneeling and the celebrant standing.
4. A sentence of Scripture may follow *(BCP, 319 or 351)*. (The deacon or assisting minister may read the Decalogue and/or the sentence of Scripture.)
5. The deacon or celebrant facing the people then says the invitation to the Confession of Sin *(BCP, 320 or 352)*.
6. It is appropriate that a period of silence follow.
7. The confession is said by the minister and people *(BCP, 320 or 352)*.
8. The bishop if present or celebrant stands alone and says the absolution *(BCP, 321 or 353)*. The sign of the cross is made over the people.
9. The liturgy continues with the Kyrie eleison, Trisagion or Gloria in excelsis (as appointed, see page 32).

Form C. When there is a solemn procession, see pages 168-169.

Form D. When the Great Litany is used at the beginning of the Eucharist, see page 163.

Note: The Kyrie eleison (or "Lord, have mercy") may be sung or said in threefold, sixfold, or ninefold form.

The Trisagion, "Holy God," may be sung or said three times, or antiphonally *(BCP, 406):*

> *Minister:* Holy God,
> Holy and Mighty,
> Holy Immortal One,
> *People:* *Have mercy upon us.*
>
> *or*
>
> *Minister:* Holy God, *People: Holy God,*
> *Minister:* Holy and Mighty, *People: Holy and Mighty,*
> *Minister:* Holy Immortal One, *People: Holy Immortal One,*
> *Minister and People: Have mercy upon us.*

Ceremonies at the Entrance

1. The celebrant, whether bishop or priest, is the last one in the procession. Assisting ministers and acolytes precede. The deacon or assisting priest may carry the Gospel Book.

2. For the entrance, whether Form A or Form B is used it is appropriate that the sacred ministers face the altar with their backs to the people. The celebrant turns and faces the people for the (Decalogue and the) salutation before the Collect of the Day (see 6 below). All else should be said or sung facing the altar.

3. When the celebrant and assisting ministers reach the altar, a reverence is made, either a genuflection (if the Sacrament is reserved) or a solemn bow. It looks better if this is done by all together, not individually. The celebrant may approach the altar and kiss it. (If the deacon is holding the Gospel Book, it is placed on the altar at this time.) The celebrant returns to the foot of the altar or to the celebrant's chair (accompanied by the deacon). Remember, the purpose is to focus the attention of the people on the liturgical action.

4. The sign of the cross may be made by the celebrant and people during the acclamation *(BCP, 319, 323 or 351, 355)*.

5. Three acclamations are given for Rite I and Rite II *(BCP, 319, 323 or 351, 355)*. These same acclamations precede the versicles and responses in the Baptismal liturgies *(BCP, 299, 413)*.
   a. The first acclamation ("Blessed be God . . .") is for general use except during Lent, Holy Week, and the Fifty Days of Easter.
   b. The second acclamation ("Alleluia. Christ is risen . . .") is for use at all celebrations of the Eucharist during the Fifty Days of Easter (from the Great Vigil through the Day of Pentecost). This acclamation replaces the first one and is not to be used in addition to it.
   c. The third acclamation ("Bless the Lord . . .") is for use during Lent and Holy Week (except for Good Friday and Holy Saturday). This acclamation may also be used on other penitential occasions such as a national day of fast or mourning or at a public service of penitence (see page 248). Again it is used in place of the first acclamation not in addition to it.
   d. The Baptismal liturgies follow the same rules (see above) for the acclamation preceding the proper versicles and responses.
   e. Advent is not a penitential season and therefore the proper acclamation throughout this season is the first ("Blessed be God . . .").

6. A deacon or assisting priest may read the Decalogue or Summary of the Law. In this case, this minister, not the celebrant, turns and faces the people.

7. The sign of the cross may be made at the conclusion of the Gloria in excelsis by the celebrant and people.

Note: It is proper to sing or say the Gloria Patri at the conclusion of a psalm used at the Entrance Rite.

The Collect of the Day

1. The celebrant turns (assisting ministers turn inward and face each other and the celebrant) and, facing the people, sings or says the salutation, and the people respond. (For singing the salutation and response, see *AB, 373*.)
2. The celebrant turns back to face the altar, and with hands extended (orans position) sings or says the Collect of the Day.
3. In some places the celebrant and assisting ministers go to the sedilia for the Collect of the Day. Although this does establish the presiding function of the celebrant, the oneness of motion and place from the entrance through the Collect of the Day is more desirable. Also, from the viewpoint of the people, the celebrant is facing in the same direction as they are, thus leading their prayer, not directing the collect to the people.
4. It is proper for the people to remain standing for the Collect of the Day.

Note: For chanting the Collect of the Day, see *AB, 374-376*.

When the collect is concluded, the celebrant and assisting ministers reverence the altar with a solemn bow and go to the sedilia for the reading of the lessons. The celebrant sits in the center chair and presides from there. Assistants sit on either side of the celebrant. (The deacon sits at the celebrant's right.)

The Word of God

The Lessons

On Sundays and major Feast Days, a Lesson, Epistle and Gospel are appointed to be read. It is desirable that all three be used when appointed.

Note: For chanting the Lessons, see *AB, 377.*
For chanting the Gospels, see *AB, 378-381.*

A. When three lessons are appointed

The Lesson is appropriately read by a lay reader from the lectern. The proper forms for announcing and concluding the lesson are given *(BCP, 325 or 357).* If there are lay readers or assisting ministers present the celebrant does not read the lessons and remains seated.

A Psalm is appointed with every proper in *The Book of Common Prayer.* This psalm may either be sung or said, but if the liturgy is sung it is appropriate that the psalm be sung:

1. By a cantor or the choir with the people singing an antiphon.
2. By the people throughout to a simple chant tune.
3. By the congregation in a metrical version (*A New Metrical Psalter;* Church Hymnal Corporation).
4. If the psalm is said, the Antiphonal and Responsive methods *(see BCP, 582)* are preferred, but unison recitation may also be used.
5. The Gloria Patri is traditionally not used at the conclusion of the psalm appointed for use after the lesson.

Note: It is preferable that the celebrant and people remain seated for the psalm.

The Epistle or Second Lesson also should be read by a lay reader or assisting minister from the lectern with proper announcement and conclusion (and response by the people). The celebrant remains seated.

Alleluia Verse or Sequence Hymn. Between the second lesson (Epistle) and the proclamation of the Holy Gospel a verse of Scripture with the acclamation "alleluia" (except during Lent) may be said or sung. If the alleluia verse is not used a "sequence" hymn is appropriate. This hymn should bear some relationship to the Gospel, as should the verse of Scripture with the alleluia.

B. When one lesson and a Gospel are appointed

1. The Lesson or Epistle is read by a lay reader or assisting minister from the lectern.
2. The celebrant remains seated at the sedilia.
3. The appointed psalm is sung or said between the Lesson and the Gospel. The Gloria Patri is traditionally not used at the conclusion. Ministers and people may remain seated for the psalm.

The Proclamation of the Gospel

1. It is appropriate that the Gospel be sung or read from a book that is set apart for this purpose.
2. The book should be on the altar.
3. After the Epistle, a deacon or assisting priest if present, or the celebrant, goes to the altar. The altar is reverenced with a solemn bow and the book is taken.

The deacon or other minister makes a solemn bow at the altar, holding the book and says silently this or some other prayer:

Purify my lips and heart, O God, that I may worthily proclaim *thy* Holy Gospel.

Note: If a bishop is present, either as celebrant or presiding, the reader, after taking the Gospel Book from the altar (and prayer), goes to the bishop for a blessing. The reader kneels or bows for this blessing.

4. It is customary and desirable that the Gospel be sung or read from a place close to the people. A Gospel procession from the altar to the congregation consists of (thurifer), two acolytes with candles, a person (subdeacon) to hold the Gospel Book, and the reader (deacon, assisting priest, or celebrant). The acolytes stand on either side of the Gospel Book. The reader faces the people and announces the Gospel *(BCP, 326 or 357)* while signing the beginning of the passage with a small cross using the thumb of the right hand.* (For the use of incense

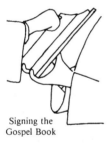

Signing the Gospel Book

at the Gospel, see page 88.) The Gospel is sung or read. At the conclusion, "The Gospel of the Lord" is said or sung *(AB, 379-381)* and the response made by the people. The book should be held high for "The Gospel of the Lord" and then lowered for the reader to kiss. It is customary for the reader to kiss the book at the place of the signing. All then return to their places. The Gospel Book is returned to the altar or other designated place before the reader returns to the sedilia.

5. If the Gospel is to be proclaimed from the pulpit or lectern, a procession is still in order. However, a person to hold the book is not necessary. See above for other ceremonies.

Note: When a portion of the congregation is composed of persons whose native tongue is other than English, a reader appointed by the celebrant may read the Gospel in the language of the people, either in place of, or in addition to, the Gospel in English (BCP, 406).

---

* It is also traditional for the deacon (or other reader of the Gospel) to make a small sign of the cross, using the thumb of the right hand, on the forehead, mouth and heart at the announcement of the Gospel following the signing of the book. The people may sign themselves in the same way.

The Sermon

It is desirable that nothing be inserted between the proclamation of the Gospel and the sermon.

A hymn at this point is out of place.

If music is needed to cover the return of the Gospel procession and to get the preacher to the pulpit, instrumental music may be played.

The sermon should follow immediately. Announcements should not be made at this point, since they break the flow of the liturgical action.

Concerning Sermons

The sermon is an important and integral part of the liturgy. Thus, careful attention should be given to the lessons for the day, especially the Gospel.

The sermon is not a break in the liturgical action as some would hold, nor does it exist apart from the liturgy. It belongs to the proclamation of the Word of God and must be approached and prepared with the appointed lessons in mind. The wealth of Scripture provided in the lectionary is the basis for sound, theological, biblical and Eucharistic preaching. It may take a little more time to prepare a sermon that fits with the liturgy, but a sermon that truly illuminates the Word of God as proclaimed in the appointed lessons is well worth the effort. As priests we must strive to ensure that our preaching is consistent with the tone and teaching of the lessons and hymns for a given occasion and does not introduce alien elements.

The Nicene Creed

On Sundays, Principal Feasts, and Holy Days the Nicene Creed follows the sermon. There is no justification for a hymn that breaks the flow from sermon to affirmation of faith. The celebrant and assisting ministers should stand at the sedilia for the Creed. It is customary to make a solemn bow (or a genuflection on the Feasts of the Nativity of Our Lord and the Annunciation) at the Incarnational affirmation ("For us and for our salvation" or "who for us men and for our salvation" . . . "was made man"). In some places this bow is continued through the affirmation of the death and burial of our Lord ("he suffered death and was buried"). It is customary in many places to make the sign of the cross at the conclusion of the Nicene Creed.

Note: The Nicene Creed is omitted at Baptisms, Confirmations and other liturgies when there is a Renewal of Baptismal Vows (i.e. the Great Vigil of Easter); it may be omitted on the Sunday of the Passion (Palm Sunday); the Nicene Creed is not traditionally used at the Burial of the Dead, but the Apostles' Creed may be said.

The Prayers of the People

Whether one is celebrating Rite I or Rite II, any of the intercessory forms given in the *BCP* may be used. The traditional "prayer for the whole state of Christ's Church," slightly modified and enriched from the 1928 Prayer Book, is given *(BCP, 328)*. The other forms (I through VI) *(BCP, 383-393)* are also appropriate within either rite.

1. If a deacon is present, it is fitting that this person lead the prayers. If not, a lay person appointed by the celebrant may do so.
2. The people stand for the Prayers of the People.
3. The concluding collect (Forms I through V) may be taken from those given *(BCP, 394-395)* or from elsewhere in the Prayer Book. This collect is *always* said or sung by the celebrant (see page 44 concerning the concluding collect).
4. When Form VI *(BCP, 392-393)* is used with its Confession of Sin, it is proper for the celebrant to conclude with an absolution *(BCP, 332 or 360)* instead of a collect.
5. In Forms I and V provision is made for asking for forgiveness of sins. These penitential suffrages should be omitted if the Confession of Sin is to follow or if the Penitential Order has been used at the beginning of the liturgy.
6. Music for chanting the Prayers of the People and concluding collects is found in *The Hymnal 1982* (Form I, *S 106;* Form III, *S 107;* Form IV, *S 108;* Form V, *S 109;* also, *HymAccEd,* Form II, *S 362;* Form VI, *S 363)* and in *The Altar Book (AB, 382-385).*

Notes on the Prayers of the People

A. Prayer for the Whole State of Christ's Church and the World *(BCP, 328-330):*

Second paragraph: provision is made for inserting the names of the Presiding Bishop and diocesan bishops.

Fourth paragraph: names of national and local leaders may be inserted. The phrase "_____, our President, the Congress, and the Courts" is a useful reminder that we have a tripartite government, not a presidential monarchy.

Sixth paragraph: provision is made to name the sick and those for whom prayers are asked.

Additional petitions and thanksgivings may be included here (BCP, 330).

Seventh paragraph: provision is made for inserting the names of the departed.

Seventh paragraph: provision is made for inserting the name of a saint whose feast is being kept, the patron saint of the parish, or as regular custom St. Mary ("so to follow the good examples of the ever-blessed Virgin Mary and of all thy saints").

This form of intercession is printed as a series of petitions with one concluding "Amen" to be said or sung by the people. However, at the conclusion of each paragraph a versicle and response may be added:

V. Lord, in thy mercy:
R. *Hear our prayer.*

If the versicle and response are used, the final paragraph of the prayer *(BCP, 330)* ends with "Amen," and no versicle and response are added.

Note: This form does not contain a Confession of Sin or a penitential suffrage; therefore the Confession of Sin and absolution may follow the "Amen" unless it has been used at the entrance rite (see pages 33 and 45).

B. Forms I through VI.

Form I *(BCP, 383-385; Hymnal, S 106)*

This form is in "traditional language" with the final response "To thee, O Lord our God." It is therefore appropriate for use with Rite I. Form I (as well as Form V) is adapted from the Liturgy of the Eastern churches.

The Presiding Bishop and diocesan bishops may be mentioned by name in the third petition:

"For *N.* our Presiding Bishop, for *N. (N. N.)* our bishop(s), for all bishops and for all the clergy and people . . ."

In the fourth petition the President of the United States is properly included by name, as are local leaders:

"For *N.* our President, for the leaders of the nations, for *N.* our governor, for *N.* our mayor, (etc.), and for all in authority . . ."

The "lined" petitions (i.e., those marked with a vertical line in the margin) may be omitted.

The sick and others for whom prayers are asked are appropriately included by name in the ninth petition:

"For the aged and infirm, for the widowed and orphans, and for the sick and the suffering, especially *N.*, *N.*, let us pray to the Lord."

The departed are appropriately included by name in the twelfth petition:

"For all who have died in the hope of the resurrection, especially *N.*, *N.*, and for all the departed, let us pray to the Lord."

The fourteenth petition, a penitential suffrage, is omitted if the Penitential Order has been used at the entrance or if the Confession of Sin is to follow the prayers.

The final petition provides for the naming of saints:

"In the communion of the ever-blessed Virgin Mary, St. (Blessed) *N.*, and all the saints, let us . . ."

The celebrant concludes with a collect after a period of silence.

Form II *(BCP, 385-387; HymAccEd, S 362)*

The insertion of the name(s) of the bishop(s) is provided for in the first petition.

The naming of the sick and those in need may be added at the conclusion of the third petition.

Provision is made to name the departed in the fifth petition.

Special prayers and thanksgivings may be added as indicated in the two lined petitions.

Saints' names may be added in the final petition.

Silence follows each petition.

After the final petition, the celebrant adds a concluding collect (see rubric, *BCP, 387*).

Note: Form II does not contain a Confession of Sin or a penitential suffrage; therefore the Confession of Sin and absolution may follow the concluding collect unless it has been used at the entrance rite (see pages 33 and 45).

Form III *(BCP, 387-388; Hymnal, S 107)*

This form is best used straight through as printed, the people making the italicized responses.

The naming of the sick, those in need, and the departed may come after the final sentence:

"Let us pray for our own needs and those of others: especially N., N., and all those who are sick; N., N., and all who are in need; N., N., and all the departed."

Provision is made for petitions from the people *(BCP, 388),* and a concluding collect by the celebrant is necessary.

Note: Form III does not contain a Confession of Sin or penitential suffrage; therefore the Confession of Sin and absolution may follow the concluding collect unless it has been used at the entrance rite (see pages 33 and 45).

Form IV *(BCP, 388-389; Hymnal, S 108)*

This form is similar to the prayer for the whole state of Christ's Church and the world *(BCP, 328-330)*.

The Presiding Bishop and diocesan bishops may be named after the first petition, before the silence.

National and local government leaders may be named at the conclusion of the second petition, before the silence.

The sick and those in need may be named at the conclusion of the fifth petition, before the silence.

The departed may be mentioned at the conclusion of the final petition, before the silence.

The celebrant adds a concluding collect.

Note: Form IV does not contain a Confession of Sin or a penitential suffrage; therefore the Confession of Sin and absolution may follow the concluding collect unless it has been used at the entrance rite (see pages 33 and 45).

Form V *(BCP, 389-391; Hymnal, S 109)*

This parallels Form I and is adapted from the Liturgy of the Eastern Churches.

The response of the people may be either in Greek or English.

The Presiding Bishop and diocesan bishops are named in the second petition.

Although many name the sick in the tenth petition, it is also appropriate that they be included in the fourteenth petition:

"For all who have commended themselves to our prayers, especially N., N.; for our families, friends . . ."

Others for whom prayers are asked are named in the fifteenth petition.

The thirteenth petition is a penitential suffrage and is omitted if the Penitential Order has been used at the entrance or if the Confession of Sin is to follow the Prayers of the People.

Names of the departed may be inserted in the sixteenth petition:

"For all who have died in the communion of your Church, especially remembering N., N.; and those whose faith is known . . ."

Other saints may be named in the final petition in addition to the Blessed Virgin Mary.

After a period of silence, the celebrant concludes either with the Doxology printed *(BCP, 391)* or some other suitable collect.

Form VI *(BCP, 392-393; HymAccEd, S 363)*

In style this intercession parallels Form III and is best used straight through with the people making the italicized responses.

Provision is made for the naming of the Presiding Bishop and diocesan bishops in the sixth petition.

The sick and others for whom prayers are asked are named after a period of silence in the seventh petition.

Thanksgivings (including thanksgiving for a saint whose feast is being observed) may be added to the eighth petition.

The departed may be remembered by name in the ninth petition.

A Confession of Sin is included at the end of this intercession. A solemn bow by celebrant and people is appropriate.

It is proper for the celebrant to conclude with an absolution rather than a collect if this confession is used.

If the form of confession printed *(BCP, 393)* is *not* used, a suitable concluding collect is inserted by the celebrant after the response:

"Who put their trust in you."

If this confession is not used, either the Penitential Order is used at the opening of the liturgy, or one of the forms of Confession of Sin *(BCP, 331-332 or 359-360)* and absolution may follow the intercession.

Ceremonies at the Prayers of the People

It is appropriate that the leader (whether deacon, lay person, or priest) face the people for the initial statement in:

The Prayer for the Whole State *(BCP, 328)*.

Form I : "With all our heart . . ." *(BCP, 383)*.

Form IV: "Let us pray for the Church and for the world." *(BCP, 388)*.

Form V : "In peace, let us pray to the Lord, saying . . ." *(BCP, 389)*.

The leader then reads or sings the remainder of the petitions facing the altar (or if the prayers are bidding in nature, i.e. Form II, the leader faces the people). All should remain standing for the prayers. At the penitential suffrages in Form I and Form V the sign of the cross may be made by celebrant and people. The confession at the end of Form VI should be accompanied by a solemn bow.

Concluding Collect at the Prayers
(BCP, 394-395)

Note: The orans position for the celebrant is appropriate at the concluding collect.

Collect 1 is appropriate at any time.

Collect 2 is appropriate during Lent and on other penitential occasions.

Collects 3 and 4 are appropriate at any time.

Collect 5 is appropriate during Lent and other penitential seasons.

Collect 6 is appropriate at any time, but especially so if the confession has occurred at the entrance or during the prayers (Form I or V) since it leads logically into the Peace. This collect is also suitable during Lent and on other penitential occasions.

Collect 7 is appropriate during Advent, on the Last Sunday after Pentecost (Christ the King), Ascension Day, during the season of Epiphany, or on other occasions where the emphasis is on the Kingdom of God or the Reign of Christ.

Collect 8 is appropriate on Saints' Days, whether they be major or minor feasts. The emphasis on the Communion of Saints is obvious.

Any suitable collect may be used at the conclusion of the Prayers of the People.

For concluding collects during the weekdays of Lent and the Fifty Days of Easter, see pages 155 and 158.

Note: There is no provision for a concluding collect to the prayers when the prayer for the whole state of Christ's Church and the world is used. The final paragraph ends with an Amen which thus concludes the Prayers of the People *(BCP, 330)*.

Note: In some places the Bishop of Rome (Pope *N.*), the Archbishop of Canterbury, the Patriarchs of the Eastern Churches, the bishops, moderators and others in authority in Protestant churches are included in the prayers. These are appropriately added in the petition for the Presiding Bishop and other bishops.

Concerning Singing the Prayers of the People

At a sung Eucharist it is appropriate that the prayers be sung. Music for Forms I, III, IV and V is found in *The Hymnal 1982 (Hymnal, S 106-109; HymAccEd,* Form II *S 362,* Form VI *S 363).* The prayer given in Rite I *(BCP, 328-330)* is sung to Collect Tone II *(AB, 375-376; Hymnal, S 108)*; also, for the versicle and response which may be inserted after each paragraph see *The Hymnal 1982 (Hymnal, S 108).* If the prayers are sung, the concluding collect is sung by the celebrant:

Form I : monotoned or Collect Tone II *(AB, 375-376)*

Form III: monotoned
Form IV: monotoned or Collect Tone II *(AB, 375-376)*
Form V : monotoned or Collect Tone I *(AB, 375-376)*
  or
concluding Doxology *(Hymnal, S 109)*

Confession of Sin

If the Penitential Order was used at the entrance, the Confession of Sin is omitted here, and the Peace follows immediately.

If the penitential suffrage in Form I or V of the Prayers of the People was used the Confession of Sin is omitted, and the Peace follows immediately.

If the Confession of Sin in Form VI was used, the absolution and the Peace follow immediately.

At other times the deacon (assisting minister) or celebrant bids the people to confess their sins *(BCP, 330 or 360);* kneeling or a solemn bow is appropriate. Silence may be kept before the confession begins. The confession is recited by minister and people, and the celebrant (bishop, if present) alone stands, if the confession has been said kneeling, to give the absolution. It is customary for the celebrant (or bishop) to make the sign of the cross over the people during the absolution.

Note: Following the absolution, a sentence of Scripture *(BCP, 332)* may be said by the deacon (assisting minister or celebrant). The rubrics do not imply that all of the sentences should be read; one sentence is quite appropriate. If the Penitential Order or a Confession of Sin has been used at the beginning of the Eucharist, the sentence(s) of Scripture is not used here.

The Peace

Although the rubric in Additional Directions *(BCP, 407)* permits the Peace to be exchanged in the position of the Roman liturgy after the Breaking of the Bread and before the administration of the Sacrament, it is desirable that the Peace follow directly after the Confession of Sin or the Prayers of the People, before the beginning of the Offertory: the symbolism of placement here is obvious (Matt. 5:23-24). On a practical note, it is less an intrusion here than before communion, especially if the people are exuberant in their greeting of one another!

Note: The Peace is the exchange of the Peace of Christ and should not be allowed to deteriorate into a visiting time.

1. The celebrant greets the people with the Peace and then exchanges a gesture of greeting in the Name of the Lord with the assisting ministers and those nearby. The celebrant and/or one or more of the assisting ministers or acolytes may go and greet the people, or the people may exchange the Peace among themselves while the celebrant and assisting ministers proceed with the Offertory.

2. It is appropriate for the celebrant to extend hands at the giving of the Peace (as at the salutation), since this is directed to the whole congregation. The manual act helps to underscore this.

3. The Peace and the response may be sung or said (see *AB, 386; Hymnal, S 110-111).*

4. Even if the Peace is not physically exchanged by the people the salutation and response may not be omitted.

5. *If there is no Communion, all that is appointed through the Prayers of the People may be said. (If it is desired to include a Confession of Sin, the service begins with the Penitential Order.) A hymn or anthem may then be sung, and the offerings of the people received. The service may then conclude with the Lord's Prayer; and with either the Grace or a blessing, or with the exchange of the Peace (BCP, 406-407).*

In the absence of a priest, all that is described above (No. 5), *except for the blessing, may be said by a deacon, or, if there is no deacon, by a lay reader (BCP, 407).*

The Holy Communion

The Offertory

Like the entrance rite, the preparation of the gifts for the Great Thanksgiving is another part of the Eucharistic liturgy that can be so crowded with extraneous elements that the action and purpose tend to be lost. A profusion of offertory sentences and anthems and hymns and presentation sentences and flag processions and additional intercessions do not in any way clarify what is happening, but rather confuse the rite. The purpose of the Offertory is very simple: the presentation (offering) of the elements for the Eucharist and the gifts of the people and the preparation of the elements. Whatever does not expedite this should be avoided.

Note: If the celebrant is vested in a cope for the Liturgy of the Word, the cope is removed and a chasuble put on at the beginning of the Offertory.

A. At a celebration without assisting ministers.

Immediately after the Peace has been exchanged the celebrant may say an offertory sentence *(BCP, 343-344, 376-377)*, and then approach the altar (and kiss the altar, if this has not been done at the entrance). A lay assistant or acolyte brings the chalice to the altar.

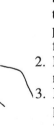

Offering the Bread

1. Place chalice to one side, remove corporal from burse and spread it on altar (folds down). Put burse to one side, flat on the altar (not on edge as a display piece), place chalice on corporal, remove veil, fold veil in thirds and put to one side, remove pall.
2. Receive and prepare enough bread for communions. Place on the paten.
3. Raise the paten slightly and offer the bread. (A silent prayer or one with a response by the people may be said. See page 274.) Place paten on the corporal.
4. Receive wine from acolyte, pour it in chalice; receive water and add a small amount. (Receive cruets from the acolyte's right hand and return them to the left hand.)

Offering the Wine

Replacing the Chalice

Offering the Money

5. Raise the chalice slightly and offer the wine. (A silent prayer or one with a response by the people may be said. See page 274.) Place chalice on the corporal.

6. If a money offering has been received from the people, take this if it is presented, and raise it slightly and offer it; then return the basin to a server.

7. Wash hands, when server presents the lavabo bowl (see page 274).

8. If desired, the elements may be received (from the server or the people) and prepared. Then, after the money offering is received, the bread and wine are offered and the lavabo follows.

B. When there is a deacon or assisting priest.

Immediately after the Peace has been exchanged the celebrant may say an offertory sentence *(BCP, 343-344 or 376-377)*.

1. The deacon or assisting priest spreads the corporal on the altar (and unveils the chalice).
2. The deacon receives (from the people or a server) and prepares enough bread for communion on the paten. It is placed on the corporal.
3. The deacon pours wine in the chalice and adds a little water. The chalice is placed on the corporal.
4. The celebrant then comes to the center (kisses the altar if this has not been done at the entrance), then offers the bread (see A.3 above) and the wine (see A.5 above).
5. The deacon receives the money offering of the people and presents it to the celebrant (see A.6).
6. The server or deacon then washes the celebrant's hands (see page 272).
7. If desired the deacon may receive the money offering first (after spreading the corporal). The celebrant then offers the money. The deacon prepares (or previously has prepared) the offerings of bread and wine. The celebrant offers these after the money offering and places the paten and chalice upon the corporal. The lavabo follows.

C. When there is an offertory procession and assisting ministers.

Immediately after the Peace has been exchanged the celebrant may say an offertory sentence (BCP, 343-344 or 376-377).

1. A deacon or an assisting priest spreads the corporal (and unveils the chalice). The celebrant comes to the center (and kisses the altar if this has not been done at the entrance).
2. The gifts of bread, wine, (water) and money are then brought to the altar by representatives of the congregation (see page 50).
3. The deacon and/or other assisting minister (or lay reader) receives the bread from the people and presents it to the celebrant, who then offers it (see A.3 above).
4. The deacon and/or other assisting minister (or lay reader) receives the cruet(s) of wine (and water) from the people. If the assisting minister is a deacon or priest, the chalice is prepared by that person (see A.4 above). If a lay person is assisting the celebrant, first the wine is presented and the celebrant pours it into the chalice; then, the water is presented and a small amount is poured into the chalice. The cup is then offered by the celebrant (see A.5 above).
5. If there is a money offering from the people this is presented to the assisting minister, who gives it to the celebrant, who then receives (and offers) it (see A.6 above).
6. The server, or deacon, or assisting minister washes the celebrant's hands.
7. If desired, the money offering may be received (and offered) first. The bread and the wine are then received, prepared and offered accordingly. The celebrant then proceeds with the lavabo.

D. At a celebration when incense is used.

All takes place as above except:

1. After the gifts (including the money) have been presented and offered the thurifer brings the thurible and boat to the celebrant; incense is prepared (and blessed) in the usual way (see page 270).
2. The celebrant then censes the gifts and the altar (see pages 84-85).
3. After the altar is censed, the deacon or thurifer may cense the celebrant and assisting ministers and then the people (see page 80).
4. The celebrant's hands are washed *after* the altar has been censed.

E. At a celebration with music.

1. If the choir sings a motet or anthem while the money offering is being received the following may take place:

   a. If there is no deacon or assisting priest, the celebrant goes to the altar, spreads the corporal (and unveils the chalice).

   b. If there is a deacon or assisting priest, the celebrant may remain at the sedilia while the deacon or assisting priest spreads the corporal (and unveils the chalice).

   c. After the anthem or motet is completed a hymn may be sung; the celebrant goes to the altar and receives and offers the gifts.

2. If there is no hymn, or only a hymn and no anthem: as soon as the money offering is taken, the gifts are brought to the altar and received, prepared and offered.

   or

   The oblations of bread and wine may be brought to the celebrant immediately, and then after the money offering has been received (during the hymn) it is brought to the altar and presented.

   or

   If there is no money offering, the bread and wine are brought to the altar and presented.

   After preparation and offering, the celebrant continues with the lavabo.

Concerning the Offertory Procession

This is a simple procession with representatives of the congregation carrying the following:

1. bread (in a suitable container)
2. cruet of wine (and cruet of water)
3. the money offerings

After the gifts have been received and offered, those who presented them return to their places in the congregation.

Note: If desired, the gifts of bread and wine (and water) may be brought to the altar immediately at the beginning of the Offertory (after the sentence of Scripture). The deacon (or celebrant) receives them and then gives the alms basins to the persons who have presented the gifts. These persons receive the money offering of the people while the gifts are being prepared and offered at the altar. The money offering is brought to the altar and received in the usual way.

Concerning Chalices

During the Great Thanksgiving, it is appropriate that there be only one chalice on the Altar, and, if need be, a flagon of wine from which additional chalices may be filled after the Breaking of the Bread (BCP, 407).

Thus, if more than one chalice is needed for communions, a flagon or extra cruet of wine (with a little water added) should be placed on the corporal during the Offertory.

Concerning the Reserved Sacrament

An adequate amount of bread should be prepared and offered for the number of people present. If the Reserved Sacrament is used, it is not brought to the altar until the anthem at the Breaking of Bread (see page 71).

Illustration of Manual Acts
during the Great Thanksgiving

Orans Position

Gesture of Thanksgiving: Bread

Gesture of Thanksgiving: Wine

Showing of Gifts: Bread

Showing of Gifts: Wine

Pointing to Gifts

Hands over Gifts

Hands on Corporal

Solemn Bow at Altar

Elevation at Great Doxology

The Great Thanksgiving

The Sursum Corda and Preface

1. The celebrant faces the people across the altar or turns and faces them. The people stand.
2. The celebrant's hands should be extended for
   "The Lord be with you."
3. Then an upward motion with extended hands for
   "Lift up your hearts."
4. Then hands together (or orans position) for
   "Let us give thanks . . ."
5. If the altar is not freestanding, the celebrant now turns, faces it, and continues with the Preface.
6. The Preface is sung or said with hands extended in the orans position. (For Eucharistic Prayer C, see page 64; for Eucharistic Prayer D, see page 67.)
7. A Proper Preface is added as directed (see pages 55-56).
8. If it is customary to bow at the Name of Jesus, the celebrant's hands are joined for this reverence and then extended for the remainder of the Preface.
9. At the Sanctus (and all other corporate sections of the Canon said or sung in unison), the celebrant joins hands. It is customary for the celebrant and assisting ministers to make a solemn bow during the Sanctus, standing upright again at the word "heaven." They may make the sign of the cross at the words, "Blessed is he..." Bells may be rung during the Sanctus.
10. At the conclusion of the Sanctus and Benedictus qui venit the celebrant continues with the Eucharistic Prayer.
11. At the conclusion of the Sanctus and Benedictus qui venit the people remain standing or kneel. Directions may be given in a service leaflet and by the example of those assisting in the Chancel. "Let us pray" should not be said here, as the entire Great Thanksgiving is one prayer.

Concerning Proper Prefaces

The Proper Prefaces given in the Prayer Book are as follows *(BCP, 344-349 or 377-382):*

Preface of the Lord's Day
(To be used on Sundays as appointed, but not on succeeding weekdays)

1. Of God the Father *(BCP, 344 or 377)*
2. Of God the Son *(BCP, 345 or 377)*
3. Of God the Holy Spirit *(BCP, 345 or 378)*

Prefaces for Seasons

(*To be used on Sundays and weekdays alike, except as otherwise appointed for Holy Days, Lesser Feasts and Fasts or Various Occasions,* see pages 95-108; 114-115)

Advent *(BCP, 345 or 378)*
Incarnation *(BCP, 345 or 378)*
*Epiphany *(BCP, 346 or 378)*
Lent *(BCP, 346 or 379)*

    a. The first Proper Preface is appropriate for Lent 1 through Lent 3.
    b. The second Proper Preface is appropriate for Lent 4 and 5.

Holy Week *(BCP, 346 or 379)*
Easter *(BCP, 346 or 379)*
Ascension *(BCP, 347 or 379)*
Pentecost *(BCP, 347 or 380)*
Weekdays after Pentecost—no Proper Preface is used unless appointed for Holy Days, Lesser Feasts and Fasts or Various Occasions.

Prefaces for Other Occasions

Trinity Sunday *(BCP, 347 or 380)*
All Saints *(BCP, 347 or 380)*
A Saint

    The first and second given are general *(BCP, 348 or 380)*.
    The third Proper Preface is especially suitable for Feasts of Martyrs *(BCP, 348 or 381)*.

Apostles and Ordinations *(BCP, 348 or 381)*
Dedication of a Church *(BCP, 348 or 381)*
Baptism *(BCP, 348 or 381)*
Marriage *(BCP, 349 or 381)*
Commemoration of the Dead *(BCP, 349 or 382)*

Notes on the Proper Preface:

1. The Proper Preface appointed is listed:
    a. after the collects *(BCP, 159-210 or 211-261)*
    b. within special liturgies of the *BCP* or *BOS*
    c. after the collects in *LFF*
    d. in *The Altar Book (AB, 22-30 or 158-166)*

2. Music for the Sursum Corda is found in *The Altar Book (AB, 21* or *157)* and in *The Hymnal 1982 (Hymnal, S 112, S 120)*.

---

*From the Feast of the Epiphany (January 6) through the Tuesday before Ash Wednesday, the Preface of the Epiphany *(BCP, 346 or 378)* is used on weekdays, except where otherwise indicated for Holy Days, Lesser Feasts and Fasts, or Various Occasions.

3. The music for singing the Proper Prefaces is found in *The Altar Book:*
   a. Rite One: Solemn Tone *(AB, 102-120)*
   b. Rite One: Simple Tone *(AB, 121-140)*
   c. Rite Two: Solemn Tone *(AB, 252-270)*
   d. Rite Two: Simple Tone *(AB, 272-290)*
4. The Proper Preface is not used with Eucharistic Prayer C *(BCP, 369-372)* nor with Eucharistic Prayer D *(BCP, 372-375).* However, music for chanting the beginning of Eucharistic Prayer D is found in *The Altar Book (AB, 184-186)* and for chanting Eucharistic Prayer C in *The Hymnal Accompaniment Edition (HymAccEd, S 369-370).*

Concerning Music for the Memorial Acclamation

The Memorial Acclamation (Rite II) may be sung as follows:
   Eucharistic Prayer A: *(Hymnal, S 132-135; HymAccEd, S 366)*
   Eucharistic Prayer B: *(Hymnal, S 136-138; HymAccEd, S 367-368)*
   Eucharistic Prayer D: *(Hymnal, S 139-141; HymAccEd, S 371-372)*
   or
   these texts may be sung to other settings;
   also
   Music for chanting Eucharistic Prayer C *(HymAccEd, S 369-370).*

Concerning Music for the Conclusion of the Eucharistic Prayer

The chants for the Doxology are as follows:
   Eucharistic Prayer I: *(AB, 34)*
   Eucharistic Prayer II: *(AB, 40)*
   Eucharistic Prayer A: *(AB, 169)*
   Eucharistic Prayer B: *(AB, 174)*
   Eucharistic Prayer C: *(AB, 180)*
   Eucharistic Prayer D: *(AB, 190)*
The Great Amen is sung as given above in *The Altar Book* or from *The Hymnal 1982 (Hymnal, S 142-147)* or from other settings.

Note: Bells may be rung during the Great Thanksgiving as follows:
   a. at the Sanctus
   b. at the elevation(s) of the Elements
   c. at the conclusion of the Eucharistic Prayer while the gifts are elevated for the Doxology and Great Amen (see above).

Eucharistic Prayer I   (BCP, 334-336)

Then the Celebrant continues

All glory be to thee, Almighty God, our heavenly Father, for that thou, of thy tender mercy, didst give thine only Son Jesus Christ to suffer death upon the cross for our redemption; who made there, by his one oblation of himself once offered, a full, perfect, and sufficient sacrifice, oblation, and satisfaction, for the sins of the whole world; and did institute, and in his holy Gospel command us to continue, a perpetual memory of that his precious death and sacrifice, until his coming again.

At the following words concerning the bread, the Celebrant is to hold it, or lay a hand upon it; and at the words concerning the cup, to hold or place a hand upon the cup and any other vessel containing wine to be consecrated.

For in the night in which he was betrayed,

1. he took bread;

2. and when he had given thanks, he broke it,

3. and gave it to his disciples, saying, "Take, eat, this is my Body, which is given for you. Do this in remembrance of me."

4.

Ceremonial Directions for the Celebrant

Orans position.

1. Take host or lay hand upon bread.

2. (Raise the right hand in a gesture of thanksgiving.)

3. Show the bread to the people (if celebrating facing the people).

4. (Optional) Elevate host or bread, replace bread on paten, genuflect or make a solemn bow.
(A period of silence may follow.)

Eucharistic Prayer II   (BCP, 341-343)

Then the Celebrant continues

All glory be to thee, O Lord our God, for that thou didst create heaven and earth, and didst make us in thine own image; and, of thy tender mercy, didst give thine only Son Jesus Christ to take our nature upon him, and to suffer death upon the cross for our redemption. He made there a full and perfect sacrifice for the whole world; and did institute, and in his holy Gospel command us to continue, a perpetual memory of that his precious death and sacrifice until his coming again.

At the following words concerning the bread, the Celebrant is to hold it, or lay a hand upon it; and at the words concerning the cup, to hold or place a hand upon the cup and any other vessel containing wine to be consecrated.

For in the night in which he was betrayed,

1. he took bread;

2. and when he had given thanks to thee, he broke it,

3. and gave it to his disciples, saying, "Take, eat, this is my Body, which is given for you. Do this in remembrance of me."

4.

Eucharistic Prayer I	Ceremonial Directions for the Celebrant	Eucharist Prayer II
Likewise after supper,		Likewise after supper,
5. he took the cup;	5. Take the chalice and lay a hand on other vessels to be consecrated.	5. he took the cup;
6. and when he had given thanks,	6. (Raise the right hand in a gesture of thanksgiving.)	6. and when he had given thanks,
7. he gave it to them, saying, "Drink ye all of this; for this is my Blood of the New Testament, which is shed for you, and for many, for the remission of sins. Do this as oft as ye shall drink it, in remembrance of me."	7. Show the chalice to the people (if celebrating facing the people).	7. he gave it to them, saying, "Drink this, all of you; for this is my Blood of the New Covenant, which is shed for you, and for many, for the remission of sins. Do this, as oft as ye shall drink it, in remembrance of me."
8.	8. (Optional) Elevate the chalice, replace the chalice on the altar, genuflect or make a solemn bow. (A period of silence may follow.)	8.
Wherefore, O Lord and heavenly Father, according to the institution of thy dearly beloved Son our Savior Jesus Christ, we, thy humble servants,		Wherefore, O Lord and heavenly Father, we thy people
9. do celebrate and make here before thy divine Majesty, with these thy holy gifts, which we now offer unto thee, the memorial thy Son hath commanded us to make; having in remembrance his blessed passion and precious death, his mighty resurrection and glorious ascension; rendering unto thee most hearty thanks for the innumerable benefits procured unto us by the same.	9. Point to the bread and wine. Orans position.	9. do celebrate and make, with these thy holy gifts which we now offer unto thee, the memorial thy Son hath commanded us to make; having in remembrance his blessed passion and precious death, his mighty resurrection and glorious ascension; and looking for his coming again with power and great glory.
And we most humbly beseech thee, O merciful Father, to hear us; and, of thy almighty goodness, vouchsafe		And we most humbly beseech thee, O merciful Father, to hear us, and,

Eucharistic Prayer I	Ceremonial Directions for the Celebrant	Eucharistic Prayer II
10. to bless and sanctify, with thy Word and Holy Spirit, these thy gifts and creatures of bread and wine; that we, receiving them according to thy Son our Savior Jesus Christ's holy institution, in remembrance of his death and passion, may be partakers of his most blessed Body and Blood.	10. Extend hands over the gifts, or make a single sign of the cross over the gifts.	10. with thy Word and Holy Spirit, to bless and sanctify these gifts of bread and wine, that they may be unto us the Body and Blood of thy dearly-beloved Son Jesus Christ.
And we earnestly desire thy fatherly goodness mercifully to accept this our sacrifice of praise and thanksgiving; most humbly beseeching thee to grant that, by the merits and death of thy Son Jesus Christ, and through faith in his blood, we, and all thy whole Church, may obtain remission of our sins, and all other benefits of his passion.	Orans position.	
11. And here we offer and present unto thee, O Lord, our selves, our souls and bodies, to be a reasonable, holy, and living sacrifice unto thee; humbly beseeching thee that we, and all others who shall be partakers of this Holy Communion, may worthily receive the most precious Body and Blood of thy Son Jesus Christ,	11. Place hands on altar with palms up.	11. And we earnestly desire thy fatherly goodness to accept this our sacrifice of praise and thanksgiving, whereby we offer and present unto thee, O Lord, our selves, our souls and bodies. Grant, we beseech thee, that all who partake of this Holy Communion may worthily receive the most precious Body and Blood of thy Son Jesus Christ,
12. be filled with thy grace and heavenly benediction, and made one body with him, that he may dwell in us, and we in him.	12. Make the sign of the cross.	12. and be filled with thy grace and heavenly benediction; and also that we and all thy whole Church may be made one body with him, that he may dwell in us, and we in him; through the same Jesus Christ our Lord;

Eucharistic Prayer I

12a. And although we are unworthy, through our manifold sins, to offer unto thee any sacrifice, yet we beseech thee to accept this our bounden duty and service, not weighing our merits, but pardoning our offenses, through Jesus Christ our Lord;

13. By whom, and with whom, in the unity of the Holy Ghost, all honor and glory be unto thee, O Father Almighty, world without end. *AMEN.*

14.

Ceremonial Directions for the Celebrant

12a. Strike the left breast with the right hand.

13. Elevate both Bread and Wine throughout the entire Doxology and Amen. The deacon or other assisting minister may elevate the chalice while the celebrant elevates the Bread. Replace the gifts on the altar.

14. Make a solemn bow or genuflection. (A period of silence may follow.)

Eucharistic Prayer II

13. By whom, and with whom, and in whom, in the unity of the Holy Ghost all honor and glory be unto thee, O Father Almighty, world without end. *AMEN.*

14.

Eucharistic Prayer B (BCP, 368-369)

Then the Celebrant continues

We give thanks to you, O God, for the goodness and love which you have made known to us in creation; in the calling of Israel to be your people; in your Word spoken through the prophets; and above all in the Word made flesh, Jesus, your Son. For in these last days you sent him to be incarnate from the Virgin Mary, to be the Savior and Redeemer of the world. In him, you have delivered us from evil, and made us worthy to stand before you. In him, you have brought us out of error into truth, out of sin into righteousness, out of death into life.

At the following words concerning the bread, the Celebrant is to hold it, or lay a hand upon it; and at the words concerning the cup, to hold or place a hand upon the cup and any other vessel containing wine to be consecrated.

On the night before he died for us, our Lord Jesus Christ

1. took bread;

2. and when he had given thanks to you, he broke it,

3. and gave it to his disciples, and said, "Take, eat: This is my Body, which is given for you. Do this for the remembrance of me."

4.

Orans position.

1. Take host or lay hand upon bread.

2. (Raise the right hand in a gesture of thanksgiving.)

3. Show the bread to the people (if celebrating facing the people).

4. (Optional) Elevate host or bread, replace bread on paten, genuflect or make a solemn bow.
   (A period of silence may follow.)

Eucharistic Prayer A (BCP, 362-363)

Then the Celebrant continues

Holy and gracious Father: In your infinite love you made us for yourself; and, when we had fallen into sin and become subject to evil and death, you, in your mercy, sent Jesus Christ, your only and eternal Son, to share our human nature, to live and die as one of us, to reconcile us to you, the God and Father of all.

He stretched out his arms upon the cross, and offered himself, in obedience to your will, a perfect sacrifice for the whole world.

At the following words concerning the bread, the Celebrant is to hold it, or lay a hand upon it; and at the words concerning the cup, to hold or place a hand upon the cup and any other vessel containing wine to be consecrated.

On the night he was handed over to suffering and death our Lord Jesus Christ

1. took bread;

2. and when he had given thanks to you, he broke it,

3. and gave it to his disciples, and said, "Take, eat: This is my Body, which is given for you. Do this for the remembrance of me."

4.

Eucharistic Prayer A

5. After supper he took the cup of wine;

6. and when he had given thanks,

7. he gave it to them, and said, "Drink this, all of you: This is my Blood of the new Covenant, which is shed for you and for many for the forgiveness of sins. Whenever you drink it, do this for the remembrance of me."

8.

8a. Therefore we proclaim the mystery of faith:

Celebrant and People
Christ has died.
Christ is risen.
Christ will come again.

The Celebrant continues

9. We celebrate the memorial of our redemption, O Father, in this sacrifice of praise and thanksgiving. Recalling his death, resurrection, and ascension, we offer you these gifts.

Ceremonial Directions for the Celebrant

5. Take the chalice and lay a hand on other vessel to be consecrated.

6. (Raise the right hand in a gesture of thanksgiving.)

7. Show the chalice to the people (if celebrating facing the people).

8. (Optional) Elevate the chalice, replace the chalice on the altar, genuflect or make a solemn bow. (A period of silence may follow.)

8a. (Optional) Elevate paten and chalice through the acclamation, or resume orans position.

9. Point to the bread and wine.

Eucharistic Prayer B

5. After supper he took the cup of wine;

6. and when he had given thanks,

7. he gave it to them and said, "Drink this, all of you: This is my Blood of the new Covenant, which is shed for you and for many for the forgiveness of sins. Whenever you drink it, do this for the remembrance of me."

8.

8a. Therefore, according to his command, O Father,

Celebrant and People
We remember his death,
We proclaim his resurrection,
We await his coming in glory.

The Celebrant continues

9. And we offer our sacrifice of praise and thanksgiving to you, O Lord of all; presenting to you, from your creation, this bread and this wine.

Eucharistic Prayer A

10. Sanctify them by your Holy Spirit to be for your people the Body and Blood of your Son, the holy food and drink of new and unending life in him.

11. Sanctify us also that we may faithfully receive this holy Sacrament, and serve you in unity, constancy, and peace; and at the last day bring us with all your saints into the joy of your eternal kingdom.

12. All this we ask through your Son Jesus Christ. By him, and with him, and in him, in the unity of the Holy Spirit all honor and glory is yours, Almighty Father, now and for ever. *AMEN.*

13.

Ceremonial Directions for the Celebrant

10. Extend hands over the gifts, or make a single sign of the cross over the gifts.

11. Make the sign of the cross.

12. Elevate both Bread and Wine throughout the entire Doxology and Amen. The deacon or other assisting minister may elevate the chalice while the celebrant elevates the Bread. Replace the gifts on the altar.

13. Make a solemn bow or genuflection. (A period of silence may follow.)

Eucharistic Prayer B

10. We pray you, gracious God, to send your Holy Spirit upon these gifts that they may be the Sacrament of the Body of Christ and his Blood of the new Covenant.

11. Unite us to your Son in his sacrifice, that we may be acceptable through him, being sanctified by the Holy Spirit. In the fullness of time, put all things in subjection under your Christ, and bring us to that heavenly country where, with [and] all your saints, we may enter the everlasting heritage of your sons and daughters; through Jesus Christ our Lord, the firstborn of all creation, the head of the Church, and the author of our salvation.

12. By him, and with him, and in him, in the unity of the Holy Spirit all honor and glory is yours, Almighty Father, now and for ever. *AMEN.*

13.

The Great Thanksgiving

Eucharistic Prayer C   (BCP, 369-372)

In this prayer, the lines in italics are spoken by the People.
The Celebrant, whether bishop or priest, faces them and sings or says

The Lord be with you.
And also with you.

Lift up your hearts.
We lift them to the Lord.

Let us give thanks to the Lord our God.
It is right to give him thanks and praise.

Then, facing the Holy Table, the Celebrant proceeds

God of all power, Ruler of the Universe, you are worthy of glory and praise.
Glory to you for ever and ever.

At your command all things came to be: the vast expanse of interstellar space, galaxies, suns, the planets in their courses, and this fragile earth, our island home.
By your will they were created and have their being.

From the primal elements you brought forth the human race, and blessed us with memory, reason, and skill. You made us the rulers of creation. But we turned against you, and betrayed your trust; and we turned against one another.
Have mercy, Lord, for we are sinners in your sight.

Again and again, you called us to return. Through prophets and sages you revealed your righteous Law. And in the fullness of time you sent your only Son, born of a woman, to fulfill your Law, to open for us the way of freedom and peace.
By his blood, he reconciled us.
By his wounds, we are healed.

And therefore we praise you, joining with the heavenly chorus, with prophets, apostles, and martyrs, and with all those in every generation who have looked to you in hope, to proclaim with them your glory, in their unending hymn:

Ceremonial Directions for the Celebrant

(see page 54)
(see *HymAccEd,* S 369-370)

(*Note:* A Proper Preface is not used with this Eucharistic Prayer)

Orans position.

Eucharistic Prayer C

Celebrant and People

Holy, holy, holy Lord, God of power and might,
heaven and earth are full of your glory.
  Hosanna in the highest.
Blessed is he who comes in the name of the Lord.
  Hosanna in the highest.

The Celebrant continues

1. And so, Father, we who have been redeemed by him,
   and made a new people by water and the Spirit, now
   bring before you these gifts.

2. Sanctify them by your Holy Spirit to be the Body and
   Blood of Jesus Christ our Lord.

*At the following words concerning the bread, the Celebrant is to hold it, or lay
a hand upon it; and at the words concerning the cup, to hold or place a hand
upon the cup and any other vessel containing wine to be consecrated.*

On the night he was betrayed he

3. took bread,

4. said the blessing, broke the bread,

5. and gave it to his friends, and said,
   "Take, eat: This is my Body, which is given for you. Do
   this for the remembrance of me.

6.

7. After supper, he took the cup of wine,

8. gave thanks, and said,

Ceremonial Directions for the Celebrant

(see page 54)

1. Point to the bread and wine.

2. Extend hands over the gifts, or make a single sign of the cross over the gifts.

3. Take host or lay hand upon bread.

4. (Raise the right hand in a gesture of thanksgiving.)

5. Show the bread to the people (if celebrating facing the people).

6. (Optional) Elevate host or bread, replace bread on paten, genuflect or make a solemn bow.

7. Take the chalice and lay a hand on other vessels to be consecrated.

8. (Raise the right hand in a gesture of thanksgiving.)

8a. "Drink this, all of you: This is my Blood of the new Covenant, which is shed for you and for many for the forgiveness of sins. Whenever you drink it, do this for the remembrance of me."

9.

10. Remembering now his work of redemption, and offering to you this sacrifice of thanksgiving,
We celebrate his death and resurrection, as we await the day of his coming.

11. Lord God of our Fathers; God of Abraham, Isaac, and Jacob; God and Father of our Lord Jesus Christ: Open our eyes to see your hand at work in the world about us. Deliver us from the presumption of coming to this Table for solace only, and not for strength; for pardon only, and not for renewal.

12. Let the grace of this Holy Communion make us one body, one spirit in Christ, that we may worthily serve the world in his name.
Risen Lord, be known to us in the breaking of the Bread.

13. Accept these prayers and praises, Father, through Jesus Christ our great High Priest, to whom, with you and the Holy Spirit, your Church gives honor, glory, and worship, from generation to generation. *AMEN.*

Ceremonial Directions for the Celebrant

8a. Show the chalice to the people (if celebrating facing the people).

9. (Optional) Elevate the chalice, replace the chalice on the altar, genuflect or make a solemn bow. (A period of silence may follow.)

10. (Optional) Elevate paten and chalice through the acclamation or resume orans position.

Orans position.

11. Make the sign of the cross.

12. Elevate both Bread and Wine throughout the entire Doxology and Amen. The deacon or other assisting minister may elevate the chalice while the celebrant elevates the Bread. Replace the gifts on the altar.

13. Make a solemn bow or genuflect.
(A period of silence may follow.)

The Great Thanksgiving

Eucharistic Prayer D   (BCP: 372-375)

The people remain standing. The Celebrant, whether bishop or priest, faces them and sings or says

        The Lord be with you.
People   And also with you.
Celebrant Lift up your hearts.
People   We lift them to the Lord.
Celebrant Let us give thanks to the Lord our God.
People   It is right to give him thanks and praise.

Then, facing the Holy Table, the Celebrant proceeds

It is truly right to glorify you, Father, and to give you thanks; for you alone are God, living and true, dwelling in light inaccessible from before time and for ever.

Fountain of life and source of all goodness, you made all things and fill them with your blessing; you created them to rejoice in the splendor of your radiance.

Countless throngs of angels stand before you to serve you night and day; and, beholding the glory of your presence, they offer you unceasing praise. Joining with them, and giving voice to every creature under heaven, we acclaim you, and glorify your Name, as we sing (say),

Celebrant and People

Holy, holy, holy Lord, God of power and might,
heaven and earth are full of your glory.
    Hosanna in the highest.
Blessed is he who comes in the name of the Lord.
    Hosanna in the highest.

The people stand or kneel.

Then the Celebrant continues

Ceremonial Directions for the Celebrant

(see page 54)

Orans position.

(*Note:* A Proper Preface is not used with this Eucharistic Prayer.)

Eucharistic Prayer D

We acclaim you, holy Lord, glorious in power. Your mighty works reveal your wisdom and love. You formed us in your own image, giving the whole world into our care, so that, in obedience to you, our Creator, we might rule and serve all your creatures. When our disobedience took us far from you, you did not abandon us to the power of death. In your mercy you came to our help, so that in seeking you we might find you. Again and again you called us into covenant with you, and through the prophets you taught us to hope for salvation.

Father, you loved the world so much that in the fullness of time you sent your only Son to be our Savior. Incarnate by the Holy Spirit, born of the Virgin Mary, he lived as one of us, yet without sin. To the poor he proclaimed the good news of salvation; to prisoners, freedom; to the sorrowful, joy. To fulfill your purpose he gave himself up to death; and, rising from the grave, destroyed death, and made the whole creation new.

And, that we might live no longer for ourselves, but for him who died and rose for us, he sent the Holy Spirit, his own first gift for those who believe, to complete his work in the world, and to bring to fulfillment the sanctification of all.

At the following words concerning the bread, the Celebrant is to hold it, or lay a hand upon it; and at the words concerning the cup, to hold or place a hand upon the cup and any other vessel containing wine to be consecrated.

When the hour had come for him to be glorified by you, his heavenly Father, having loved his own who were in the world, he loved them to the end;

at supper with them

1. he took bread,

2. and when he had given thanks to you, he broke it,

Ceremonial Directions for the Celebrant

Orans position.

1. Take host or lay hand upon bread.
2. (Raise the right hand in a gesture of thanksgiving.)

Eucharistic Prayer D

3. and gave it to his disciples, and said,
"Take, eat: This is my Body which is given for you. Do this in remembrance of me."

4.

5. After supper he took the cup of wine;

6. and when he had given thanks,

7. he gave it to them, and said,
"Drink this, all of you: This is my Blood of the new Covenant, which is shed for you and for many for the forgiveness of sins. Whenever you drink it, do this for the remembrance of me."

8.

9. Father, we now celebrate this memorial of our redemption. Recalling Christ's death and his descent among the dead, proclaiming his resurrection and ascension to your right hand, awaiting his coming in glory;

10. and offering to you, from the gifts you have given us, this bread and this cup, we praise you and we bless you.

Celebrant and People

We praise you, we bless you,
we give thanks to you,
and we pray to you, Lord our God.

11.

The Celebrant continues

Lord, we pray that in your goodness and mercy

Ceremonial Directions for the Celebrant

3. Show the bread to the people (if celebrating facing the people).

4. (Optional) Elevate host or bread, replace bread on paten, genuflect or make a solemn bow. (A period of silence may follow.)

5. Take the chalice and lay a hand on other vessels to be consecrated.

6. (Raise the right hand in a gesture of thanksgiving.)

7. Show the chalice to the people (if celebrating facing the people).

8. (Optional) Elevate the chalice, replace the chalice on the altar, genuflect or make a solemn bow. (A period of silence may follow.)

9. Orans position.

10. Raise paten and chalice throughout this and the following acclamation; or point to the bread and wine.

11. Replace paten and chalice on the altar.

Eucharistic Prayer D

12. your Holy Spirit may descend upon us,

13. and upon these gifts, sanctifying them and showing them to be holy gifts for your holy people, the bread of life and the cup of salvation, the Body and Blood of your Son Jesus Christ.

13a. Grant that all who share this bread and cup may become one body and one spirit, a living sacrifice in Christ, to the praise of your Name.

14. Remember, Lord, your one holy catholic and apostolic Church, redeemed by the blood of your Christ. Reveal its unity, guard its faith, and preserve it in peace.

14a. [Remember (*NN.* and) all who minister in your Church.] [Remember all your people, and those who seek your truth.]
[Remember _____ .]
[Remember all who have died in the peace of Christ, and those whose faith is known to you alone; bring them into the place of eternal joy and light.]
And grant that we may find our inheritance with [the Blessed Virgin Mary, with patriarchs, prophets, apostles, and martyrs, (with _____) and] all the saints who have found favor with you in ages past. We praise you in union with them and give you glory through your Son Jesus Christ our Lord.

15. Through Christ, and with Christ, and in Christ, all honor and glory are yours, Almighty God and Father, in the unity of the Holy Spirit, for ever and ever. *AMEN.*

16.

Ceremonial Directions for the Celebrant

12. Make the sign of the cross.

13. Extend hands over gifts, or make a single sign of the cross over the gifts.

13a. (Optional) Make the sign of the cross.

14. Join hands at breast.

14a. A deacon or other assisting minister may sing or say commemorations.

Note: These commemorations are intended for optional use. They are all appropriately used if the Prayers of the People have been omitted (i.e., at a Baptism, Confirmation, Ash Wednesday, etc.). One or more of the commemorations may be used to heighten a particular liturgy (i.e., Ordination, Burial of the Dead, etc.).

15. Elevate both Bread and Wine throughout the entire Doxology and Amen. The deacon or other assisting minister may elevate the chalice while the celebrant elevates the Bread. Replace the gifts on the altar.

16. Make a solemn bow or genuflection.
(A period of silence may follow.)

The Lord's Prayer

After the Doxology and the Great Amen the celebrant sings or says the introduction to the Lord's Prayer *(AB, 34, 40, 170, 174, 180, 190)* and continues with the Our Father; hands may be either extended or folded. Music for chanting the Lord's Prayer is found in *The Hymnal 1982 (Hymnal, S 148-150)* or in other settings.

The Breaking of the Bread

At the conclusion of the Lord's Prayer a solemn bow by the celebrant is appropriate. There should be a marked period of silence and then the Bread is broken in silence.

1. If a large host is used, it is held high and broken in two and then broken into smaller pieces on the paten.
2. If a loaf is used it is broken on the paten.
3. The Fraction Anthem *(Confractoria)* is then either sung or said.
    a. "Christ our Passover" is sung or said by the celebrant (or Cantor) with the people responding (see *AB, 386; Hymnal, S 151-154).*
    or b. "Christ our Passover" is sung throughout by all or by the choir (see *Hymnal, S 152-156).*
    or c. Another Fraction Anthem is sung or said *(see BOS, 17-21; Hymnal, S 157-172; HymAccEd, S 373-374).*
    d. In some places both "Christ our Passover" and Agnus Dei are used regularly.
4. During the singing or saying of the anthem, the remainder of the Bread is broken or placed on the paten. If a second chalice is to be used, it is placed on the corporal and the consecrated Wine from the flagon or cruet poured into it.
5. If the Reserved Sacrament is to be used, it is placed on the corporal at this point.
6. If more than one anthem is used at the fraction (i.e. "Christ our Passover" and Agnus Dei) the Agnus Dei *(BCP, 337 or 407)* may be sung after the invitation.

Administration of Communion

1. After the anthem(s) are concluded the Prayer of Humble Access may be said *(BCP, 337)*. The celebrant and assisting ministers bow for this prayer.
2. The chalice and paten are elevated (deacon or assisting minister may hold the cup) while the celebrant facing the people says or sings the invitation:

   "The Gifts of God . . ." *(BCP, 338 or 363-364; for music, AB, 387)*

Elevation at the Invitation

3. The celebrant and assisting ministers receive the Sacrament after the invitation is said.
4. After the invitation, the celebrant may genuflect or make a solemn bow before receiving the Sacrament.
5. *While the people are coming forward to receive Communion, the celebrant receives the Sacrament in both kinds. The bishops, priests and deacons at the Holy Table then communicate, and after them the people (BCP, 407).*
6. The words for administration *(BCP, 338 or 365)*.
7. During the ministration of Communion, hymns, psalms or anthems may be sung.

Concerning the Administration of Holy Communion

The shorter form of administration sentence directed to each communicant is desirable. This provides an opportunity for the person receiving the consecrated Bread and the Wine to respond with "Amen," which is an important affirmation of faith.

When the celebrant is assisted by a deacon or another priest, it is customary for the celebrant to administer the consecrated Bread and the assistant the Chalice. When several deacons or priests are present, some may administer the Bread and others the Wine. In the absence of sufficient deacons and priests, lay persons licensed by the bishop according to the canon may administer the Chalice (BCP, 408).

Ablutions

The cleansing of the vessels may be done in a number of ways. Whichever method is used, it should be done reverently, simply and quickly. Ablutions are not an edifying part of liturgy and little purpose is served by doing this facing the people.

The celebrant returns to the altar and places the paten or ciborium on the corporal. The chalice(s) are placed on the corporal. The remaining Bread is either consumed or placed in the tabernacle or aumbry; the Wine remaining in the chalices is reverently consumed by the celebrant and/or assisting ministers. If there is any consecrated Wine left in the cruet or flagon it is either poured into the chalice and consumed or placed in the tabernacle or aumbry.

The deacon (or celebrant) then cleanses the vessels.

(The deacon or other minister may face the celebrant across the altar.)

1. Wine may first be poured into the chalice(s) and then consumed; then wine and water poured into the chalices and consumed; the chalices are then returned to the credence (veiled): the corporal is folded (and put back into the burse).
2. The celebrant may place the thumb and index finger of each hand over the chalice, and the wine and water are poured over them. If another minister is doing the ablutions, a server may wash the celebrant's fingers as at the lavabo.

Note: If the ablutions are done at the altar, the priest or assisting minister faces the altar with back to the people.

3. The vessels may be taken to the credence or chapel altar where the remaining Elements are reverently consumed and the vessels cleansed as above.
4. Water only may be used in the cleansing of the vessels.
5. If there is no deacon or assisting priest(s), the ablutions are done by the celebrant.
6. When all of the cleansing is completed, the vessels are returned to the credence (or left on the chapel altar if ablutions are done there) and the celebrant moves to the center of the altar for the postcommunion prayer.

Postcommunion Prayer

The prayer given for Rite I *(BCP, 339),* Rite II *(BCP, 365-366)* and various occasions (see page 74) should not in any way be confused with The Great Thanksgiving. Prefacing the prayer with "Let us give thanks . . ." is misleading; likewise, listing this prayer in a service program as "The Thanksgiving" only assists in leading people to confusion. "Let us pray" (followed by a brief period of silence) and the postcommunion prayer is what is given in the *BCP*. The celebrant leads the people in this prayer with hands extended (orans position).

Note: There are four proper postcommunion prayers appointed for various occasions:

at marriages	*(BCP, 432; AB, 45 or 195)*
for the sick	*(BCP, 457; AB, 46 or 196)*
for the departed	*(BCP, 482 or 498; AB, 46 or 196)*
at ordinations, and at the induc- tions of priests and deacons	*(BCP, 535; AB, 46 or 196)*

Blessing and Dismissal

The celebrant faces the people and gives the blessing (in Rite I) or *may* give a blessing (in Rite II) *(BCP, 339 or 366; for music see AB, 387-389; Hymnal, S 173)*. The deacon (or celebrant) then dismisses the people with one of the dismissals provided *(BCP, 339-340 or 366; for music see AB, 390; Hymnal, S 174)*. During the Fifty Days of Easter alleluias are added to the dismissal *(AB, 390-391; Hymnal, S 175-176)*.

Concerning Hymns at the Conclusion of the Eucharist

Ideally, the liturgy concludes with the dismissal.

1. A hymn may be sung at the end of Communion or after the post-communion prayer before the blessing; or after the blessing and before the dismissal. The celebrant and ministers reverence the altar and return to the sacristy.
2. After the retiring procession, a prayer may be said in the sacristy by the celebrant and ministers (see page 273), but this should not involve the congregation. The dismissal is the conclusion of the liturgy; there is no need to add anything else.

Concerning Intinction

Opportunity is always to be given to every communicant to receive the consecrated Bread and Wine separately. The Sacrament may be received in both kinds simultaneously, in a manner approved by the bishop (BCP, 407-408).

Concerning the Consecration of additional Elements

If the consecrated Bread or Wine does not suffice for the number of communicants, the celebrant is to return to the Holy Table, and consecrate more of either or both, by saying

Hear us, O heavenly Father, and with thy (your) Word and Holy Spirit bless and sanctify this bread (wine) that it, also, may be the Sacrament of the precious Body (Blood) of thy (your) Son Jesus Christ our Lord, who took bread (the cup) and said, "This is my Body (Blood)." Amen. (BCP, 408; also, AB, 37, 43 or 193).

Note: The above formula for the Consecration of the Elements is to be used only in the context of a celebration of the Holy Eucharist, not separately.

Concerning Announcements

Necessary announcements may be made before the service, after the Creed, before the Offertory, or at the end of the service, as convenient (BCP, 407).

Concerning Reservation of the Sacrament

If any of the consecrated Bread or Wine remain, apart from any which may be required for the Communion of the sick, or of others who for weighty cause could not be present at the celebration, or for the administration of Communion by a deacon to a congregation when no priest is available . . . (BCP, 408-409).

See also:

1. Maundy Thursday (*BCP, 275;* also pages 188-189).
2. Good Friday (*BCP, 282;* also page 197).
3. Communion under Special Circumstances (*BCP, 396;* also page 76).
4. Ministration to the Sick (*BCP, 457;* also pages 233-235).

The Blessed Sacrament is reserved:

1. in a tabernacle affixed to the altar.
2. in an aumbry either in the wall or on a shelf (on the gospel side of the sanctuary).
3. in a chapel or other place of devotion.
4. A white candle in a clear glass, or an oil lamp, is kept burning before the Reserved Sacrament at all times.
5. The tabernacle or aumbry is fixed with a door and lock; the inside (traditionally lined in cedar) is covered completely with cloth or at least a linen corporal is laid on the bottom; the vessels containing the consecrated Elements are covered with a white cloth; two candles may flank an aumbry and are lighted during celebrations of the Holy Eucharist and other devotions or offices; the Sacrament may be reserved in one or both kinds. Reserved Elements should be replaced regularly to prevent spoilage.

The place of reservation should be one of devotion (i.e., a drawer or shelf in the sacristy or the desk drawer of the priest are not appropriate places).

Note: Nothing else should be kept in the tabernacle or aumbry where the Sacrament is reserved, but a small container of water and a cloth may be kept on the shelf for cleansing one's fingers. It is preferable to provide a separate aumbry for the holy oils.

Communion under Special Circumstances

This form *(BCP, 396-399)* is intended for pastoral situations in which a person or several members of a congregation cannot be present for a regular celebration of the Holy Eucharist. It applies also to the Ministration to the Sick and Communion from the Reserved Sacrament (see page 235).

The officiant may be a priest or deacon.

Scripture	A passage appropriate to the day or one of those provided *(BCP, 396-397)*.
Homily	*After the Reading, the celebrant may comment on it briefly (BCP, 397).*
The Prayers	*Suitable prayers may be offered, concluding with [that given] or some other collect (BCP, 397).*
Confession of Sin	Any of the forms in the *BCP* are used or that given *(BCP, 397-398)*. A deacon uses the form for the absolution as prescribed (see *BCP, 398*). A priest pronounces the absolution.
The Peace	
The Lord's Prayer	
The Invitation	"The Gifts of God . . ." *(BCP, 399)*.
Communion from the Reserved Sacrament	The sentence of administration as given *(BCP, 399)*.
Postcommunion Prayer	That given *(BCP, 399)* or one of the usual prayers *(BCP, 339 or 365-366)*.
Blessing and/or Dismissal	*(BCP, 399)*.

An Order for Celebrating the Holy Eucharist

1. This form *(BCP, 400-405)* may be used, but not as the principal Sunday or weekly celebration of the Holy Eucharist.
2. Although seen by many as a means to add informality in worship, careful preparation is necessary lest chaos ensue.
3. The structure of the service is outlined carefully *(BCP, 400-401)*. This form works best with small groups of people who are able to interrelate with ease. No one should feel uncomfortable or made to be an observer. It would be far better to celebrate a Rite I or Rite II Eucharist than to impair the community spirit of the Celebration and the opportunity for all to participate. The celebrant must be sensitive to this, and the planning and make-up of a "Rite III" Eucharist must ensure that all things are done decently and in order.
4. The Proclamation of the Word of God must have a cohesiveness.
   a. The lessons may be those appointed in the lectionary or *Lesser Feasts and Fasts*.
   b. The lessons may be chosen from other portions of Scripture (or non-Scriptural Christian literature), but a reading from the Gospels must always be included.
   c. Music, silence or dance must be carefully planned and chosen to fit the situation.
   d. The Prayers of the People follow the outline given *(BCP, 383)*. They may either utilize one of the authorized forms (I through VI) or be in free form but still following the general outline.
5. The preparation of the gifts and the setting of the table should be done in a dignified manner.
6. The Great Thanksgiving is the high point of the liturgy.
7. The Eucharistic Prayer must be taken either from Rite One (I or II), Rite Two (A, B, C, or D), or one of the two forms given with the instructions *(BCP, 402-405)*. These are the only alternatives permitted in *The Book of Common Prayer*, and it is presumed that these directions will be followed faithfully.
8. At the Breaking of the Bread, one of the anthems provided in Rite I or Rite II may be used or some other anthem *(BOS, 17-21)*.
9. Communion is administered and received in a reverent manner. Care regarding crumbs should be observed.
10. The vessels are cleansed in a dignified manner after the remaining elements have been consumed.
11. A postcommunion prayer is appropriate or simply a period of silent thanksgiving.
12. A (blessing and) dismissal concludes the Eucharist, or "Let us bless the Lord" with the response "Thanks be to God" if the people are to remain for a common meal or Agapé.

13. *An Order for Celebrating the Holy Eucharist* is not a license to do whatever comes into your head. Nor is such a celebration meant to be an informal picnic! The Eucharist is to be celebrated with dignity and devotion, allowing as much room as the celebrant deems appropriate for spontaneity.

Concerning Concelebration

It is appropriate that the other priests present stand with the celebrant at the Altar, and join in the consecration of the gifts, in breaking the Bread, and in distributing Communion (BCP, 322 or 354). When several priests are present for the celebration of the Eucharist, it is fitting that they concelebrate. If a bishop is present, the bishop is always the principal celebrant.

Concelebration is especially appropriate on Maundy Thursday and at the Great Vigil of Easter. Also on various special occasions, either for the parish or in the life of a priest, concelebration is fitting.

Unless the parish possesses a set of matching chasubles, it is better that only the principal celebrant be vested in a chasuble and the concelebrants in alb and stole (of the same color as the vestments of the principal celebrant). If no deacon is present, the concelebrants may perform the duties that a deacon would normally do; however, if a deacon is present, the deacon should perform those acts of the Eucharist assigned to this order.

The concelebrants sit together for the Liturgy of the Word, with the principal celebrant sitting in the center. Care must be taken that movement and space are used in such a way as not to give the impression from the congregation of a "crowd" scene. When standing at the altar, the principal celebrant stands in the center and the concelebrants on either side.

Although in some places, the Eucharistic Prayer is broken up by giving a paragraph to each of the concelebrants, this has proven to be very distracting and confusing to the people. "Silent concelebration" is more appropriate. The concelebrants should not say anything with the principal celebrant, unless it is part of the liturgy that is sung or said by the people.

1. During the Great Thanksgiving, the normal position for the hands of the concelebrants is folded. A number of persons all using the orans position looks bad. The principal celebrant is the only one who uses the orans position and performs other manual acts (see pages 52-53).

2. At the Words of Institution, the concelebrants extend their right hands over the bread and likewise the cup. The concelebrants make the solemn bow or genuflection with the principal celebrant.

Words of Institution: Concelebration

3. At the epiclesis, the concelebrants again extend their right hands over the Elements.
4. At the elevation during the great Doxology, one of the concelebrants may elevate the chalice while the principal celebrant elevates the paten.
5. The concelebrants assist the principal celebrant in breaking the Bread and in pouring the Wine from the cruets or flagons into additional chalices.
6. It is appropriate for the concelebrants to elevate the Elements they will be administering during the invitation to Communion, which is said by the principal celebrant.
7. It is not appropriate for licensed lay persons to administer the chalice when enough ordained persons are either concelebrating or assisting in the sanctuary.
8. After the administration of Communion, the concelebrants may assist with the ablutions.
9. The principal celebrant alone gives the blessing, and if no deacon is present one of the concelebrants says the dismissal.

Concerning the Use of Incense at the Eucharist

Incense is traditionally used in the Eucharistic Liturgy:

1. at the entrance or during the song of praise.
2. at the Gospel.
3. at the Offertory.
4. at the Great Thanksgiving.

1. At the entrance the thurifer precedes the celebrant to the altar. The altar is reverenced and the celebrant fills the thurible (and blesses the incense). The altar may be censed immediately.

   or

   During the Gloria or other song of praise it is appropriate for the celebrant to cense the altar (see pages 82-83) if not censed at the entrance.

2. During the alleluia verse or hymn preceding the Gospel, incense is brought to the celebrant, who fills the thurible (and blesses the incense). The thurifer then precedes the deacon or other reader to the place of the proclamation of the Gospel. The Gospel Book may be censed by the reader after the announcement before the reading commences.

3. At the Offertory incense is brought to the celebrant after the gifts have been presented and prepared (and offered)—but before the lavabo. The celebrant fills the thurible (blesses incense), and then censes the gifts (see pages 84-85) and the altar. The thurifer (or deacon or assisting priest) may then cense the celebrant and the other ministers and cense the congregation.

Note on the Censing of the Ministers and People:

After the altar is censed, either at the Offertory in the Eucharist, or during some other Office, the ministers and people may be censed. The celebrant or officiant gives the thurible to the deacon (or thurifer); this person censes the celebrant and others in the sanctuary and then censes the people. Although in some places it is customary to cense each person individually, a corporate censing is less distracting. The person with the thurible faces those in the sanctuary, bows, and with a single swing censes those in the center, then those to the left, then those to the right. The person then turns to the people, bows, and censes them, again with one swing to the center, then to the left, and finally to the right.

4. At the Great Thanksgiving:
   a. the thurifer may gently swing the thurible during the Sanctus.
   b. the Consecrated Elements may be censed:
      1. at the elevation(s) following the Words of Institution.
      2. at the elevation during the Doxology at the conclusion of the
      Great Thanksgiving and during the Great Amen.

Note: If a bishop is present and is not the celebrant, it is traditional that the
thurifer bring the thurible to the bishop whenever the thurible is filled (and
incense blessed). This applies at the Eucharist or any other office or liturgy.

Filling the Thurible

Blessing the Incense

The Censing of the Altar

A. A Freestanding Altar

At the entrance of the Eucharist or during one of the canticles at the Office or at other times apart from the Offertory of the Eucharist (for Offertory, see page 84).

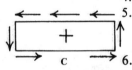
Censing Freestanding Altar

1. The thurifer brings incense and thurible to the celebrant.
2. The celebrant fills the thurible (and blesses incense).
3. The celebrant goes to the center of the altar facing the cross and with back to the people.
4. The celebrant reverences the altar with a solemn bow.
5. The celebrant censes the altar cross:
   a. with a simple single swing of the thurible,
   b. or with three swings of the thurible.
6. The celebrant bows and then walks slowly to the right. The thurible is swung gently as the celebrant walks, censing both the top and sides of the altar.
7. The celebrant keeps turning left, circling the altar until the entire altar has been censed.
8. The celebrant then reverences the altar again with a solemn bow and returns the thurible to the thurifer.

Note: For the sake of simplicity, everyone else in the sanctuary stays in place. There is no need to hold the celebrant's cope or chasuble or to follow the celebrant around the altar.

B. An Altar Fixed to the "East" Wall

At the entrance of the Eucharist or during one of the canticles at the Office or at other times including the Offertory of the Eucharist.

1. The thurifer brings incense and thurible to the celebrant.
2. The celebrant fills the thurible (and blesses incense).
3. If at the Offertory, the gifts are censed first (see page 84).
4. The celebrant reverences the altar with a solemn bow.
5. The celebrant censes the altar cross:
   a. with a simple single swing of the thurible,
   b. or with three swings of the thurible.
6. The celebrant bows and then walks to the right, censing the top of the altar.
7. The celebrant then returns to the center, censing the front of the altar.
8. At center, the celebrant bows again.
9. The celebrant then walks to the left, censing the top of the altar.
10. The celebrant then returns to the center, censing the front of the altar.
11. At center the celebrant bows again.
12. The celebrant returns the thurible to the thurifer.

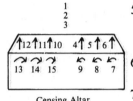

Censing Altar
Affixed to Wall

Note: The motions of censing should be dignified. The walk should be slow, the bows full and reverent. There is no prescribed way of censing the altar, no "magical" number of swings. Slow, constant motion is always in order. Let simplicity prevail, at the same time making sure that what you are doing is clear to the congregation.

The Censing of the Gifts at the Offertory

After the gifts have been presented and offered, the thurifer comes to the celebrant with incense and thurible. The celebrant fills the thurible (and blesses the incense). Then the celebrant censes the gifts.

A. Simple Censing of the Gifts

A slow, gentle swinging of the thurible at the gifts on the altar. Three swings, one to the center, one to the left and one to the right might be used, or simply a circle over the gifts.

B. The Traditional Censing of the Gifts

Caution must be observed here, especially if the celebrant is facing the people. This action must not look fussy or "magical," but there is a pattern that may be observed.

1. The celebrant makes three signs of the cross over the gifts with the thurible in the following way:

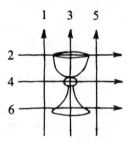

Sign of Cross over Gifts

2. The celebrant then makes two circles counterclockwise and one circle clockwise:

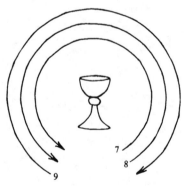

Circles over Gifts

The celebrant then continues with the censing of the altar.

A. At a freestanding altar:

1. The celebrant walks slowly to the right, swinging the thurible gently and censing both the top and sides of the altar.
2. The celebrant keeps turning left, circling the altar until the entire altar has been censed, but stopping in front of the altar at the center, bowing to the cross, and then censing the altar cross. This may be done,
   a. with a simple swing of the thurible,
   b. or with three swings of the thurible.
3. Upon returning to the center behind the altar, the celebrant gives the thurible back to the thurifer.
4. The deacon (or thurifer) may cense the ministers and the people, see page 80.

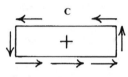

Censing Freestanding Altar

B. At an altar fixed to the wall, the celebrant follows the procedure as outlined on page 83, B.4-12.

After the altar is censed, the deacon (or thurifer) may cense the ministers and the people, see page 80.

Note: See appendix, page 270, for suggested forms for blessing incense.

Use of Incense in Other Ways

The use of incense to signify a blessing or a setting apart of things (palms on Palm Sunday, ashes on Ash Wednesday, Gospel Book at the Eucharist, etc.) has a long tradition. Again, simplicity should govern and a simple gesture of three swings—one to the center, one to the left and one to the right over or at the objects helps to signify this setting apart.

At the Daily Offices—See Solemn Evensong, pages 142-144.

At An Order of Worship for the Evening—See pages 132-135.

During Processions:

The celebrant fills the thurible (and blesses the incense) at the start of a solemn procession, and the thurifer leads the procession, swinging the thurible while walking. If a station is made, the celebrant may fill the thurible again at this point and cense the object of the station (e.g. the creche at Christmas, the font at a Baptism or on Easter). (See page 168.)

Solemn Eucharist

The Solemn Eucharist is a celebration in which the celebrant is assisted by a deacon (or assisting priest) and a lay person (subdeacon). Other assisting servers are a thurifer and two acolytes. The subdeacon may double as a crucifer, or the processional cross may be omitted, or there may be a server as crucifer.

Traditionally, the ministers are vested as follows:

Celebrant	Eucharistic vestments (or alb, cincture, stole and cope for the [procession and] Liturgy of the Word. The celebrant changes into a chasuble at the Offertory).
Deacon	Alb, cincture, stole (worn over the left shoulder, and tied or fastened under the right arm) and dalmatic. In some places the deacon follows the tradition of the Eastern Church and wears the stole over the dalmatic.
Subdeacon	A tunicle worn over alb and cincture. If the subdeacon is a cleric, a stole may be worn under the tunicle according to order.
Thurifer and Acolytes	Cassock and surplice; or amice, alb and cincture or cassock-alb.
(Crucifer)	The crucifer is vested as the acolytes or may wear a tunicle over an alb.

The Entrance

The order for the entrance procession is:

Thurifer

Acolyte (Crucifer) Acolyte

(Assisting Ministers)

Subdeacon

Deacon

(Subdeacon) Celebrant (Deacon)

The thurifer goes to the celebrant's left (facing the altar), the acolytes put their candles in the usual place, and assistant ministers, after reverencing the altar, go to their designated places. The subdeacon stands next to the thurifer (at the celebrant's immediate left), the deacon to the celebrant's immediate right, and the celebrant in the center. When all three are in place, facing the altar, the usual reverence is made.

After reverencing the altar, the thurifer brings the thurible to the celebrant for the preparation of incense (and blessing) (see page 270). Then one of the following takes place:

1. The celebrant sings or says the acclamation (for music, see *AB, 372; Hymnal, S 76-83*). (The Collect for Purity, and Summary of the Law may follow.) The Kyrie eleison may be sung. On a Sunday (except in Advent or Lent) or Feast Day the Gloria in excelsis (or other song of praise) or the Kyrie eleison and song of praise follows. The celebrant may intone the song of praise. During the song of praise the celebrant takes the thurible, which has been previously filled with incense (and blessed) and censes the altar (see pages 82-83). After the altar has been censed:

   a. the celebrant, deacon and subdeacon remain in place facing the altar for the Collect of the Day, *or*
   b. go to the sedilia for the collect (see page 35).

   or

2. Immediately after reaching the altar and filling the thurible, the celebrant censes the altar during the entrance hymn, psalm or anthem (see pages 82-83). The celebrant, deacon and subdeacon remain at the altar, or after reverencing the altar, go to the sedilia.

   or

3. If a solemn procession precedes the Eucharist (see pages 168-169), the altar may be censed either prior to the procession or after the procession, or during the song of praise.

   or

4. If the Litany is to be sung in procession preceding the Eucharist, see pages 163-164.

(If a bishop is present and is not the celebrant, see note on page 81.)

The Lessons

The reader appointed (lay person) reads or chants the lesson at the lectern or other designated place. (See *AB, 377* for instructions on chanting.) The ministers remain seated at the sedilia (deacon to the right of the celebrant, subdeacon to the left).

All remain seated for the psalm.

Traditionally, the subdeacon reads or chants the Epistle from the lectern or other designated place. (See *AB, 377* for instructions on chanting the Lesson and Epistle.) At the conclusion of the Epistle the subdeacon returns to the sedilia. (The subdeacon may go to the celebrant or bishop for a blessing after the Epistle.)

The sacred ministers stand. If the celebrant is a bishop, the bishop remains seated. The thurifer brings the thurible to be filled (and incense blessed). The deacon goes to the altar and takes the Gospel Book. (See page 37 for Gospel procession.) The thurifer leads the procession; the subdeacon walks in front of the deacon. At the place designated for the proclamation of the Gospel, the deacon first announces the Gospel and may then cense the book. The subdeacon holds the book for the deacon. Traditionally, the deacon censes the book with three swings: first to the center, then to the left, and finally, to the right. The thurible is returned to the thurifer, and the deacon chants (see *AB, 378-381*) or reads the Gospel. At the conclusion, after the deacon kisses the book the procession returns, the thurifer leading, the deacon carrying the book. The Gospel Book is returned to the altar or other designated place. The deacon and subdeacon return to the sedilia.

Note: It is traditional for the deacon to go to the celebrant (or bishop) for a blessing. The deacon receives this blessing after taking the book from the altar, and before the Gospel procession. In some places the Gospel Book is brought to the celebrant or bishop to be kissed following the reading of the Gospel.

The Sermon

The sacred ministers, except for the preacher, sit at the sedilia for the sermon.

The Creed

The sacred ministers stand at the sedilia for the singing or reciting of the Creed (if appointed for the day or occasion).

The Prayers of the People

1. Traditionally the deacon leads the prayers. This may be done:
    a. from the center, facing the altar
    b. from the center, facing the people
    c. from the lectern or other designated place

The celebrant and subdeacon remain standing at the sedilia. (Some other person may be appointed to lead the prayers.)

2. The celebrant sings or says the concluding collect.

(Concerning the Prayers of the People, see page 39-44.)
For singing the prayers and responses:
Forms I and V (see *AB, 382-385*)
Forms I, III, IV, V (see *Hymnal, S 106-109;* also page 44)
Form II (see *HymAccEd, S 362*)
Form VI (see *HymAccEd, S 363*)

Confession of Sin

The deacon faces the people for the invitation to the Confession of Sin *(BCP, 330 or 360)*. If the liturgy began with the Penitential Order or if the penitential suffrage from Forms I or V was used in the Prayers of the People, the confession is omitted. The deacon either bows or kneels for the confession. The deacon may return to the sedilia after the invitation. The celebrant (or bishop) gives the absolution (making the sign of the cross over the people). The deacon and subdeacon remain bowing or kneeling until the conclusion of the absolution.

If a sentence of Scripture *(BCP, 332)* follows the absolution, it is appropriate that the deacon read it.

The Peace

The sacred ministers either remain at the sedilia or come before the altar, bow, and turn to the people (deacon and subdeacon should face the celebrant). The celebrant, after saying (or singing, see *AB, 386; Hymnal, S 110-111)* the Peace, first greets the deacon and then the subdeacon (and others in the sanctuary). The celebrant or assisting ministers may then exchange the Peace with the people.

The Offertory

The celebrant may begin with one of the sentences *(BCP, 343-344 or 376)* or with some other sentence of Scripture.

For the ceremonies at the preparation of the gifts, see pages 47-50.

For the censing of the gifts by the celebrant, see pages 84-85.

For the censing of the ministers and the people, see page 80.

The Great Thanksgiving

The celebrant stands either at the altar or behind it, facing the people. If standing at the altar, the deacon stands to the celebrant's right, and the subdeacon to the left. All may stand at the same level, or the subdeacon may stand on a lower step. If standing behind the altar, the deacon stands to the celebrant's right and the subdeacon to the left.

For the Great Thanksgiving see pages 52-70, and for notes on incense during the Great Thanksgiving see page 81. For music see *Hymnal, S 112-147.*

The Lord's Prayer

The celebrant sings (for music see *AB 34, 40 or 169, 174, 180, 190)* or says the introduction to the Lord's Prayer, and the people join in the singing (or saying) of the Lord's Prayer (for music see *Hymnal, S 148-150)*.

The Breaking of the Bread

See page 71. (For music see *AB, 386; Hymnal, S 151-172; HymAccEd, S 373-374.*)

Facing the people the celebrant sings or says the invitation (for music see *AB, 287*).

It is appropriate for the deacon to elevate the chalice and the celebrant to elevate the Bread during the invitation.

At the ministration of Holy Communion, the celebrant administers the Bread and the deacon the Wine. If licensed, the subdeacon may administer a second chalice (see page 72).

Ablutions and Postcommunion Prayer

See pages 73-74.

The Dismissal

The celebrant (or bishop) may sing or say the blessing (for music, see *AB, 387-389; Hymnal, S 173*).

The deacon sings or says the dismissal (for music, see *AB, 390-391; Hymnal, S 174-176*).

After reverencing the altar (the three sacred ministers together, as at the entrance), the procession leaves in the same order in which it came in.

Morning or Evening Prayer as the Liturgy of the Word at the Eucharist

In places where there has been a strong tradition of Morning Prayer as the principal service, its use as the Liturgy of the Word at the Eucharist is becoming more common on "Morning Prayer Sundays." This usage is permitted *(BCP, 142)*. Also, this combination of the Office and Eucharist may be used at weekday celebrations.

The impression of two services should by all means be avoided. The balance between Word and Sacrament should not be lost in an attempt to have a "complete" service of Morning Prayer with a truncated Eucharist.

In general, the following order is both in accord with *The Book of Common Prayer* and maintains the desired balance:

Outline

(Hymn)
(Opening Sentence)
Confession of Sin and Absolution
Invitatory (Venite, Jubilate, *or* Pascha Nostrum)
Appointed Psalm(s): either that appointed in the Eucharistic Lectionary
                  for the day or from the Daily Office Lectionary
(Lesson)
(Canticle)
Lesson: preferably from the Eucharistic Lectionary
Canticle
Gospel: that appointed in the Eucharistic Lectionary for the day
Sermon: either at this point or after the prayers
Nicene or Apostles' Creed
Salutation and response
Collect of the Day (only)
The Prayers of the People *(BCP, 383 to 393)*
The Peace
Preparation and Offering of Gifts
The Great Thanksgiving
Breaking of the Bread
Conclusion of the Liturgy

Note: At the principal Sunday service, the lessons are always those appointed in the Eucharistic Lectionary for Year A, B or C, whichever is current. On other days (except Major Feasts) the lessons may be taken from the Daily Office Lectionary.

Note: The combination of Evening Prayer and Eucharist follows the same pattern.

Notes

1. The "shape" of the Office, with canticles, psalms and lessons, should be retained, *but* collect upon collect, hymn upon hymn, must be avoided. Also, the sermon should be in proportion to the entire liturgy. The service is not Morning Prayer, Sermon and Eucharist. It is a complete Liturgy of the Word and Liturgy of the Holy Communion in itself.
2. Intercessions are made in the Prayers of the People. Additional "concluding" collects are unnecessary and interfere with the Prayers of the People.
3. If the Confession of Sin is used at the beginning of the Office, it is omitted later in the service.
4. Once the Holy Communion begins, with the Offertory, the flow should continue to the end. It is undignified and irreverent to give an opportunity for people to leave after the Offertory. The Offertory is the preparation for the Eucharistic action, not the conclusion of the Daily Office. Therefore, closing hymns, collects, blessings, the grace, or anything that might give an impression of finality are to be avoided.

Ceremonial Guidelines

1. The officiant at the Office should preside from a prominent place either in the choir or chancel, or at the sedilia.
2. The officiant should not be vested in chasuble for the Office. The chasuble should be put on before the beginning of the Offertory when the altar is approached.
3. It is fitting, although not essential, that the Gospel lesson at the Office be read by a deacon, assisting priest, or celebrant.
   a. The Gospel may be read either from the lectern, or a Gospel procession may be formed (see page 37) and the Gospel proclaimed either from the midst of the people or the pulpit.
   b. The people should stand for the Gospel lesson.
4. A song of praise such as the Gloria in excelsis (except in Advent and Lent) is appropriately used as one of the canticles, preferably the one before the Gospel reading for the day.
5. A suitable hymn may be substituted for the canticle following the reading that precedes the Gospel.
6. If three readings are used, two may be taken from the Daily Office Lectionary, or all three from the Eucharistic lections appointed for the day. The Gospel is taken from the Eucharistic Lectionary for the day. However, if this is the principal celebration of the Sunday or Major Feast or Holy Day, the three readings are always taken from the appointed Eucharistic lections.
7. The most appropriate place for the sermon in this combination of Office and Eucharist is after the reading of the Gospel.

The Calendar

The Calendar of the Church Year

Introduction

The Prayer Book gives the order of precedence for the celebration of Feast Days (see *BCP, 15-18*).

1. Principal Feasts, which take precedence over any other day or observance (including Sundays).
2. Sundays, as the regular celebration of the Resurrection of our Lord Jesus Christ, and feasts and other observances that may take precedence.
3. Holy Days, which have precedence over Sundays, except *from the Last Sunday after Pentecost through the First Sunday after the Epiphany, or from the Last Sunday after the Epiphany through Trinity Sunday (BCP, 16).*
4. Days of Special Devotion: Ash Wednesday, weekdays of Lent (except the Feast of the Annunciation), and Holy Week, Good Friday and all other Fridays of the year, except for Fridays in the Christmas and Easter seasons, and any Feasts of our Lord which occur on a Friday, are observed by special acts of discipline and self-denial *(BCP, 17).*
5. Provisions for other commemorations, Ember Days, Rogation Days and Various Occasions.

During Lent, the observance of a commemoration should follow the suggested pattern (see page 155).

During the Fifty Days of Easter, the observance of a commemoration should follow the suggested pattern (see page 158).

Concerning Transferring a Feast

Feasts appointed on fixed days in the Calendar are not observed on the days of Holy Week or of Easter Week. Major Feasts falling in these weeks are transferred to the week following the Second Sunday of Easter, in the order of their occurrence.

Feasts appointed on fixed days in the Calendar do not take precedence of Ash Wednesday.

Feasts of our Lord and other Major Feasts appointed on fixed days, which fall upon or are transferred to a weekday, may be observed on any open day within the week (BCP, 17).

The Feasts of the Holy Name, the Presentation, and the Transfiguration take precedence over Sundays.

Color	Day	Collect	Lessons and Psalms			Proper Preface
			Year A	Year B	Year C	
	Advent Season					
Blue	The First Sunday of Advent	(BCP,159 or 211)	(BCP,889)	(BCP,900)	(BCP,911)	Advent
or	The Second Sunday of Advent	(BCP,159 or 211)	(BCP,889)	(BCP,900)	(BCP,911)	Advent
Violet	The Third Sunday of Advent	(BCP,160 or 212)	(BCP,889)	(BCP,900)	(BCP,911)	Advent
	The Fourth Sunday of Advent	(BCP,160 or 212)	(BCP,889)	(BCP,900)	(BCP,911)	Advent
	Christmas Season					
White	The Nativity of Our Lord Jesus Christ: Christmas Day, *December 25*	(BCP,160-161 or 212-213)	(BCP,889-890)	(BCP,900-901)	(BCP,911)	Incarnation
	The First Sunday after Christmas Day	(BCP,161 or 213)	(BCP,890)	(BCP,901)	(BCP,911)	Incarnation
	The Holy Name of Our Lord Jesus Christ, *January 1*	(BCP,162 or 213)	(BCP,890)	(BCP,901)	(BCP,912)	Incarnation
	The Second Sunday after Christmas Day	(BCP,162 or 214)	(BCP,890)	(BCP,901)	(BCP,912)	Incarnation
	Epiphany Season					
White	The Epiphany, *January 6*	(BCP,162 or 214)	(BCP,890)	(BCP,901)	(BCP,912)	Epiphany
White	The First Sunday after the Epiphany: The Baptism of Our Lord Jesus Christ	(BCP,163 or 214)	(BCP,890)	(BCP,901)	(BCP,912)	Epiphany
Green	The Second Sunday through the Eighth Sunday after the Epiphany	(BCP,163-165 or 215-217)	(BCP,890-891)	(BCP,901-902)	(BCP,912-913)	Epiphany, *or of the Lord's Day*
White	The Presentation, *February 2*	(BCP, 187 or 239)	—	(BCP, 922)	—	Epiphany

Color	Day	Collect	Lessons and Psalms			Proper Preface
			Year A	Year B	Year C	
White	The Last Sunday after the Epiphany (The Transfiguration)	(BCP,165 or 217)	(BCP,891)	(BCP,902)	(BCP,913)	Epiphany
	(The alleluias may be added to the dismissal on this Sunday (AB,390) and/or on the Monday or Tuesday before Ash Wednesday, see page 159.)					
	Lenten Season					
Lenten Array or Violet	Ash Wednesday	(Proper Liturgy, BCP,264-269) (Rite I Collect, BCP,166)				Lent (1)
	The First Sunday in Lent	(BCP,166 or 218)	(BCP,891)	(BCP,902)	(BCP,913)	Lent (1)
	The Second Sunday in Lent	(BCP,166-67 or 218)	(BCP,891)	(BCP,902)	(BCP,913)	Lent (1)
	The Third Sunday in Lent	(BCP,167 or 218)	(BCP,892)	(BCP,902)	(BCP,913)	Lent (1)
	The Fourth Sunday in Lent	(BCP,167 or 219)	(BCP,892)	(BCP,903)	(BCP,913)	Lent (2)
	The Fifth Sunday in Lent	(BCP,167 or 219)	(BCP,892)	(BCP,903)	(BCP,913)	Lent (2)
	Holy Week					
Passiontide Red	The Sunday of the Passion: Palm Sunday	(Proper Liturgy, BCP,270-273) (Rite I Collect, BCP,168)				Holy Week
	Monday in Holy Week	(BCP,168 or 220)	(BCP,892)	(BCP,903)	(BCP,914)	Holy Week
	Tuesday in Holy Week	(BCP,168 or 220)	(BCP,892)	(BCP,903)	(BCP,914)	Holy Week
	Wednesday in Holy Week	(BCP,169 or 220)	(BCP,892)	(BCP,903)	(BCP,914)	Holy Week
	Maundy Thursday	(Proper Liturgy, BCP,274-275) (Rite I Collect, BCP,169)				Holy Week
	Good Friday	(Proper Liturgy, BCP,276-282) (Rite I Collect, BCP,169)				(No Eucharist)
	Holy Saturday	(Proper Liturgy, BCP,283) (Rite I Collect, BCP,170)				(No Eucharist)
	Easter Season					
White	The Great Vigil of Easter	(Proper Liturgy, BCP,284-295) (Rite I Collect, BCP,170)				Easter

THE CALENDAR OF THE CHURCH YEAR
SUNDAYS AND PRINCIPAL FEASTS

Color	Day	Collect	Lessons and Psalms			Proper Preface
			Year A	Year B	Year C	
White	The Sunday of the Resurrection: Easter Day	(BCP,170-171 or 222)	(BCP,893)	(BCP,904)	(BCP,915)	Easter
	Monday in Easter Week	(BCP,171 or 222)	(BCP,894)	(BCP,905)	(BCP,915)	Easter
	Tuesday in Easter Week	(BCP,171 or 223)	(BCP,894)	(BCP,905)	(BCP,915)	Easter
	Wednesday in Easter Week	(BCP,171 or 223)	(BCP,894)	(BCP,905)	(BCP,915)	Easter
	Thursday in Easter Week	(BCP,172 or 223)	(BCP,894)	(BCP,905)	(BCP,915)	Easter
	Friday in Easter Week	(BCP,172 or 224)	(BCP,894)	(BCP,905)	(BCP,916)	Easter
	Saturday in Easter Week	(BCP,172 or 224)	(BCP,894)	(BCP,905)	(BCP,916)	Easter
	The Second Sunday of Easter	(BCP,172 or 224)	(BCP,894)	(BCP,905)	(BCP,916)	Easter
	The Third Sunday of Easter	(BCP,173 or 224)	(BCP,894)	(BCP,905)	(BCP,916)	Easter
	The Fourth Sunday of Easter	(BCP,173 or 225)	(BCP,895)	(BCP,905)	(BCP,916)	Easter
	The Fifth Sunday of Easter	(BCP,173 or 225)	(BCP,895)	(BCP,906)	(BCP,916)	Easter
	The Sixth Sunday of Easter (Rogation Sunday)	(BCP,174 or 225)	(BCP,895)	(BCP,906)	(BCP,916)	Easter
	Ascension Day	(BCP,174 or 226)	(BCP,895)	(BCP,906)	(BCP,917)	Ascension
	The Seventh Sunday of Easter	(BCP,175 or 226)	(BCP,895)	(BCP,906)	(BCP,917)	Ascension
	Vigil of Pentecost (see page 277)	(BCP,175 or 227)	(BCP,896)	(BCP,906)	(BCP,917)	Pentecost
Red	The Day of Pentecost: Whitsunday	(BCP,175 or 227)	(BCP,896)	(BCP,906-907)	(BCP,917)	Pentecost
	The Season After Pentecost					
White (White)	Trinity Sunday (Corpus Christi)	(BCP,176 or 228)	(BCP,896)	(BCP,907)	(BCP,918)	Trinity Sunday

(see appendix, page 264.)

Note: The Paschal Candle is lighted at all services through the Fifty Days of Easter, that is from the Great Vigil of Easter through the Day of Pentecost.

THE CALENDAR OF THE CHURCH YEAR
SUNDAYS AND PRINCIPAL FEASTS

Color	Day	Collect	Lessons and Psalms			Proper Preface
			Year A	Year B	Year C	
Green	The Second through the Twenty-Seventh Sunday after Pentecost	(BCP,176-185 or 228-236)	*(The Sundays after Pentecost use the Propers closest to the date given. See pages 113-115 for further details.)* (BCP,896-900)	(BCP,907-910)	(BCP,918-921)	Of the Lord's Day
White	The Transfiguration, *August 6*	(BCP, 191 or 243)		(BCP, 924)		Epiphany
White	All Saints' Day	(BCP,194 or 245)	(BCP,925)	(BCP,925)	(BCP,925)	All Saints
White	The Sunday after All Saints' Day		*(All Saints' Day may always be observed on the Sunday following November 1, in addition to its observance on the fixed date, BCP,15.)*			
White	The Last Sunday after Pentecost *(Christ the King)*	(BCP,185 or 236)	(BCP,900)	(BCP,910)	(BCP,921)	Baptism or of the Lord's Day

HOLY DAYS AND NATIONAL DAYS

Color	Day	Date	Collect	Lessons and Psalms	Proper Preface
Red	St. Andrew	November 30	(BCP, 185 or 237)	(BCP, 921)	Apostles
Red	St. Thomas	December 21	(BCP, 185 or 237)	(BCP, 921)	Apostles
Red	St. Stephen	December 26	(BCP, 186 or 237)	(BCP, 922)	Incarnation
White	St. John	December 27	(BCP, 186 or 238)	(BCP, 922)	Incarnation
Red	The Holy Innocents	December 28	(BCP, 186 or 238)	(BCP, 922)	Incarnation
White	Confession of St. Peter	January 18	(BCP, 187 or 238)	(BCP, 922)	Apostles
Red	St. Matthias	February 24	(BCP, 188 or 239)	(BCP, 922)	Apostles
White	St. Joseph	March 19	(BCP, 188 or 239)	(BCP, 922)	Epiphany
White	The Annunciation	March 25	(BCP, 188 or 240)	(BCP, 922)	Epiphany
Red	St. Mark	April 25	(BCP, 188 or 240)	(BCP, 923)	All Saints
Red	St. Philip and St. James	May 1	(BCP, 189 or 240)	(BCP, 923)	Apostles
White	The Visitation	May 31	(BCP, 189 or 240)	(BCP, 923)	Epiphany
Red	St. Barnabas	June 11	(BCP, 189 or 241)	(BCP, 923)	Apostles
White	Nativity of St. John the Baptist	June 24	(BCP, 190 or 241)	(BCP, 923)	Advent
Red	St. Peter and St. Paul	June 29	(BCP, 190 or 241)	(BCP, 923)	Apostles
White	Independence Day	July 4	(BCP, 190, 207 or 242, 258)	(BCP, 923 or 930)	Trinity Sunday
White	St. Mary Magdalene	July 22	(BCP, 191 or 242)	(BCP, 923)	All Saints
White	St. Mary the Virgin	August 15	(BCP, 192 or 243)	(BCP, 924)	Incarnation
Red	St. Bartholomew	August 24	(BCP, 192 or 243)	(BCP, 924)	Apostles
Red	Holy Cross Day	September 14	(BCP, 192 or 244)	(BCP, 924)	Holy Week

THE CALENDAR OF THE CHURCH YEAR
HOLY DAYS AND NATIONAL DAYS

Color	Day	Date	Collect	Lessons and Psalms	Proper Preface
Red	St. Matthew	September 21	(BCP,192 or 244)	(BCP,924)	Apostles
White	St. Michael and All Angels	September 29	(BCP,193 or 244)	(BCP,924)	Trinity Sunday
Red	St. Luke	October 18	(BCP,193 or 244)	(BCP,924)	All Saints
Red	St. James of Jerusalem	October 23	(BCP,193 or 245)	(BCP,924)	All Saints
Red	St. Simon and St. Jude	October 28	(BCP,194 or 245)	(BCP,925)	Apostles
White	All Saints' Day	November 1	(BCP,194 or 245)	(BCP,925)	All Saints
White	Thanksgiving Day		(BCP,194 or 246)	(BCP,925)	Trinity Sunday

OTHER FEASTS AND FASTS IN THE CALENDAR   *General Conventions through 1997. The Proper for each day, including the collect, is found in the Appendix as indicated.*

Color	Day	Date	Collect, Lessons and Psalms	Proper Preface
White	Nicholas Ferrar	December 1	(LFF, 89)	Saint (1)
White	Channing Moore Williams	December 2	(LFF, 91)	Pentecost
White	John of Damascus	December 4	(LFF, 93)	Easter
White	Clement of Alexandria	December 5	(LFF, 95)	Baptism
White	Nicholas	December 6	(LFF, 97)	Saint (1)
White	Ambrose	December 7	(LFF, 99)	Saint (1)
White*	Thomas B. Becket	December 29	(LFF, 112)	Saint (1)
White	Julia Chester Emery	January 9	(LFF, 119)	Saint (2)
White	William Laud	January 10	(LFF, 121)	Saint (2)
White	Aelred	January 12	(LFF, 123)	Saint (2)
White	Hilary	January 13	(LFF, 125)	Trinity Sunday
White	Antony	January 17	(LFF, 127)	Saint (2)
White	Wulfstan	January 19	(LFF, 131)	Baptism
Red	Fabian	January 20	(LFF, 133)	Saint (3)
Red	Agnes	January 21	(LFF, 135)	Saint (3)
Red	Vincent	January 22	(LFF, 137)	Saint (3)
White	Phillips Brooks	January 23	(LFF, 139)	Saint (1)
White	Timothy and Titus	January 26	(LFF, 143)	Pentecost
White	John Chrysostom	January 27	(LFF, 145)	Saint (2)
White	Thomas Aquinas	January 28	(LFF, 147)	Trinity Sunday
White	Brigid (Bride)	February 1	(LFF, 149)	Saint (2)
White	Anskar	February 3	(LFF, 153)	Apostles
White	Cornelius	February 4	(LFF, 155)	Pentecost
Red	The Martyrs of Japan	February 5	(LFF, 157)	Holy Week
White	Absalom Jones	February 13	(LFF, 159)	Saint (1)
White	Cyril and Methodius	February 14	(LFF, 161)	Apostles
White	Thomas Bray	February 15	(LFF, 163)	Pentecost
White	Martin Luther	February 18	(LFF, 165)	Trinity Sunday
Red	Polycarp	February 23	(LFF, 167)	Saint (3)
White	George Herbert	February 27	(LFF, 171)	Saint (1)

THE CALENDAR OF THE CHURCH YEAR
OTHER FEASTS AND FASTS IN THE CALENDAR

Color	Day	Date	Collect, Lessons and Psalms	Proper Preface
White	David	March 1	(LFF, 173)	Apostles
White	Chad	March 2	(LFF, 175)	Saint (2)
White	John and Charles Wesley	March 3	(LFF, 177)	Pentecost
Red	Perpetua and her Companions	March 7	(LFF, 179)	Saint (3)
White	Gregory of Nyssa	March 9	(LFF, 181)	Trinity Sunday
White	Gregory the Great	March 12	(LFF, 183)	Apostles
White	Patrick	March 17	(LFF, 185)	Apostles
White	Cyril	March 18	(LFF, 187)	Dedication of a Church
White	Cuthbert	March 20	(LFF, 191)	Saint (2)
White	Thomas Ken	March 21	(LFF, 193)	Saint (2)
White	James De Koven	March 22	(LFF, 195)	Saint (1)
White	Gregory the Illuminator	March 23	(LFF, 197)	Apostles
White	Charles Henry Brent	March 27	(LFF, 201)	Pentecost
White	John Keble	March 29	(LFF, 203)	Saint (1)
White	John Donne	March 31	(LFF, 205)	Epiphany
White	Frederick Denison Maurice	April 1	(LFF, 207)	Baptism
White	James Lloyd Breck	April 2	(LFF, 209)	Pentecost
White	Richard	April 3	(LFF, 211)	Saint (2)
White	Martin Luther King, Jr.	April 4	(LFF, 213)	Baptism
White	William Augustus Muhlenberg	April 8	(LFF, 215)	Saint (1)
White	Dietrich Bonhoeffer	April 9	(LFF, 217)	Saint (2)
White	William Law	April 10	(LFF, 219)	Saint (2)
White	George Augustus Selwyn	April 11	(LFF, 221)	Apostles
Red	Alphege	April 19	(LFF, 223)	Saint (3)
White	Anselm	April 21	(LFF, 225)	Epiphany
White	Catherine of Siena	April 29	(LFF, 229)	Saint (2)

Color	Day	Date	Collect, Lessons and Psalms	Proper Preface
White	Monnica	May 4	(LFF, 235)	Baptism
White	Dame Julian of Norwich	May 8	(LFF, 237)	Epiphany
White	Gregory of Nazianzus	May 9	(LFF, 239)	Trinity Sunday
White	Dunstan	May 19	(LFF, 241)	Dedication of a Church
White	Alcuin	May 20	(LFF, 243)	Saint (1)
White	Jackson Kemper	May 24	(LFF, 245)	Pentecost
White	Bede the Venerable	May 25	(LFF, 247)	Saint (1)
White	Augustine of Canterbury	May 26	(LFF, 249)	Apostles
White	The First Book of Common Prayer	a weekday following the Day of Pentecost	(LFF, 253)	Pentecost
Red	Justin	June 1	(LFF, 255)	Saint (3)
Red	The Martyrs of Lyons	June 2	(LFF, 257)	Saint (3)
Red	The Martyrs of Uganda	June 3	(LFF, 259)	Holy Week
Red	Boniface	June 5	(LFF, 261)	Apostles
White	Columba	June 9	(LFF, 263)	Apostles
White	Ephrem of Edessa	June 10	(LFF, 265)	Saint (1)
White	Basil the Great	June 14	(LFF, 269)	Trinity Sunday
White	Evelyn Underhill	June 15	(LFF, 271)	Dedication of a Church
White	Joseph Butler	June 16	(LFF, 273)	Saint (1)
Red	Bernard Mizeki	June 18	(LFF, 275)	Holy Week
Red	Alban	June 22	(LFF, 277)	Saint (3)
White	Irenaeus	June 28	(LFF, 281)	Epiphany
White	Benedict of Nursia	July 11	(LFF, 287)	Saint (2)
White	William White	July 17	(LFF, 289)	Saint (1)
White	Macrina	July 19	(LFF, 291)	Saint (2)
White	Bloomer, Stanton, Truth, Tubman	July 20	(LFF, 295)	Baptism
White	Thomas a Kempis	July 24	(LFF, 293)	Saint (2)

Color	Day	Date	Collect, Lessons and Psalms	Proper Preface
White	Parents of the Blessed Virgin Mary	July 26	(LFF, 303)	Incarnation
White	William Reed Huntington	July 27	(LFF, 305)	Baptism
White	Mary and Martha of Bethany	July 29	(LFF, 307)	Epiphany
White	William Wilberforce	July 30	(LFF, 309)	Saint (2)
White	Ignatius of Loyola	July 31	(LFF, 311)	Saint (3)
White	Joseph of Arimathaea	August 1	(LFF, 313)	Commemoration of the Dead
White	John Mason Neale	August 7	(LFF, 317)	Dedication of a Church
Red	Dominic	August 8	(LFF, 319)	Saint (2)
White	Laurence	August 10	(LFF, 321)	Saint (3)
White	Clare	August 11	(LFF, 323)	Saint (2)
White	Jeremy Taylor	August 13	(LFF, 325)	Saint (1)
White	Jonathan Myrick Daniels	August 14	(LFF, 327)	Saint (2)
White	William Porcher DuBose	August 18	(LFF, 331)	Epiphany
White	Bernard	August 20	(LFF, 333)	Saint (1)
White	Louis	August 25	(LFF, 337)	Baptism
White	Thomas Gallaudet with Henry Winter Syle	August 27	(LFF, 339)	Pentecost
White	Augustine of Hippo	August 28	(LFF, 341)	Baptism
White	Aidan	August 31	(LFF, 343)	Apostles
White	David Pendleton Oakerhater	September 1	(LFF, 345)	Apostles
Red	The Martyrs of New Guinea	September 2	(LFF, 347)	Holy Week
White	Paul Jones	September 4	(LFF, 349)	Saint (3)
White	Constance, Nun, and her companions	September 9	(LFF, 350)	Saint (1)
White	Alexander Crummell	September 10	(LFF, 353)	Saint (2)
White	John Henry Hobart	September 12	(LFF, 355)	Saint (1)
Red	Cyprian	September 13	(LFF, 357)	Saint (3)
White	Ninian	September 16	(LFF, 361)	Pentecost
White	Hildegard	September 17	(LFF, 363)	Epiphany
White	Edward Bouverie Pusey	September 18	(LFF, 365)	Saint (2)
White	Theodore of Tarsus	September 19	(LFF, 367)	Saint (1)
Red	John Coleridge Patteson	September 20	(LFF, 369)	Holy Week

OTHER FEASTS AND FASTS IN THE CALENDAR

Color	Day	Date	Collect, Lessons and Psalms	Proper Preface
White	Jerome	September 30	*(LFF, 379)*	Pentecost
White	Remigius	October 1	*(LFF, 381)*	Saint (1)
White	Francis of Assisi	October 4	*(LFF, 383)*	Saint (3)
White	William Tyndale	October 6	*(LFF, 385)*	Epiphany
White	Robert Grosseteste	October 9	*(LFF, 387)*	Saint (1)
White	Samuel I.J. Schereschewsky	October 14	*(LFF, 389)*	Pentecost
White	Teresa of Avila	October 15	*(LFF, 391)*	Baptism
White*	Latimer, Ridley, Cranmer	October 16	*(LFF, 395)*	Saint (1)
Red	Ignatius of Antioch	October 17	*(LFF, 397)*	Saint (3)
White	Henry Martyn	October 19	*(LFF, 401)*	Saint (2)
White	Alfred the Great	October 26	*(LFF, 405)*	Baptism
Red	James Hannington	October 29	*(LFF, 409)*	Holy Week
Violet or Black	All Faithful Departed *(All Souls' Day)*	November 2	*(LFF, 413)* (see also page 160)	Commemoration of the Dead
White	Richard Hooker	November 3	*(LFF, 415)*	Baptism
White	Willibrord	November 7	*(LFF, 417)*	Apostles
White	Leo the Great	November 10	*(LFF, 419)*	Epiphany
White	Martin of Tours	November 11	*(LFF, 421)*	Saint (2)
White	Charles Simeon	November 12	*(LFF, 423)*	Saint (1)
White	Consecration of Samuel Seabury	November 14	*(LFF, 425)*	Apostles
White	Margaret of Scotland	November 16	*(LFF, 427)*	Baptism
White	Hugh of Lincoln	November 17	*(LFF, 429)*	Saint (2)
White	Hilda of Whitby	November 18	*(LFF, 431)*	Saint (1)
White	Elizabeth of Hungary	November 19	*(LFF, 433)*	Saint (2)
White	Edmund	November 20	*(LFF, 435)*	Baptism
White	Clement	November 23	*(LFF, 437)*	Saint (2)
White	James Otis Sargent Huntington	November 25	*(LFF, 441)*	Saint (2)
White	Kamehameha and Emma	November 28	*(LFF, 442)*	Baptism

THE CALENDAR OF THE CHURCH YEAR
COMMEMORATIONS NOT LISTED IN THE CALENDAR

Saints and Commemorations not listed in the Calendar, but which may be observed as "other Commemorations, using the Common of Saints" (BCP,18): "At the discretion of the Celebrant, and as appropriate, . . . Any of the sets of Lessons assigned to a given Common (BCP,925-927) may be used with any of the Collects . . . at the patronal festival or commemoration of a saint not listed in the Calendar." (LFF,392)

Color	Day	Date	Collect, Lessons and Psalms	Proper Preface
White	Francis Xavier, Missionary	December 3	Of a Missionary II (BCP,196 or 248, 926)	Pentecost
White	Conception of the Blessed Virgin Mary	December 8	The Visitation (May 31) (BCP,189 or 240, 923)	Incarnation or Epiphany
Red	Lucy, Martyr	December 13	Of a Martyr III (BCP,196 or 247, 925)	Saint (3)
White	John of the Cross, Theologian	December 14	Of a Theologian I (BCP,197 or 248, 926)	Saint (1)
White	John Wycliffe	December 31	Of a Martyr I (BCP,195 or 246, 925)	Saint (3)
White	Sylvester, Bishop	December 31	Of a Pastor I (BCP,196 or 248, 926)	Saint (1)
White	Elizabeth Ann Seton, Teacher	January 4	Of a Teacher II (BCP,197 or 249, 926)	Saint (1)
White	Francis de Sales, Bishop	January 24	Of a Pastor II (BCP,197 or 248, 926)	Saint (1)
Red	Charles, Martyr	January 30	See page 264	Saint (3)
Red	Agatha, Martyr	February 6	Of a Martyr III (BCP,196 or 247, 925)	Saint (3)
White	Scholastica, Monastic	February 10	Of a Monastic II (BCP,198 or 249, 926)	Saint (2)

COMMEMORATIONS NOT LISTED IN THE CALENDAR

Color	Day	Date	Collect, Lessons and Psalms	Proper Preface
Red	The Forty Martyrs of Sebaste	March 10	Of a Martyr I (BCP,195 or 246, 925)	Holy Week
White	Vincent Ferrer, Priest	April 5	Of a Monastic I (BCP,198 or 249, 926)	Saint (2)
Red	George, Martyr	April 23	Of a Martyr II (BCP,195 or 247, 925)	Saint (3)
Red	Thomas More, Martyr	July 9	Of a Martyr I (BCP,195 or 246, 925)	Saint (3)
White	Bonaventure, Bishop	July 14	Of a Pastor II (BCP,197 or 248, 926)	Saint (1)
White	Swithun, Bishop	July 15	Of a Pastor II (BCP,197 or 248, 926)	Saint (1)
Red	Margaret, Martyr	July 20	Of a Martyr III (BCP,196 or 247, 925)	Saint (3)
White	Jean-Baptiste Vianney, Priest	August 4	Of a Pastor I (BCP,196 or 248, 926)	Saint (1)
White	Stephen of Hungary	August 16	Of a Saint I (BCP,198 or 250, 926)	Saint (1)
White	Helena	August 19	Of a Saint I (BCP,198 or 250, 926)	Saint (1)
White	Jane Frances de Chantal, Teacher	August 21	Of a Teacher II (BCP,197 or 249, 926)	Saint (1)
White	Giles, Monastic	September 1	Of a Monastic II (BCP,198 or 249, 926)	Saint (2)
White	Nativity of the Blessed Virgin Mary	September 8	The Visitation (May 31) (BCP,189 or 240, 923)	Incarnation

THE CALENDAR OF THE CHURCH YEAR
COMMEMORATIONS NOT LISTED IN THE CALENDAR

Color	Day	Date	Collect, Lessons and Psalms	Proper Preface
White	Ninian, Bishop	September 16	Of a Missionary I (BCP, 196 or 247)	Saint (1)
White	Vincent de Paul, Teacher	September 27	Of a Teacher, II (BCP, 197 or 249, 926)	Saint (1)
White	The Holy Guardian Angels	October 2	Of the Holy Angels (BCP, 200 or 251, 927)	Trinity Sunday
Red	Denis, Martyr	October 10	Of a Martyr II (BCP, 195 or 247, 925)	Saint (3)
White	Wilfred, Bishop	October 12	Of a Pastor II (BCP, 197 or 248, 926)	Saint (1)
White	Edward the Confessor	October 13	Of a Saint I (BCP, 198 or 250, 926)	Saint (2)
White	Teresa of Avila, Monastic	October 14	Of a Monastic II (BCP, 198 or 249, 926)	Saint (2)
Red	Isaac Jogues and Jean Brébeuf, Martyrs	October 20	Of a Martyr II (BCP, 195 or 247, 925)	Saint (3)
White	Charles Borromeo, Theologian	November 4	Of a Theologian I (BCP, 197 or 248, 926)	Trinity Sunday
White	Albert the Great, Bishop	November 15	of a Pastor II (BCP, 197 or 248, 926)	Saint (1)
Red	Edmund, Martyr	November 20	Of a Martyr II (BCP, 195 or 247, 925)	Saint (3)
Red	Cecilia, Martyr	November 22	Of a Martyr III (BCP, 196 or 247, 925)	Saint (3)

The Lectionary

The Lectionary

Introduction

The ordering of Scripture in the celebration of the Church Year, both for the Holy Eucharist and the Daily Offices, is vital to the Church's liturgical worship. Collects, lessons and psalms are appointed for all the days of the Church Year and are intended to order the flow of the year from Sunday to Sunday, from season to season, from feast to feast, from fast to fast.

The Lectionary in *The Book of Common Prayer* is found in three places: the collects and appointed proper prefaces *(BCP, 157-261);* the Eucharistic Lectionary for Sundays, Principal Feasts, Holy Days, Commons and Various Occasions *(BCP, 887-931);* and the Daily Office Lectionary *(BCP, 933-1001).* These are discussed in the following pages, along with the lectionary for Lesser Feasts and Fasts and other commemorations not listed in the calendar of the Church Year, but following the rubrics governing their celebration.

The importance of scriptural readings in the liturgy must not be under-estimated. The common worship of the Church demands a balance between Word and Sacrament. The random choosing of lessons only leads to irrelevant reading; an established lectionary provides Scripture that will pertain to the liturgy of the day or season, while at the same time using the Bible to the fullest possible extent in the daily offering of prayer and praise. We must be aware of the Presence of Christ in both Word and Sacrament. As we pray in the evening collect, "be our companion in the way, kindle our hearts, and awaken hope, that we may know *thee* as *thou art* revealed in Scripture and the breaking of bread" *(BCP, 70 or 124).*

The following should be noted for all lessons, either from the Eucharistic Lectionary or Daily Office Lectionary:

1. In the opening verses, omit initial conjunctions which refer only to what has preceded;
2. Substitute nouns for pronouns when the referent is not otherwise clear;
3. Preface the reading with some such introduction as *"N.* said (to *N.)"* when it will clarify the context.

Note: The lessons as printed in *Lectionary Texts* for each of the years, or in *Lectionary Texts for the Lesser Feasts and Fasts,* or in *Lectionary Texts for Various Occasions and Occasional Services,* or in *The Book of Gospels* (Years A, B, C, Holy Days and Special Occasions) have all been edited for liturgical use (public reading) according to the rules given above.

Scriptural citations throughout *The Book of Common Prayer* (and in both lectionaries), except the psalms, follow the verse divisions of the Revised Standard Version of the Bible *(BCP, 14).* If other authorized versions are used, they should be carefully compared with the RSV, since the versification may be different.

Eucharistic Lectionary

Sundays

The lectionary is arranged in a three year cycle, *in which Year A always begins on the First Sunday of Advent in years evenly divisible by three (BCP, 888).*

Examples:
Advent I, 1986, divided by 3 is 662 = Year A *(BCP, 889-900)*
Advent I, 1987, not divisible by 3 = Year B *(BCP, 900-910)*
Advent I, 1988, not divisible by 3 = Year C *(BCP, 911-921)*
Advent I, 1989, divided by 3 is 663 = Year A *(BCP, 889-900)*
The cycle always runs Year A, Year B, Year C, Year A, etc.

Note: Unlike the Daily Office Lectionary (see page 118) the Sunday cycle is fixed in reference to the First Sunday of Advent in the calendar year in which it falls, not in reference to the following year.

For each Sunday a psalm (or alternate psalm) is appointed. This is intended to be sung or said after the first lesson. The Gloria Patri is not sung or said at the conclusion of this psalm.

Three lessons are appointed for each Sunday:

1. From the Old Testament or Apocrypha. (During the Easter Season, a reading from the Acts of the Apostles is given as a first reading, with an optional Old Testament lesson that may be used in place of the lesson from Acts if desired.)
2. From the Epistles or Acts or Revelation. (During the Easter Season, if Acts is read as the first lesson, then the optional Epistle is read as the second lesson.)
3. From the Gospels (Year A is usually Matthew; Year B is usually Mark; Year C is usually Luke; John is used in all three years for various occasions).

Note: Any Reading may be lengthened at discretion. Suggested lengthenings are shown in parentheses (BCP, 888).

Concerning Precedence of Sundays and Holy Days, see page 94.

Holy Days

Three lessons and the psalm(s) are appointed for each major Holy Day *(BCP, 921-925).* Their use is the same as on Sundays (see above). The lessons are printed in each volume of *Lectionary Texts* (A, B, and C—RSV); *Eucharistic Readings* (NRSV); *Lectionary Texts for the Lesser Feasts and Fasts; The Book of Gospels* (RSV); and *Gospel Readings* (NRSV).

Lesser Feasts and Fasts

Proper collect, lessons, psalm and Preface are appointed for each of the minor saints' days and commemorations as listed in the calendar of the Church Year. These are found in *Lesser Feasts and Fasts* along with a short biography or explanation of the day being observed.

A commemoration of a saint or other occasion in *LFF* may be observed on any day during the week when the Eucharist is celebrated, provided that it is not a Principal Feast or Holy Day.

For use at the Eucharist, the biography or explanation may be read as a homily after the Gospel. For use at the Daily Offices, see page 121. During Lent and the Fifty Days of Easter, see pages 155 and 158. For a list of the commemorations in LFF and the appropriate color for the vestments and the Proper Preface appointed, see pages 101-105.

The Common of Saints

Three lessons and the psalm(s) *(BCP, 925-927)* are given for each of the commons and are used as given above for Sundays. These are also found in *Lectionary Texts for the Lesser Feasts and Fasts,* which are edited for liturgical use.

Various Occasions

Three lessons and the psalm(s) *(BCP, 199-210, 251-261, 927-931)* are given for these "votive" Eucharists and also for special occasions such as Baptism, Confirmation, Ember Days, Rogation Days, and for special intentions. (*Note:* At the principal service on a Sunday or Major Holy Day it is preferable that the lessons appointed for the day be used rather than those for Baptism or Confirmation.) They are used as on Sunday (see above). These are also found in *Lectionary Texts for Various Occasions and Occasional Services* and are edited for liturgical use. The following Gospels are also found in *The Book of Gospels:*

Baptism	*(BOG,* 246-247)	*(GR,* 225-226)
Confirmation	*(BOG,* 247-249)	*(GR,* 226-228)
The Celebration and Blessing of a Marriage	*(BOG,* 249-251)	*(GR,* 228-230)
A Funeral or Commemoration of the Dead	*(BOG,* 252-254)	*(GR,* 231-233)
The Ordination of a Bishop	*(BOG,* 255-256)	*(GR,* 233-234)
The Ordination of a Priest	*(BOG,* 257-258)	*(GR,* 235-236)
The Ordination of a Deacon	*(BOG,* 258-259)	*(GR,* 236-237)
The Celebration of a New Ministry	*(BOG,* 259-260)	*(GR,* 237-238)
The Dedication and Consecration of a Church	*(BOG,* 260-261)	*(GR,* 239-240)

The Anniversary of the Dedication
of a Church (*BOG,* 261-262) (*GR,* 240)
A Church Convention (*BOG,* 262) (*GR,* 241)
Note: See page 262 for the Propers for World Hunger, Human Rights, and
Oppression approved by General Convention, 1979.

Concerning Weekday Eucharists

At a weekday celebration of the Holy Eucharist, the collect, lessons and
psalm of the previous Sunday are used when there is no Major Holy Day or
other occasion observed. However, the following should be noted:

1. Major Feasts (except Christmas Day, the Epiphany, and All Saints'
   Day) may be transferred and celebrated on any day during the week
   when there is a Eucharist, but not during the days of Holy Week or
   of Easter Week.
2. Other holy days and saints' days may be observed on a day when there
   is a Eucharist provided that a Major Feast or Fast is not appointed for
   that day.
3. Propers for Various Occasions *(BCP, 199-210, 251-261, 927-931)* may
   be used on any day at the discretion of the celebrant provided that a
   Major Feast or Fast is not appointed for that day.
   a. "Of the Holy Eucharist" is especially suitable for Thursdays.
   b. "Of the Holy Cross" is especially suitable for Fridays.
   c. "For all Baptized Christians" or "Of the Incarnation" are especially suitable for Saturdays.
4. Other commemorations (*BCP, 17-18;* also pages 106-108) may be observed provided that a Major Feast or Fast is not appointed for that day.
5. On the weekdays between Pentecost and Trinity Sunday the numbered
   Proper *(BCP, 176-178 or 228-230)* which corresponds most closely to
   the date of Pentecost in that year is used. The lessons and psalm are
   found in the lectionary for the given year and correspond to the collects
   cited above. No Proper Preface is used.
6. On the weekdays between Trinity Sunday and the following Sunday,
   the numbered Proper *(BCP, 176-178 or 228-230)* which corresponds
   most closely to the date of Trinity Sunday in that year is used. The
   lessons and psalm are found in the lectionary for the given year and
   correspond to the collects cited above. No Proper Preface is used.
7. On weekdays in Epiphany and Pentecost the collect is that of the
   preceding Sunday, but the lessons and psalm may be taken from
   those appointed for the same Sunday in another year, provided that
   a Major Feast or Fast is not appointed for that day.
   Example: A weekday in Year B following the Second Sunday after
   Epiphany.
   The collect is that of the Second Sunday after Epiphany, but the
   lessons and psalm may be chosen from those appointed either for
   Year A or Year C for the Second Sunday after Epiphany.

CONCERNING WEEKDAY EUCHARISTS AND THE SEASONS OF THE CHURCH YEAR

Season	Proper	Proper Preface
Advent	For Collects, see *BOS, page 20* For Lessons, see *LFF, pages 21-26*	Advent
Christmas		
a. the weekdays between Holy Innocents' Day and the First Sunday after Christmas Day	Collect: Christmas Day (3) Lessons: any of the sets appointed for Christmas Day.	Incarnation
b. the weekdays between the First Sunday after Christmas Day and the Epiphany	see 1-5, page 113	Incarnation
Epiphany		
a. the weekdays between Epiphany and the following Sunday (The Baptism of our Lord)	Collect: the Epiphany and the appointed lessons and psalm *or* the collect and the appointed lessons and psalm of the Second Sunday after Christmas	Epiphany Epiphany
b. the weekdays between the First Sunday after the Epiphany through the Tuesday before Ash Wednesday	see 1-4 and 7, page 113	Epiphany
Lent		
the weekdays between Ash Wednesday and the Saturday before the Sunday of the Passion	*LFF, 29-61*; (see note, *LFF, 28*; also page 113) *or* The collect, lessons, and psalms appointed for Ash Wednesday are used on Thursday, Friday, and Saturday following and then for the remaining weeks, see 5, page 113.	Lent (see page 53)

CONCERNING WEEKDAY EUCHARISTS AND THE SEASONS OF THE CHURCH YEAR

Season	Proper	Proper Preface
Holy Week (Monday, Tuesday, Wednesday, Maundy Thursday)	as appointed (*BCP, 168-169 or 220; 892, 903, 914;* also, see pages *181-189*).	Holy Week
Easter Week	as appointed (*BCP, 171-172 or 222-224; 894, 905, 915-916)*	Easter
Easter		
a. from Monday until after the Second Sunday of Easter until the Saturday before the Fourth Sunday of Easter	(*LFF, 65-68; 76-77*) *or* 1-4 and 7, page 113	Easter
b. from Monday after the Fourth Sunday of Easter until Ascension Day	(*LFF, 68-73; 78-80*) *or* 1-4 and 7, page 113	Easter
c. from the Friday after Ascension Day until Pentecost	(*LFF, 73-75; 80-81*) *or* as appointed for Ascension Day (for Friday and Saturday and the weekdays following the Seventh Sunday of Easter, see 5, page 113)	Ascension
		Ascension
After Pentecost		
the weekdays from the Monday after the Day of Pentecost until the Saturday before the First Sunday of Advent	see 1-7, page 113	No Proper Preface unless appointed for a Holy Day or Various Occasion

Concerning Ember Days

Spring	The Wednesday, Friday and Saturday following the First Sunday in Lent
Summer	The Wednesday, Friday and Saturday following the Day of Pentecost
Fall	The Wednesday, Friday and Saturday successively following Holy Cross Day (September 14)
Winter	The Wednesday, Friday and Saturday successively following December 13

Propers	Collect	Lessons and Psalm	Preface
Wednesday	No. 15. For the Ministry I. For those to be ordained *(BCP, 205 or 256)*	For the Ministry I *(BCP, 929)*	Of the Apostles
Friday	No. 15. For the Ministry II. For the choice of fit persons for the ministry *(BCP, 205 or 256)*	For the Ministry II *(BCP, 929)*	Of the Season
Saturday	No. 15. For the Ministry III. For all Christians in their vocation *(BCP, 206 or 256-257)*	For the Ministry III *(BCP, 929)*	Of Baptism *or* Of the Season

Note: Any of the Propers appointed "For the Ministry" may be used on the Ember Days or on other days that do not have a Proper assigned to them.

Concerning Rogation Days

The Rogation Days are traditionally observed on the Monday, Tuesday and Wednesday following the Sixth Sunday of Easter (and are the weekdays preceding Ascension Day).

For the Rogation Procession see pages 166-167.

On Monday
Collect
    No. 19. For Rogation Days
    I. For fruitful seasons *(BCP, 207 or 258)*
Lessons and Psalm
    For Rogation Days I *(BCP, 930)*
Preface
    Easter

On Tuesday
Collect
    No. 19. For Rogation Days
    II. For commerce and industry *(BCP, 208 or 259)*
Lessons and Psalm
    For Rogation Days II *(BCP, 930)*
Preface
    Easter

On Wednesday
Collect
    No. 19. For Rogation Days
    III. For stewardship of creation *(BCP, 208 or 259)*
Lessons and Psalm
    For Rogation Days III *(BCP, 930)*
Preface
    Easter

Suggested collects to be used at the conclusion of the Prayers of the People:

On Monday or Wednesday

1. For Joy in God's Creation *(BCP, 814)*
29. For Agriculture *(BCP, 824)*
38. For the Right Use of God's Gifts *(BCP, 827)* (Wednesday)
40. For Knowledge of God's Creation *(BCP, 827)*
41. For the Conservation of Natural Resources *(BCP, 827)* (Wednesday)
42. For the Harvest of Lands and Waters *(BCP, 828)* (Monday)
43. For Rain *(BCP, 828)* (Monday)
44. For the Future of the Human Race *(BCP, 828)*
8. Thanksgiving for the Beauty of the Earth *(BCP, 840)*
9. Thanksgiving for the Harvest *(BCP, 840)*

On Tuesday

24. For Vocation in Daily Work *(BCP, 210 or 261)*
25. For Labor Day *(BCP, 210 or 261)*

Note: proper hymn for Rogation Days *(Hymnal, 292)*

Daily Office Lectionary

The Lessons

The two-year cycle for the psalms and lessons at the Daily Office may seem confusing to many. Detailed rubrics are found preceding the lectionary *(BCP, 934-935)*. The following may be helpful in figuring out which lessons are appointed for which day.

    A. Year One (the left-hand or even-numbered pages of the lectionary) begins on the First Sunday of Advent preceding odd-numbered years. *Example:* On the first Sunday of Advent in 2000 Year One begins.

    B. Year Two (the right-hand or odd-numbered pages of the lectionary) begins on the First Sunday of Advent preceding even-numbered years. *Example:* On the first Sunday of Advent in 2001 Year Two begins.

    C. The first numbers cited in the lectionary are the psalms. The first number or set is intended for Morning Prayer. The second number or set following the asterisk is intended for Evening Prayer.

    D. Three lessons are appointed for each day:

        1. Two readings may be used in the morning and one in the evening. It is suggested that the Gospel reading oe used in the evening in Year One and in the morning in Year Two.

        2. If only one office is read, all three lessons may be used at this office.

        3. If two readings are used at both Morning and Evening Prayer, the Old Testament reading for the alternate year is suggested as the first reading at Evening Prayer.

        Note: The Gospel reading appointed for the day is used in the evening in Year One and in the morning in Year Two.

    Example: Monday in Week of 1 Advent (see *BCP, 936-937*)

Year One	Year Two
MP Isaiah 1:10-20	MP Amos 2:6-16
1 Thessalonians 1:1-10	Matt. 21:1-11 (see note above)
EP Amos 2:6-16 (from Year Two)	EP Isaiah 1:10-20 (from Year One)
Luke 20:1-8 (see note above)	2 Peter 1:1-11

        4. When more than one reading is used either at Morning Prayer or Evening Prayer, the first is always that appointed from the Old Testament (or the Apocrypha).

        5. Major Feast Days have their own appointed psalms and lessons for both Morning and Evening Prayer *(BCP, 996-1000)*. Also, there are psalms and lessons appointed for Special Occasions *(BCP, 1000-1001)*. In both cases the psalms and lessons are the same for either Year One or Year Two, and are used in place of the Daily Office Lectionary.

6. Eves of certain Feast Days (e.g. Presentation, Annunciation, Visitation, St. John the Baptist, Transfiguration, Holy Cross Day and All Saints' Day) have special psalms and lessons appointed, and are used at Evening Prayer on the day before the appointed feast (see pages 122-123).

7. The following days may be observed with a special Eve using the first set of psalms and lessons appointed:

> Eve of St. Mary the Virgin (August 15)
> Psalm 45
> Lessons: Jeremiah 31:1-14; John 19:23-27 (or Acts 1:6-14)
> Eve of St. Michael and All Angels (September 29)
> Psalms 34, 150
> Lessons: Daniel 12:1-3; Mark 13:21-27 (or Revelation 5:1-4)

8. The Eves of Apostles and Evangelists have special psalms and lessons *(BCP, 1001;* note exceptions) as does the Eve of the Dedication of a Church and the Eve of the Patronal Feast *(BCP, 1000;* see pages 122-123).

9. On Sundays:

   a. If Morning Prayer is said in its entirety not as the principal service of the day or as the Liturgy of the Word at the Eucharist, the lessons appointed in the lectionary are used according to the appropriate year.
   b. If Morning or Evening Prayer is the Liturgy of the Word at the Eucharist, then the psalm and lessons from the Eucharistic Lectionary *(BCP, 889-931)* are read.
   c. If Morning or Evening Prayer is the principal service of the day, the psalms and lessons appointed for the Eucharist of the Sunday are used in place of the Daily Office Lectionary.
   d. At Evening Prayer (provided it is not the Liturgy of the Word at the Eucharist), in place of the appointed Daily Office Lectionary for the Sunday, the lessons may be taken from the following or the preceding year of the Sunday Eucharistic Lectionary. (This is appropriate if Evening Prayer is not read on a daily basis, because in this case the course reading from the Old Testament may not always be suitable.)

   Example: Week of 1 Advent (Daily Office Year One; Eucharistic Lectionary Cycle, Year B)
   At Sunday Evening Prayer:

   > Amos 1:1-5, 13—2:8 (taken from Year Two, see 3 above)
   > Matthew 25:1-13 (see *Note* in 3 above)
   > *or*

From Eucharistic Lectionary Cycle, Year C (the year following Year B)

Zechariah 14:4-9

1 Thessalonians 3:9-13 or Luke 21:25-31

(If rubric in *Note* in 3 above is followed, Luke should be used.)

e. Concerning Evening Prayer (d. above), the psalm(s) are ordinarily taken from the Daily Office Lectionary, but the psalm appointed in the Eucharistic Lectionary may be used.

Example: Week of 1 Advent (Daily Office Year One; Eucharistic Lectionary Cycle, Year B)

At Sunday Evening Prayer:

Psalms, 111, 112, 113 (from Daily Office Lectionary)

or

Psalm 50 (from Eucharistic Lectionary, Year C)

f. If Sunday evening is the Eve of a Major Feast Day (see 6, 7, and 8 above), the psalms and lessons appointed for the Eve may be used in place of those appointed in the Daily Office Lectionary, or the option of d. and e. above.

Concerning Proper Collects at the Daily Offices

The Collect of the Day may follow the suffrages at Morning and Evening Prayer, after the Lord's Prayer at the Noonday Office, or preceding the blessing or dismissal at An Order of Worship for the Evening (unless the Eucharist follows this Order, *see BCP, 112*). This collect is used according to these rules:

1. At Morning Prayer or the Noonday Office, the Collect of the Day is that of the Sunday or Feast Day being celebrated, or, if no special collect is appointed, that of the preceding Sunday is used. (For the weekdays of Lent see *LFF, 29-61;* for the weekdays of Easter Season see *LFF, 65-75;* for Sundays, see *BCP 159-185* or *211-237;* for Major Feast Days see *BCP 185-194* or *237-246;* for Saints' Days see *LFF 87ff*, or *BCP 195-199* or *246-250;* for Various Occasions see *BCP 199-210* or *251-261* [these include Ember Days and Rogation Days].)

2. At Evening Prayer or at An Order of Worship for the Evening, if the psalms and lessons are not those of a Major Feast Day Eve, the Collect of the Day is that of the Sunday or Feast Day being celebrated, or if no special collect is appointed, that of the preceding Sunday is used (see 1 above for sources).

3. At Evening Prayer or at An Order of Worship for the Evening on Saturdays, the Collect of the next Day (Sunday) is used.

4. At Evening Prayer or at An Order of Worship for the Evening on Eves of Major Feast Days, the Collect of the Feast is used.

Lesser Feasts and Fasts at the Daily Office

If there is no celebration of the Eucharist on a day of observance appointed in the calendar, it is appropriate that the commemoration be made at one of the Daily Offices in the following way:

A. The Office is read in the usual fashion with the lessons appointed from the lectionary *(BCP, 934-1001).*

B. If a third lesson is desired at the Daily Office, it may appropriately be selected from the lessons appointed in *Lesser Feasts and Fasts* for the day.

C. The name of the person being commemorated is appropriately added to the suffrages (Form B) in Evening Prayer.

D. The hagiography from *Lesser Feasts and Fasts* or the reading from *The Prayer Book Office* (for a Major Feast) may be added after the final canticle, after the collects and intercession, or before the final "Let us bless the Lord" (or as a third reading after the biblical readings *[BCP, 142]*).

E. The collect appointed in *Lesser Feasts and Fasts* or *The Book of Common Prayer* is used as a first collect after the suffrages. A collect for the morning or evening may be added (see pages 129 and 138) followed by intercessions and conclusion of the Office.

Feast Days with Eves and Vigils

St. Andrew   Eve *(BCP, 1001)*
November 30

St. Thomas   Eve *(BCP, 1001)*
December 21

Christmas Eve   Vigil *(BOS, 35)*
December 24

St. John   Eve *(BCP, 1001)*
December 27

Vigil for the Baptism of Our Lord: Vigil *(BOS, 51-52)*
First Sunday after the Epiphany

Confession of St. Peter   Eve *(BCP, 1001)*
January 18

Conversion of St. Paul   Eve *(BCP, 1001)*
January 25

Presentation of Our Lord: Eve *(BCP, 996)*
Candlemas
February 2

St. Matthias   Eve *(BCP, 1001)*
February 24

The Annunciation   Eve *(BCP, 997)*
March 25

St. Mark   Eve *(BCP, 1001)*
April 25

SS. Philip & James   Eve *(BCP, 1001)*
May 1

The Visitation   Eve *(BCP, 997)*
May 31

St. Barnabas   Eve *(BCP, 1001)*
June 11

Nativity of St. John the Baptist   Eve *(BCP, 998)*
June 24

SS. Peter & Paul   Eve *(BCP, 1001)*
June 29

The Transfiguration   Eve *(BCP, 998)*
August 6

St. Mary the Virgin *August 15*	Eve: first psalm and first set of lessons at EP *(BCP, 999)*
St. Bartholomew *August 24*	Eve *(BCP, 999)*
Holy Cross Day *September 14*	Eve *(BCP, 999)*
St. Matthew *September 21*	Eve *(BCP, 1001)*
St. Michael and All Angels *September 29*	Eve: first psalms and first set of lessons at EP *(BCP, 999)*
St. Luke *October 18*	Eve *(BCP, 1001)*
St. James of Jerusalem *October 23*	no Eve prescribed or *(BCP, 1001)*
SS. Simon and Jude *October 28*	Eve *(BCP, 1001)*
All Saints' *November 1*	Eve *(BCP, 1000)* Vigil *(BOS, 106)*
Sunday after All Saints' Day	Vigil *(BOS, 106)*
Thanksgiving Day	no Eve prescribed
Eve of the Dedication of a Church	Eve *(BCP, 1000)*
Eve of the Patronal Feast	Eve *(BCP, 1000)*

For a Vigil on the Eve of Baptism *(BOS, 131-135)*.

For a Service on New Year's Eve *(BOS, 42-46)*.

For a Service (other than the Eve and Vigil given above) for All Hallow's
    Eve *(October 31)* *(BOS, 108-110)*.

For the Great Vigil of Easter (*BCP, 284-295;* also pages 200ff.).

For the Vigil of Pentecost (*BCP, 175 or 277; 896, 906, 917;* see also page 277).

The Daily Office

The Daily Office
Introduction

The Daily Offices (Morning Prayer, An Order of Service for Noonday, Evening Prayer, An Order of Worship for the Evening, and Compline) are the regular offering of prayer and praise by the Church. Clergy and many lay persons use the Daily Office as a regular form of private prayer. What follows is intended for ordering the public recitation of the offices, but the same rules may be applied to private recitation.

Note: For a richer and expanded office, *The Prayer Book Office* offers a full choice of antiphons, psalmody, readings, office hymns and other material.

Morning Prayer

The officiant, either clerical or lay, may be vested in cassock and surplice, or cassock-alb. A priest or deacon may wear a tippet over the surplice. The officiant enters, reverences the altar, and goes to the place from which the Office is to be led.

One or more of the opening sentences may be said by the officiant or may be sung *(BCP, 37-41 or 75-79)*.

The Confession of Sin (with either the long or short invitation) may be said *(BCP, 41-42 or 79-80)*. Only a priest stands and pronounces the absolution *(BCP, 42 or 80)*. A deacon or lay person who officiates at the Office remains kneeling, *and substitutes "us" for "you" and "our" for "your" (BCP, 42 or 80)* when saying the absolution.

The Invitatory and Psalter

All stand and the officiant sings or says the Preces, the people responding *(BCP, 42 or 80; Hymnal, S 1 or S 33)*. (*Note:* The Office may begin immediately with this versicle and response, eliminating either the opening sentence(s) or the Confession of Sin or both.)

It is traditional for the officiant and the people to trace a cross, using the thumb of the right hand, on the lips at the versicle. The Gloria Patri is sung or said by all, and "alleluia" may be added except during Lent and Holy Week *(Hymnal, S 1 or S 33)*.

Invitatory

Antiphons are provided *(BCP, 43-44 or 80-82;* for music see *HymAccEd, S 289-294)* to be used with the Invitatory Psalm. These may be sung or said:

a. at the beginning and the conclusion of the Invitatory;
b. at the beginning, after each of the single or double verses of the Invitatory, and at the conclusion;
c. as a congregational response during the Invitatory either after each verse, or after each double verse.

The choices for the Invitatory are:

1. the Venite *(BCP, 44-45 or 82; Hymnal, S 2-7 or S 34-40);*
2. Psalm 95 *(BCP, 146 or 724; Hymnal, S 8-10 or S 36-40)* especially suitable on Fridays (except during the Fifty Days of Easter), during Lent, during the days of Holy Week, and other penitential occasions;
3. the Jubilate *(BCP, 45 or 82-83; Hymnal, S 11-15 or S 41-45);*
4. Christ our Passover *(BCP, 46 or 83; Hymnal, S 16-20 or S 46-50).* This canticle is used in place of one of the above as the Invitatory during Easter Week and may be used daily throughout the Fifty Days of Easter, until the Day of Pentecost.

The Psalm(s)

The officiant and people may sit or stand for the psalm(s).

The psalm(s) are said or sung as appointed in the Daily Office Lectionary *(BCP, 936-1001).*

The following rubrics concerning the psalms should be noted *(BCP, 934-935):*

In the citation of the Psalms, those for the morning are given first, and then those for the evening. At the discretion of the officiant, however, any of the Psalms appointed for a given day may be used in the morning or in the evening. Likewise, Psalms appointed for any day may be used on any other day in the same week, except on major Holy Days.

Brackets and parentheses are used (brackets in the case of whole Psalms, parentheses in the case of verses) to indicate Psalms and verses of Psalms which may be omitted. In some instances, the entire portion of the Psalter assigned to a given Office has been bracketed, and alternative Psalmody provided. Those who desire to recite the Psalter in its entirety should, in each instance, use the bracketed Psalms rather than the alternatives.

Antiphons drawn from the Psalms themselves, or from the opening sentences given in the Offices, or from other passages of Scripture, may be used with the Psalms and biblical Canticles. The antiphons may be sung or said at the beginning and end of each Psalm or Canticle, or may be used as refrains after each verse or group of verses.

On Special Occasions, the officiant may select suitable Psalms and Readings.

A Note on the Psalms: In addition to the psalms appointed in the Daily Office Lectionary, the Psalter itself is arranged so that it may be read "in course" over a thirty-day period. This arrangement of the psalms may be used in place of those appointed in the lectionary.

The appointed psalm(s) are sung or said according to one of the following methods:

> direct recitation
> antiphonal recitation
> responsorial recitation
> responsive recitation

For an explanation of each of these ways see *BCP, 582.*

The Gloria Patri (BCP, 46 or 84) is always sung or said at the conclusion of the entire portion of the Psalter; and may be used . . . after each Psalm, and after each section of Psalm 119 (BCP, 141).

For the pointing of the Gloria Patri, see *BCP, 141.*

The Lessons and Canticles

The officiant and people sit for the lessons (the reader stands) and stand for the canticles.

The appointed lessons are read. They are announced by the reader *(BCP, 47 or 84)* and concluded with the optional response *(BCP, 47 or 84).*

It is appropriate that the lessons be read by lay persons (other than the officiant).

One or two lessons are read, but *if three Lessons are used, the Lesson from the Gospel is read after the second Canticle (BCP, 47 or 84).* (For instructions on the use of the lectionary and the appointed psalms and lessons, see pages 118-120).

Silence may follow each reading, and then a canticle is sung or said. A table of canticles for use at Morning Prayer is given *(BCP, 144; for music see Hymnal, S 177-288).*

The sign of the cross may be made by the officiant and people at the beginning of the canticles taken from the Gospels:

> Magnificat (Canticle 3 *or* 15)
> Benedictus Dominus Deus (Canticle 4 *or* 16)
> Nunc dimittis (Canticle 5 *or* 17)

On occasion, at the discretion of the Minister, a reading from non-biblical Christian literature may follow the biblical Readings (BCP, 142). In special circumstances, in place of a Canticle, a hymn may be sung (BCP, 142).

After the final canticle (or the Gospel, if three lessons have been read) the Apostles' Creed is sung or said. The officiant and people remain standing. (If the Eucharist is to be celebrated after the Office, and the Nicene Creed is to be said, the Apostles' Creed is omitted. Also, if more than one Office is said daily, the Apostles' Creed may be omitted at one of the Offices on weekdays.)

If Morning Prayer is used as the Liturgy of the Word for the Eucharist, see pages 91-92.

The Prayers

The people stand or kneel for the prayers.

Salutation and The Lord's Prayer *(BCP, 54 or 97; Hymnal, S 21 or S 51).*

The Lord's Prayer may be omitted from the Office when the Litany or the Eucharist is to follow immediately (BCP, 142).

The suffrages are sung or said following the Lord's Prayer (or after the final canticle, see above). Either set A or set B *(BCP, 55 or 97-98; Hymnal, S 22-23 or S 52-53)* may be used; set B is particularly suitable for use when the Te Deum is the final canticle after the lessons.

One or more collects are sung or said after the suffrages:

1. If a full celebration of the Eucharist is to follow, the Collect of the Day should not be used since it will be used at the Eucharist.
2. The "daily" collects may follow. Those for Sundays, Fridays and Saturdays are so indicated *(BCP, 56 or 98-99)*. The other collects are appropriately used as follows:

   For the Renewal of Life—Monday *(BCP, 56 or 99)*
   For Peace—Tuesday *(BCP, 57 or 99)*
   For Grace—Wednesday *(BCP, 57 or 100)*
   For Guidance—Thursday *(BCP, 57 or 100)*

The Great Litany may be sung or said at this point *(BCP, 148;* also see page 163). The Supplication may be sung or said after the Great Litany or alone *(BCP, 154)*. Unless the Eucharist or a form of general intercession (i.e., Great Litany or Supplication) is to follow, one of the three prayers for mission is added *(BCP, 57-58 or 100-101)*.

A hymn or anthem suitable for the morning *(Hymnal, 1-11)* or the season or the feast may be sung.

Authorized intercessions and thanksgivings may follow (BCP, 58 or 101). In the Intercessions and Thanksgivings, opportunity may be given for the members of the congregation to express intentions or objects of prayer and thanksgiving, either at the bidding, or in the course of the prayers; and opportunity may be given for silent prayer (BCP, 142).

Before the close of the Office either the General Thanksgiving *(BCP, 58 or 101)* or the Prayer of St. Chrysostom or both *(BCP, 59 or 102)* may be said by the officiant and people. If a Eucharist is to follow, the General Thanksgiving is not appropriate since the Great Thanksgiving is the central Eucharistic prayer.

The Office concludes with "Let us bless the Lord" and the response *(BCP, 59 or 102; Hymnal, S 24 or S 54)*. During the Fifty Days of Easter "Alleluia, alleluia" is added *(Hymnal, S 25 or S 55)*.

A closing sentence of Scripture may be added *(BCP, 59-60 or 102)*.

It is traditional for the officiant and the people to make the sign of the cross at the closing sentence.

If there is to be a sermon at the Office, it may be preached:

1. after the Office
2. within the Office, after the readings
3. within the Office, after the collects (preceding or following the hymn or anthem)

An offering may be received and presented at the Office (BCP, 142).

At the conclusion of the Office, the officiant reverences the altar and returns to the sacristy.

An Order of Service for Noonday

The officiant, either clerical or lay, may be vested in cassock and surplice, or cassock-alb. A priest or deacon may wear a tippet over the surplice. The officiant enters, reverences the altar, and goes to the place from which the Office is to be led.

The officiant sings or says the opening versicle; the people respond *(BCP, 103)*.

It is traditional to make the sign of the cross at the opening versicle.

The Gloria Patri is sung or said by all.

The alleluia is added except in Lent and during Holy Week.

A hymn of the day, of the season, of the hour, or any suitable hymn may be sung (see *Hymnal, 12-23;* also, *HymAccEd, S 296-304*).

The Psalms

One or more of the psalms given *(BCP, 103-105)* is sung or said.

Other suitable selections include Psalms 19, 67, one or more sections of Psalm 119, or a selection from Psalms 120 through 133 (BCP, 103).

Or the following pattern may be used *(PBO, 37-57):*

Day	Psalm(s)
Sunday	23 and 67
	or 118 (This is especially appropriate on the Sundays of Easter. It may also be used when Psalm 23 or 67 has been used earlier on the same day.)
Monday	119:1-8, 17-24
Tuesday	119:89-96, 105-112
Wednesday	121 and 122
Thursday	124 and 126
Friday	119:81-88 and 130 (except in the seasons of Christmas and Easter)
	23 and 67 (during the seasons of Christmas and Easter)
Saturday	132 (except during Lent)
	119:137-144, 169-176 (during Lent)
	(For Holy Week see page 183 for proper psalms.)

The Gloria Patri is sung or said at the conclusion of the psalm(s) *(BCP, 105)*.

The Short Reading

One of the passages of Scripture *(BCP, 105-106)* or some other suitable passage is read.

The passages may be read on ordinary days as follows *(PBO, 55):*

Romans 5:5 *(BCP, 105)*	Mondays and Thursdays
2 Cor. 5:17-18 *(BCP, 106)*	Sundays and Wednesdays
Malachi 1:11 *(BCP, 106)*	Tuesdays and Saturdays
2 Timothy 2:11b-12a	Fridays

It is appropriate that the reading be read without announcement.

At the conclusion of the passage of Scripture, the people respond, "Thanks be to God."

A meditation, silent or spoken, may follow (BCP, 106).

The Prayers

The Kyrie and Lord's Prayer follow *(BCP, 106)*.

After the versicle and response one of the collects *(BCP, 107)* is sung or said. *If desired, the Collect of the Day may be used (BCP, 107)*.

Intercessions may be offered either freely or using one of the authorized forms.

The Office concludes with the final versicle and response *(BCP, 107)*.

An Order of Worship for the Evening

This Order provides a form of evening service or vespers for use on suitable occasions in the late afternoon or evening. It may be used as a complete rite in place of Evening Prayer, or as the introduction to Evening Prayer, or some other service, or as the prelude to an evening meal or other activity. It is appropriate also for use in private houses (BCP, 108).

Note: This order is not for use on Monday, Tuesday or Wednesday in Holy Week, or on Good Friday (see page 183). For the Great Vigil of Easter and the Lighting of the Paschal Candle see pages 201-210.

The Entrance

A musical prelude is inappropriate and a processional or hymn should not be used.

The church is dark or partially so.

The people may be given unlighted candles or tapers when they arrive.

The officiant may be vested in a cope of the color of the feast or season.

The minister(s) enter in silence. Two torches may be carried before the officiant. If incense is used, the thurifer leads the procession. *From Easter Day through the Day of Pentecost, the Paschal Candle, if used, should be burning in its customary place before the people assemble (BCP, 143).* After reverencing the altar, the officiant faces the people. The torchbearers stand on either side of the officiant. (During the Fifty Days of Easter, the officiant goes to a place near the Paschal Candle to begin the service by its light.)

The officiant sings or says the proper greeting *(BCP, 109; Hymnal, S 56-57)*, the people responding.

Any part or parts of this service may be led by lay persons. A priest or deacon, when presiding, should read the Prayer for Light and the Dismissal at the end. A bishop or priest gives the final blessing (for deacon or lay person, see rubric *BCP, 114* concerning the blessing).

The Short Lesson

If one or more Scripture lessons are to be read later (e.g. at Evening Prayer or at the Eucharist), the Short Lesson may be omitted *(BCP, 143)*.

This reading is chosen from:

      1. one of the three appointed *(BCP, 109-110)*
      2. one of the seasonal passages *(BCP, 108)*
      3. some other suitable passage of Scripture

The lesson is chanted or read without announcement or conclusion and response.

The Prayer for Light

The officiant sings or says the Prayer for Light, first singing or saying "Let us pray." The orans position of the hands (for priest or bishop) is appropriate for this prayer.

1. One of the four general prayers may be used *(BCP, 110-111)*.
2. One of the seasonal prayers may be used *(BCP, 111)*.
3. Some other suitable prayer may be used.

The candles on the altar are lighted. During the Fifty Days of Easter the light is taken from the burning Paschal Candle; during Advent, the lighting of the Advent Wreath may take place before lighting the altar candles. The candles of the people and any other candles are lighted. *During the candle-lighting, an appropriate anthem or psalm may be sung, or silence kept (BCP, 112).*

Suggested anthems *(Lucernaria)* are found in *The Book of Occasional Services*. Music for the *Lucernaria* is found in *HymAccEd*.

1. For general use, Nos. 1-4 *(BOS, 10-12; HymAccEd, S 305-308)*
2. For seasonal use, *(BOS, 10-16; HymAccEd, S 309-320)*
3. One of the evening psalms may be sung or said *(BCP, 143)*:

Psalms 8, 23, 27, 36, 84, 93, 113, 114, 117, 121, 134, 139, 141, 143

The Hymn

When all the candles have been lighted, *Phos hilaron (BCP, 64 or 112; Hymnal, S 59-61)* is sung. A metrical version of this may be used or some other suitable hymn (see *Hymnal, 25-26, 36-37, [176]*).

If incense is used the officiant fills the thurible (and blesses the incense). The altar is censed (see pages 82-83); during the Fifty Days of Easter the Paschal Candle is censed; other objects may be censed; and the people may be censed (see page 80). (See *BCP, 143.*)

After the hymn has been sung (and the censing completed) the service may continue in any of the following ways:

A. On Major Feast Days or their Eves, a solemn procession may take place (see pages 168-169), followed by the Eucharist (or any of the other options given below). The procession begins with the versicle "Let us go forth in peace" and the response. The Eucharist begins after the procession with the salutation and collect (preceded by the Gloria in excelsis or other song of praise).

B. With Evening Prayer, beginning with the psalms (omitting the opening sentences, Confession of Sin, and Invitatory). The psalm(s) and lesson(s) are those appointed for the day.

C. With the Great Litany (and Supplication) (*BCP, 148-155;* see also page 164).

D. With some other office or devotion *(BCP, 112).*

E. With the celebration of the Holy Eucharist, beginning with the salutation and Collect of the Day.

F. It may be followed by a meal or other activity, in which case *Phos hilaron* (or other hymn) may precede the Lord's Prayer and a grace or blessing *(BCP, 112).* When a meal is to follow, a blessing over food may serve as the conclusion of this form of service *(BCP, 143).* For blessings over food see *BCP, 835;* also, *BOS, 97-98* for use during the Easter Season.

G. It may continue as a complete evening Office:

1. Psalm(s)—either those appointed for the day or feast or other suitable psalm(s).
2. A reading from Scripture.
3. A sermon or homily, a passage from Christian literature, or a brief silence may follow the reading.
4. The Magnificat or other canticle or some other song of praise.

5. The Prayers (one or more of the following):

    a. a litany or other suitable devotion or the Lord's Prayer (Suffrage B, *BCP, 68 or 122* is appropriate);

    b. on feasts or other days of special significance the Collect of the Day or a seasonal collect;

    c. one of the two collects appointed *(BCP, 113);*

    d. one of the collects from Evening Prayer or from Compline *(BCP, 69-70, 123-124, 133).*

6. A hymn may be sung at this point (during which an offering may be received and presented).

7. Blessing and/or dismissal *(BCP, 114).*

8. *The Peace may then be exchanged (BCP, 114).*

9. The ministers reverence the altar and return to the sacristy.

Any of the prayers in contemporary language may be adapted to traditional language by changing the pronouns and the corresponding verbs (BCP, 108).

Evening Prayer

The officiant, either clerical or lay, may be vested in cassock and surplice or cassock-alb. A priest or deacon may wear a tippet over the surplice.

The officiant enters, reverences the altar, and goes to the place from which the Office is to be led.

One or more of the opening evening sentences may be said by the officiant or may be sung *(BCP, 61-62 or 115-116)*, or the seasonal opening sentences from Morning Prayer may be used *(BCP, 37-41 or 75-78)*.

or

An Order of Worship for the Evening may be used as the beginning of Evening Prayer (see page 134; also *BCP, 109-112*).

The Confession of Sin (with either the long or short invitation) may be said *(BCP, 62-63 or 116-117)*. Only a priest stands and pronounces the absolution *(BCP, 63 or 117)*. A deacon or lay person who officiates at the Office remains kneeling, *and substitutes "us" for "you" and "our" for "your" (BCP, 63 or 117)* when saying the absolution.

The Invitatory and Psalter

All stand and the officiant sings or says the Preces, the people responding *(BCP, 63 or 117; Hymnal, S 26 or S 58)*. (The Office may begin immediately with this versicle and response, eliminating either the opening sentence or the Confession of Sin or both.)

It is traditional for the officiant and people to make the sign of the cross at the opening versicle. The Gloria Patri is sung or said by all, and alleluia may be added except during Lent and Holy Week.

Invitatory

The *Phos hilaron (BCP, 64 or 118)* is sung or said by all *(Hymnal, S 27 or S 59-61).*

or

A metrical version of this hymn may be sung *(Hymnal, 25-26, 36-37, [176]).*

or

Some other suitable hymn either of the season or of the Feast may be sung.

or

An Invitatory Psalm may be sung or said (see *BCP, 44-46 or 82-83; Hymnal, S 2-20 or S 34-50;* also page 127).

The Psalm(s)

The officiant and people sit or stand for the psalms. The psalm(s) appointed are found in the lectionary or are read as appointed "in course" (see pages 127-128; also, *BCP, 936-1001*). For the manner for singing or reciting the psalms, see *BCP, 582.* For the use of the Gloria Patri, see page 128.

The Lessons and Canticles

The officiant and people sit for the lessons (the reader stands) and stand for the canticles.

The appointed lessons are read. They are announced by the reader *(BCP, 64 or 118)* and concluded with the optional response *(BCP, 65 or 119).*

It is appropriate that the lessons be read by lay persons (other than the officiant).

One or two lessons are read, but *if three Lessons are used, the Lesson from the Gospel is read after the second Canticle (BCP, 65 or 119).*

Silence may follow each reading, and then a canticle is sung or said.

A table of canticles for use at Evening Prayer is given *(BCP, 145; Hymnal, S 177-288),* or traditional evening canticles (Magnificat and Nunc Dimittis: *BCP, 65-66 or 119-120; Hymnal, S 185-189, S 196-200 or S 247, S 253-261)* are used.

The sign of the cross may be made by the officiant and people at the beginning of the canticles taken from the Gospel (i.e., Magnificat and Nunc Dimittis).

On occasion, especially the Eves of Major Feast Days, at the discretion of the minister, a reading from non-biblical Christian literature may follow the biblical readings *(BCP, 142)*:

1. On the Eves of Major Feast Days and other Occasions, see *PBO, 714-771*, for appropriate non-scriptural readings. (These may also be used at Evening Prayer on the Feast or Day itself as a second or third reading or as a homily or meditation.)
2. One Major Feast Days or Lesser Feasts and Fasts the hagiography or commentary may be read *(LFF, 86-442)* as a second or third reading or as a homily or meditation.

In special circumstances, in place of a Canticle, a hymn may be sung (BCP, 142).

After the final canticle (or Gospel reading, if three lessons are read) the Apostles' Creed is sung or said. The officiant and people remain standing. (If the Eucharist is to be celebrated after the Office, and the Nicene Creed is to be said, the Apostles' Creed is omitted. Also, if more than one Office is said daily, the Apostles' Creed may be omitted at one of the Offices on weekdays.)

If Evening Prayer is used as the Liturgy of the Word for the Eucharist, see pages 91-92.

The Prayers

The people stand or kneel for the prayers.

Salutation and The Lord's Prayer *(BCP, 67 or 121; Hymnal, S 28 or S 62)*.

The Lord's Prayer may be omitted from the Office when the Litany or the Eucharist is to follow immediately (BCP, 142).

The suffrages are sung or said following the Lord's Prayer (or after the final canticle, see above). Either set A *(BCP, 67 or 121; Hymnal, S 22 or S 52)* or Set B *(BCP, 68 or 122; Hymnal, S 29-30 or S 63-64)* may be used.

One or more collects are sung or said after the suffrages:

1. If a full celebration of the Eucharist is to follow, the Collect of the Day is not used, since it will be used at the Eucharist.
2. On Saturday at Evening Prayer and Eves of Major Feast Days (see pages 122-123), the collect of the next Sunday or the feast is used.
3. The "daily" collects may follow. Those for Sundays, Fridays and Saturdays are so indicated *(BCP, 69 or 123)*. The other collects are appropriately used as follows:

   For Peace—Monday *(BCP, 69 or 123)*
   For Aid against Perils—Tuesday *(BCP, 70 or 123)*
   For Protection—Wednesday *(BCP, 70 or 124)*
   For the Presence of Christ—Thursday *(BCP, 70 or 124)*

The Great Litany may be sung or said at this point (*BCP, 148; Hymnal, S 67;* see also page 163). The Supplication may be sung or said after the Great Litany or alone (*BCP, 154;* also page 165). Unless the Eucharist or a form of general intercession (i.e., Great Litany or Supplication) is to follow, one of the three prayers for mission is always added *(BCP, 70-71 or 124-125).*

A hymn or anthem suitable for the evening or the season or the feast may be sung (see *Hymnal, 24-37, 163-184).*

Authorized intercessions and thanksgivings may follow (BCP, 71 or 125). In the Intercessions and Thanksgivings, opportunity may be given for the members of the congregation to express intentions or objects of prayer and thanksgiving, either at the bidding, or in the course of the prayers; and opportunity may be given for silent prayer (BCP, 142).

Before the close of the Office either the General Thanksgiving *(BCP, 71-72 or 125)* or the Prayer of St. Chrysostom or both *(BCP, 72 or 126)* may be said by the officiant and people. If a Eucharist is to follow, the General Thanksgiving is not appropriate since the Great Thanksgiving is the central Eucharistic prayer.

The Office concludes with "Let us bless the Lord" and the response *(BCP, 59 or 102; Hymnal, S 24 or S 54).* During the Fifty Days of Easter "Alleluia, alleluia" is added *(Hymnal, S 25 or S 55).* A closing sentence of Scripture may be added *(BCP, 59-60 or 102).*

It is traditional for the officiant and the people to make the sign of the cross at the closing sentence.

If there is to be a sermon at the Office, it may be preached:

1. after the Office
2. within the Office, after the readings
3. within the Office after the collects (pre-ceding or following the hymn or anthem)

An offering may be received and presented at the Office (BCP, 142).

At the conclusion of the Office, the officiant reverences the altar and returns to the sacristy.

Compline

The officiant, either clerical or lay, may be vested in cassock and surplice or cassock-alb. A priest or deacon may wear a tippet over the surplice.

The officiant enters, reverences the altar, and goes to the place from which the Office is to be led.

All standing, the officiant sings or says the opening sentence followed by the versicle and response *(BCP, 127)*. It is traditional to make the sign of the cross at the versicle.

The Confession of Sin may follow. A period of silence should be kept between the invitation and the confession. The people may stand or kneel. If the people kneel, the officiant remains kneeling for the absolution *(BCP, 128)*; if the officiant is a bishop or priest, the absolution is pronounced standing and the sign of the cross is made over the people.

The next versicle and response is said or sung, all standing. All then sing or say the Gloria Patri with the alleluia added at the conclusion except during Lent and Holy Week.

(Music for the Preces, Psalms, and Lessons, see *HymAccEd, S 321-330*).

The Psalm(s)

Any or all of the psalms given are sung or said, and suitable antiphons may be used with the psalm(s) *(BCP, 128-131)*. Other psalm(s) may be substituted at the discretion of the minister.

The people may sit or stand for the psalm(s).

At the conclusion of the psalm(s) the Gloria Patri is sung or said *(BCP, 131)*.

The Short Reading

One of the selections of Scripture given *(BCP, 131-132)* is read without announcement and the people respond, "Thanks be to God."
Some other suitable passage of Scripture may be read.

The following suggested lessons may be used in daily recitation of the Office *(PBO, 95-96)*:

Sunday	Revelation 22:3c-5
Monday	1 Thessalonians 5:9-10
Tuesday	1 Peter 5:8-9a
Wednesday	Matthew 11:28-30
Thursday	1 Thessalonians 5:23
Friday	Jeremiah 14:9, 22
Saturday	Hebrews 13:20-21

A hymn suitable for the evening may be sung *(BCP, 132; Hymnal, 38-46 or 24-37, [163-184])*.

The Prayers

The people and officiant stand. The versicles and responses, Kyrie and Lord's Prayer are sung or said *(BCP, 132-133; HymAccEd, S 331-335)*.

The next versicle and response is sung or said, and the officiant sings or says one of the collects *(BCP, 133);* note the proper collect for Saturday night *(BCP, 134)*.

One of the prayers *(BCP, 134)* may be added.

Silence may be kept, and free intercessions and thanksgivings may be offered (BCP, 134).

The Song of Simeon (Nunc dimittis) with the proper antiphon is sung or said *(BCP, 134-135; HymAccEd, S 336)*. The antiphon is intended to be sung or said by both officiant and people (with the triple alleluia added during the Fifty Days of Easter). At the beginning of the canticle it is customary to make the sign of the cross. At the conclusion of the canticle, the antiphon is repeated.

The concluding versicle and response is sung or said *(BCP, 135)*.

The officiant concludes the Office with the sentence *(BCP, 135)*.

The sign of the cross may be made during this sentence.

Solemn Evensong

Evening Prayer, sung and celebrated with the use of incense, is appropriate on Saturdays and Sundays, Feast Days, and the Eves of Feast Days (when an Eve is observed, see pages 122-123).

The officiant vests in cassock and surplice, or cassock-alb (with stole) and cope. Assisting ministers are vested as for a Solemn Eucharist (dalmatic and tunicle or in copes).

Servers will be needed to assist.

The officiant is preceded into the sanctuary by the thurifer, two torches, (processional cross), and assisting ministers.

The Office begins in one of the following ways:

1. All reverence the altar and the officiant goes to the sedilia or other place from which the celebrant presides at the Eucharist. The assisting ministers go to their places with the officiant. The officiant begins the Office with the Preces *(BCP, 63 or 117)*. These and the Gloria Patri (and the alleluia) are sung *(Hymnal, S 26 or S 58)*.

   During the *Phos hilaron (Hymnal, S 27 or S 59-61; also, 25-26, 36-37, [176])* or other suitable hymn, the thurifer brings incense to the officiant. The thurible is filled (and the incense blessed). The officiant alone takes the thurible and censes the altar (see pages 82-83). (During the Fifty Days of Easter, the Paschal Candle should be censed first and then the altar.) The officiant returns to the sedilia. The deacon then censes the officiant and the people (see page 80). The Office then continues with the singing of the psalms.

2. All reverence the altar. The officiant and assisting ministers remain facing the altar, and the officiant begins the Office with the Preces *(BCP, 63 or 117)*. These and the Gloria Parti (and the alleluia) are sung *(Hymnal, S 26 or S 58)*.

   During the *Phos hilaron (Hymnal, S 27 or S 59-61; also, 25-26, 36-37, [176])* or other suitable hymn, the thurifer brings incense to the officiant. The thurible is filled (and the incense blessed). The officiant alone takes the thurible and censes the altar (see pages 82-83). (During the Fifty Days of Easter, the Paschal Candle should be censed first and then the altar.) The officiant and ministers then go to the sedilia. The deacon censes the officiant and the people (see page 80). The Office then continues with the singing of the psalms.

3. All reverence the altar. The Office begins with An Order of Worship for the Evening (see page 132). After the candles are lighted, the officiant fills the thurible (and blesses incense). During the singing of the *Phos hilaron (Hymnal, S 27 or S 59-61; also, 25-26, 36-37, [176])* or other suitable hymn, the officiant takes the thurible and censes the altar (see pages 82-83). (During the Fifty Days of Easter, the Paschal Candle should be censed first and then the altar.) The officiant and ministers go to the sedilia. The deacon censes the officiant and the people (see page 80). After the hymn is completed, Evensong continues with the appointed psalms.

Note: If a bishop is present in the sanctuary and is not the officiant at the Office, it is customary that the thurifer bring the thurible to the bishop; the bishop then fills it (and blesses the incense). The thurifer then brings the thurible to the officiant, who censes the altar.

After the altar is censed, the deacon or thurifer may cense the bishop before censing those in the sanctuary and the people. (See page 80.)

The Psalm(s)

The appointed psalm(s) are sung or said. The officiant and people may sit or stand. The Gloria Patri is sung at the conclusion of the psalm(s).

The Lesson(s)

One or two lessons are read or chanted as appointed. A person or persons other than the officiant should read or chant the lessons. A canticle follows each lesson. If only one lesson is used, the Magnificat should be sung as the canticle at Evensong. On certain Eves, another canticle may be more appropriate as the first canticle (if there are two lessons); thus, the Magnificat would be the final canticle (see pages 122-123).

Note: In some places the tradition of censing the altar during the Magnificat is observed. This is in place of the censing at the *Phos hilaron* or in addition as a second censing. If the officiant, assisting ministers, and people have been censed at the *Phos hilaron*, they should not be censed again during the Magnificat; or, the censing of the ministers and people may be omitted at the *Phos hilaron* and done after the censing of the altar at the Magnificat.

The Apostles' Creed is sung.

The Prayers

The officiant sings the salutation and the officiant and people together sing the Lord's Prayer *(Hymnal, S 28 or S 62)*. The officiant, assisting ministers, and servers remain standing. All others may stand or kneel according to local custom. It is traditional for the acolytes to take their torches and stand on either side of the book, either facing each other or the officiant for the prayers.

Following the Lord's Prayer the suffrages are sung *(Hymnal, S 22, S 29-30, or S 63-64)*. It is appropriate for a cantor to sing the suffrages (either set A or set B).

The officiant sings the Collect of the Day (see page 138 for the collects) and may add other collects.

A cantor (or the officiant) sings "Let us bless the Lord" ("Alleluia, alleluia") *(Hymnal, S 31 or S 65)*.

The officiant may conclude with one of the closing sentences.

After reverencing the altar, all leave in the same way as at the entrance. (It is not necessary that the thurifer lead the procession.)

Solemn Te Deum

On days of special thanksgiving, the Te Deum may be sung in a solemn manner. This may be done at one of the following times:

1. After the postcommunion prayer at the Eucharist, before the blessing and dismissal.
2. After the collects at Morning or Evening Prayer at the place where a hymn or anthem may be sung.
3. After the Prayer for Light and *Phos hilaron* at An Order of Worship for the Evening, or if desired in place of the *Phos hilaron*.
4. As a separate service of thanksgiving.
5. At the Great Vigil of Easter (see page 209).

The officiant is vested in cope. Assisting ministers may also be vested in copes. The thurifer and acolytes precede the ministers to the altar. The altar is reverenced, and the officiant prepares incense. If the Te Deum is to be intoned the officiant sings the intonation.

During the singing of the Te Deum bells may be rung.

The officiant censes the altar at the beginning of the Te Deum (see pages 82-83). Following the censing, the thurible is given to the thurifer, who stands to the right of the altar, swinging the thurible. (If desired, two thurifers, with thuribles, may stand one to the right of the altar and the other to the left and swing the thuribles after the officiant has censed the altar.) All remain standing in front of the altar facing it. A solemn bow (or genuflection) is traditionally made at the words "We therefore pray *thee* . . ." Unless the musical setting precludes it, the Te Deum should end before the suffrages *(BCP, 53 or 96)*.

The suffrages (set B, *BCP, 55 or 98*) are then sung as versicles and responses by the officiant and people *(Hymnal, S 23 or S 53)*.

At the conclusion of the suffrages appropriate collects of thanksgiving may be sung (see *BCP, 836-841*).

The service ends with a (blessing and) dismissal.

After reverencing the altar, the officiant and assisting ministers return to the sacristy, led by the thurifer and acolytes with lighted torches.

Proper Liturgies
for Special Days
and other Occasions

Proper Liturgies for Special Days and other Occasions

Introduction

The Book of Common Prayer gives proper liturgies for Ash Wednesday and Holy Week; *The Book of Occasional Services* gives liturgies for other days. Special ceremonies and devotions have always been part of the liturgy of the Church. They have emerged either from historical sources or from the spiritual needs of the people. They are aids in heightening the awareness that this day or season is different from other days or seasons of the Church Year.

The observances and liturgies that follow (and commentaries on Lent and Eastertide) are taken either from *The Book of Common Prayer* or *The Book of Occasional Services.* In some instances traditional practices or devotions have been noted from other sources for optional use.

The intent in this section is to outline these services so that they can be celebrated either solemnly or simply, in their fullest traditional form or adapted with good judgment and taste to local and pastoral needs. For example, the Lighting of the Advent Wreath is mentioned both in *The Book of Common Prayer* and *The Book of Occasional Services* with minimal rubrical directions given; here these have been put in a way that can be used in a ceremony that will serve as a visual guide to the approaching celebration of the Nativity of Our Lord Jesus Christ. Likewise, Lent has its own various traditions (such as the Sarum Lenten Array) to emphasize the austerity of the season, as the use of the alleluia and the special quality of celebration of the Fifty Days of Easter underline the festive celebration of the Resurrection.

The following section incorporates most of these days, except for Holy Week. Holy Week (including the Great Vigil of Easter) follows as a separate section (see page 172*ff*).

The Lighting of the Advent Wreath

The Advent Wreath is a visual symbol marking the progress of the season of Advent. If it is lit at the beginning of a Sunday service (or at the announcement time if children are not present at the beginning), the ceremony should be brief. The Advent antiphon (BCP, page 43 or page 80) may be said in unison or responsively and followed with this prayer, said while the candles are lit:

Lord, grant us your light, that being rid of the darkness of our hearts, we may come to the true light which is Christ.

On the Saturday evening, before the First Sunday of Advent, the following form may be used:

An Order of Worship for the Evening (*BCP, 109ff.;* also pages 132-135)
Entrance
Greeting
Scripture reading (Isaiah 60:19-20 *or* Luke 12:35-37)
Prayer for Light (Collect for the First Sunday of Advent)
(If holy water is used, the wreath is sprinkled after the prayer.)
The lighting of the first candle of the Advent Wreath
During the lighting, the appropriate anthem *(Lucernarium)* for Advent, *(BOS, 10)* may be sung or said.
The hymn "Creator of the stars of night" *(Hymnal, 60)* is appropriate, or some other Advent hymn, or the *Phos hilaron.*
The order then continues as described on page 134.

The above may be used on any Saturday evenings during Advent (lighting the correct number of candles each Saturday) or on any other evening.

At morning services, the appropriate number of candles is lighted before the service begins.

At evening services, when the above Order of Worship for the Evening is not used, the appropriate number of candles is lighted before the service begins.

Concerning Advent

"Blessed be God . . ." is the proper acclamation at the Eucharist *(Hymnal, S 76-77).*

The "alleluia" is used during Advent at the Eucharist or Daily Office.

The Great "O" Antiphons may be used with the Magnificat *(The Song of Mary)* beginning on December 17. The text and music are found in *The Hymnal 1982, 56:*

December 17	O Wisdom	Stanza 2
December 18	O Lord of Might	Stanza 3
December 19	O Branch of Jesse	Stanza 4
December 20	O Key of David	Stanza 5
December 21	O Dayspring	Stanza 6
December 22	O Desire of Nations	Stanza 7
December 23	O Emmanual	Stanza 1 or 8, [Stanza 1]

The Presentation of Our Lord Jesus Christ in the Temple

Candlemas

(February 2)

The traditon of (blessing and) lighting candles and a procession on this feast is an ancient and venerable one. An order is found in *The Book of Occasional Services (53-55)* and is intended to be used immediately before the celebration of the Holy Eucharist on this day or if desired on the eve of the day.

Preparations

The people are given unlighted candles when they arrive. If possible, the congregation gathers at a place apart from the church, and the procession then moves to the church; or the procession may take place within the church. *In this case it is suitable that the celebrant begin the rite standing just inside the door of the church (BOS, 53).*

The Entrance

The celebrant and assisting ministers enter in the usual way (unless the rite begins at the door, see above). If incense is used, the thurifer leads the procession followed by (crucifer), acolytes (with lighted candles), and assisting ministers and the celebrant.

During the entrance, a hymn, psalm or anthem may be sung (Psalm 48:8-9 is appropriate concluding with the Gloria Patri).

After reverencing the altar, the celebrant turns and sings or says the greeting *(BOS, 53).*

The Blessing and Lighting of Candles

All hold their unlighted candles, or a table with unlighted candles for the celebrant and others is placed in the center of the chancel or some other convenient place in full sight of the congregation.

One of the following forms may be used:

Form A. After the greeting, the celebrant sings (or says) the collect provided *(BOS, 54)*, or the following:

> Almighty and everlasting God who on this day *didst* present *thine* only-begotten Son in the holy temple to be received in the arms of blessed Simeon; we humbly entreat *thee* to bless, hallow and kindle with the light of *thy* heavenly benediction these candles which we *thy* servants desire to carry, lighted in honor of *thy* Holy Name. May we be filled with the fire of *thy* love, and made worthy to be presented in the holy temple of *thy* glory; through Jesus Christ our Lord. *Amen.*

If incense and/or holy water are used, the candles may be censed and/or sprinkled after the prayer.

The candles on the table are distributed, and the celebrant lights the candles of the assisting ministers (taking the light from one of the acolytes' torches), and the light is passed to the people.

During the lighting of the candles, the Song of Simeon (Nunc dimittis) is sung with the third verse used as a antiphon (see *BOS, 51-52; or BCP, 66; see HymAccEd, S 341*).

When the candles are all lighted, preparations are made for the solemn procession (see page 168). *During the procession, all carry lighted candles; and appropriate hymns, psalms, or anthems are sung (BOS, 52; see Hymnal, 259, [115]).*

A station may be made at a suitable place. (See page 251 for versicle, response and collect; also *BOS, 53*.)

As the procession resumes and approaches the altar, the antiphon and psalm (see *BOS, 53*) may be sung, or some other suitable hymn, psalm or anthem (see *HymAccEd, S 343*).

When the procession reaches the sanctuary, the altar is reverenced and the Eucharist begins with the Gloria in excelsis. (The altar may be censed during this song of praise, see pages 82-83; or the altar may be censed before the song of praise, at the conclusion of the procession.)

After the Collect of the Day, all extinguish their candles. In some places, the tradition is observed of lighting the candles again for the proclamation of the Gospel and for the Great Thanksgiving, extinguishing them after the Breaking of the Bread.

If desired, the candles of the congregation may be lighted again at the time of the dismissal, and borne by them as they leave the church (BOS, 53).

Form B. After the greeting, the Song of Simeon (Nunc dimittis; see *HymAccEd, S 341*) with the antiphon (see above) is sung while the candles are lighted. At the conclusion, the celebrant sings or says the prayer given *(BOS, 52)*, or the variant given in Form A. The procession follows (see page 168).

During the procession, all carry lighted candles; and appropriate hymns, psalms, or anthems are sung (BOS, 52; see Hymnal, 259, [115]). A station may be made at a suitable place using the collect given *(BOS, 52)* or that on page 251. As the procession continues and approaches the altar, the antiphon and psalm (see *BOS, 53*) may be sung or some other suitable hymn, psalm or anthem (see *HymAccEd, S 343*).

When the procession reaches the sanctuary, the altar is reverenced and the Eucharist begins with the Gloria in excelsis. (The altar may be censed during this song of praise, see pages 82-83; or the altar may be censed before the song of praise at the conclusion of the procession.)

After the Collect of the Day, all extinguish their candles. In some places, the tradition is observed of lighting the candles again for the proclamation of the Gospel and for the Great Thanksgiving, extinguishing them after the Breaking of the Bread.

If desired, the candles of the congregation may be lighted again at the time of the dismissal, and borne by them as they leave the church (BOS, 53).

The collect *(BCP, 187 or 239)* and the lessons and psalm *(BCP, 922)* are those appointed for the feast. The Nicene Creed is said and the Proper Preface is that of the Epiphany.

Shrove Tuesday

The venerable custom of a pancake supper or some sort of Mardi Gras celebration is in many places part of parish life, but should be seen in the context of the next day, as a preparation for Ash Wednesday and the days of the Lenten discipline.

A celebration of the Eucharist or Evening Prayer would be appropriate at the beginning of the evening.

A "farewell" to the alleluia is fitting since the word will not be used again until the Easter Vigil (see pages 96 and 159).

It is fitting that the Exhortation *(BCP, 316-317;* also page 231) be read on this day and followed by the Confession of Sin, either in the Eucharist or at the Office. This solemn call to repentance, with its fine statement of Eucharistic theology, should not be overlooked and this is a most suitable day to use it. It may be followed by either the traditional Decalogue *(BCP, 317-318),* the contemporary Decalogue *(BCP, 350),* A Penitential Order (Rite I *or* II), or by the Confession of Sin in the Eucharist or the Confession from Morning or Evening Prayer. This will help keep Shrove Tuesday in its proper perspective as a day of preparation for Ash Wednesday. Time could be allowed after the Exhortation for people to make a private confession to a priest if they so desire (see pages 248-249).

Note: In some places it is customary to veil all crosses throughout Lent and/or to hang a Lenten Array. This is done after the liturgy on Shrove Tuesday.

Note: Shrove Tuesday (from the old English word "shrive"—to forgive) is a day for individual confession to a priest. Ash Wednesday, with its proper liturgy, is a day of public penitence for common sins.

The Preparation of Ashes for Ash Wednesday

Ashes, for imposition on Ash Wednesday, should be prepared well ahead of time. Some "palm dealers" include packets of ashes in the shipments for Palm Sunday; these may be kept and used the following Ash Wednesday. If you "make your own":

1. Ask the people of the parish to bring in palms from last year. It is still a common custom to save the palms from Palm Sunday.
2. These will naturally be quite dry and should be burned in a safe container outside. They will burn quite easily and furiously.
3. After the palms are burned and the ashes have cooled, they need to be put through a sieve to break down the larger particles.
4. The ashes should then be ground—a mortar and pestle work quite well —into a powder.
5. The ashes should then be put into a small bowl or other container for imposition. This container should be of such size that it will be easy for the priest to hold in the palm of the left hand while imposing the ashes with the thumb of the right hand.

Imposition of Ashes

Note: It is appropriate that the Paschal Candle be removed from the church (or baptistry) before the Liturgy of Ash Wednesday. It may be kept in the sacristy or other place in case it is needed for funerals or baptisms.

Ash Wednesday

The Entrance: Either in silence or with a penitential psalm (Ps. 69) or hymn. If incense is used, the altar may be censed during this psalm or hymn, or in silence.

The salutation and collect *(BCP, 166 or 264)* follow immediately (no acclamation, or other song of praise).

The Word of God:
Lesson	Joel 2:1-2, 12-17 *or* Isaiah 58:1-12
Psalm	103, *or* 103:8-14
Epistle	2 Corinthians 5:20b—6:10
(Hymn or Tract)	
Gospel	Matthew 6:1-6, 16-21
Sermon	

The Bidding: *(BCP, 264-265)*
Silence (all, including the ministers, kneeling)

The Blessing
of Ashes: The ashes may be sprinkled with holy water and/or censed after the blessing.

The Imposition
of Ashes: The people come to the celebrant and assisting ministers, and the ashes are imposed. During this it is appropriate that Psalm 51 be sung or recited, or Psalm 51 may be recited by all after the imposition of ashes.

The Litany
of Penitence: *(BCP, 267-269)* The people and celebrant and ministers all kneel.

The Absolution: *(BCP, 269)* The celebrant stands alone and gives the absolution.

The Peace follows, and the service then continues with the Offertory, Proper Preface of Lent (1), the Great Thanksgiving, Breaking of the Bread and Communion. The Prayer over the People *(BOS, 24-25)* may be used after the postcommunion prayer. The liturgy concludes with a dismissal.

Note: After the imposition of ashes, before the Litany of Penitence, the ministers should wash their hands. A cruet of water, lavabo bowl and towel should be available for this purpose.

Note: It is inappropriate to distribute or impose ashes outside of the above liturgy. For serious pastoral reasons, ashes may be imposed at other times in a setting of penitence and confession. The act of receiving ashes must not become the focal point of this day but rather a *sign* of the day, a sign that is part of the penitential beginning of the season of Lent.

Concerning Lent

Eucharistic Propers (collect, lessons and psalms) are given in *Lesser Feasts and Fasts* for all of the weekdays from Ash Wednesday until the Saturday before the Sunday of the Passion. *In keeping with ancient tradition, the observance of Lenten weekdays ordinarily takes precedence over Lesser Feasts occurring during this season. It is appropriate, however, to name the saint whose day it is in the Prayers of the People, and, if desired, to use the Collect of the saint to conclude the Prayers (BCP, 394).* Also, the biography of the saint may be read after the Gospel (see page 112).

1. The alleluia is omitted throughout Lent (see page 159).
2. The Gloria in excelsis is omitted throughout Lent. (On major Holy Days, another song of praise is more suitable, such as the Te Deum on the Feast of St. Joseph [March 19] and the Magnificat on the Feast of the Annunciation [March 25].) This reserves the use of the Gloria for the Great Vigil of Easter.
3. The appropriate color for the vestments and other hangings during Lent is violet or a Lenten Array. The Lenten Array is sackcloth or similar unbleached fabric with orphreys of deep red and black borders. Symbols of the Passion of our Lord may be on the vestments and hangings. In some places it is customary that the Lenten Array cover all decorations during Lent and Holy Week. In place of the usual processional cross, a simple wooden cross of dark red with black edges is substituted.
4. In place of or before the blessing at the Eucharist, a solemn Prayer over the People may be used (see *BOS,* 24-26).
5. The Great Litany (see pages 163-164) is suitable on the First Sunday in Lent and the following Sundays until the Sunday of the Passion.
6. Stations of the Cross (see pages 156-157; also *BOS, 56-73*) is an appropriate devotion during the season of Lent.
7. At the Daily Office or as a separate devotion, it is traditional that the Great Litany be sung or said on Wednesdays and Fridays from the Friday after Ash Wednesday through the Friday before Palm Sunday (see pages 163-164).
8. For the Burial of the Dead and Requiem Eucharists during Lent, see page 162.
9. The Penitential Acclamation is used at the Eucharist throughout Lent *(Hymnal, S 80-83).* This is used in place of the first acclamation ("Blessed be God . . .").

The Way of the Cross (Stations of the Cross)

The devotion known as the Way of the Cross is an adaptation to local usage of a custom widely observed by pilgrims to Jerusalem: the offering of prayer at a series of places in that city traditionally associated with our Lord's passion and death. The number of stations, which at first varied widely, finally became fixed at fourteen. Of these, eight are based directly on events recorded in the Gospels. The remaining six (numbers 3, 4, 6, 7, 9 and 13) are based on inferences from the Gospel account or from pious legend (BOS, 56).

The order for the Way of the Cross as given in *The Book of Occasional Services (BOS, 57-73)* is suitable for use at any time, but especially appropriate as an "extra-liturgical" devotion during Lent and on Good Friday. (Note that on Good Friday this devotion should not take the place of a public celebration of the Proper Liturgy appointed for the day.)

The stations are fourteen (or fewer if desired) wooden crosses which are placed around the church or some other suitable place. There may also be a pictorial representation of the event being commemorated. It is desirable that in addition to the officiant the people walk in the procession from station to station rather than staying in their places. The physical as well as the contemplative nature of walking the Way of the Cross is important.

The hymn Stabat Mater ("At the cross her station keeping") has frequently been associated with this service, but is not an integral part of it. Selected stanzas of this hymn may appropriately be sung at the entrance of the ministers, and (after the opening devotions before the Altar) as the procession approaches the first station (BOS, 59). In the form given in *BOS* the Trisagion is printed at the end of each station, and this may be sung as the procession moves from station to station, or verses of the Stabat Mater may be used *(Hymnal, 159).*

The officiant may be either an ordained or a lay person. The officiant leads the opening devotions, the versicle and response at the beginning of each station, and the concluding collect. The Scripture readings and the versicle and response following are appropriately read by another person. The officiant leads the concluding prayers *(BOS, 73).*

The officiant may be vested in cassock and surplice (with stole) or cassock-alb (and stole) and may also wear a cope. A crucifer may lead the procession using a plain Lenten (red with black edges) processional cross. Two acolytes with lighted candles may accompany the crucifer. The crucifer and acolytes may be vested in cassock and surplice or cassock-alb.

At the entrance of the officiant (and servers), silence may be kept or a hymn sung. The officiant (and other ministers) reverence the altar. The Opening Devotions *(BOS, 57-58)* are read standing before the altar and facing it. After the collect *(BOS, 57)* the procession moves to the first station. The people follow the officiant.

At each Station:

1. The officiant announces the station and reads the title. ("The First Station: Jesus is condemned to death.")
2. It is traditional that a genuflection or solemn bow be made by the officiant and the people at the opening versicle and response ("We adore . . .").
3. A period of silence is kept either immediately following the reading or after the versicle, response and "Let us pray." All remain standing.
4. After the collect, as the procession moves to the next station, either the Trisagion or some other suitable hymn (see above) is sung. The Trisagion may be said at the station, and a hymn sung as the procession moves.
5. At the Twelfth Station it is traditional to kneel at the end of the reading for a period of silent prayer. All stand after the versicle is said ("Christ for us became obedient unto death . . .").
6. After the Fourteenth Station the people return to their places and the officiant leads the concluding prayers standing facing the altar. The people remain standing.

The devotion may end with the final prayer *(BOS, 73).*

or

A hymn may follow.

or

A sermon or meditation may follow.

or

Other suitable devotions may follow.

In some places Devotions before the Sacrament are customary (see pages 265-266).

Concerning the Fifty Days of Easter

1. The Paschal Candle is lighted for all services from the Vigil of Easter through the Day of Pentecost. (It is not to be extinguished after the Gospel on Ascension Day.)
2. The alleluia is used throughout the season (see page 159).
3. The color of the vestments and hangings is white (or gold).
4. The Pascha Nostrum *(BCP, 46 or 83; Hymnal, S 16-20 or S 46-50)* may be used at the Breaking of the Bread or during the administration of Holy Communion throughout the Fifty Days of Easter.
5. The Pascha Nostrum *(BCP, 46 or 83)* is used as the Invitatory at Morning Prayer throughout Easter Week and may be used daily until the Day of Pentecost.
6. The Great Paschal Vespers may be used in place of Evening Prayer on Easter Day, the days of Easter Week, and the Second Sunday of Easter (see *PBO, 350-361*).
7. Propers are provided for weekday celebrations of the Eucharist throughout the Fifty Days of Easter (see *LFF, 64-81*). Unlike the weekdays of the Lenten Season (see page 155), it is suitable that the saints' days be observed as appointed in the calendar. *Since the triumphs of the saints are a continuation and manifestation of the Paschal victory of Christ, the celebration of saints' days is particularly appropriate during this season. On such days, therefore, the Collect, Lessons, Psalm and Preface are ordinarily those of the saint. Where there is a daily celebration, however, the weekday Lessons and Psalm may be substituted (LFF, 64).* See also page 112.
8. A Rogation Procession may be held on the Sixth Sunday of Easter (see pages 166-167).
9. A Vigil may be held on the Eve of the Day of Pentecost (see *BCP, 175 or 227; 896, 906, 917;* see also page 277).
10. At the Vigil of Pentecost, it is appropriate to read one or more of the lessons in several languages or to divide a reading among several persons who speak other languages.
11. The Paschal Candle is extinguished after Evening Prayer on the Day of Pentecost.
12. The Easter Acclamation is used at the Eucharist throughout the Fifty Days of Easter *(Hymnal, S 78-79)*.

Concerning the Alleluia

This exclamation of joy and praise, whether in the Latin form "alleluia" or the Hebraic form "hallelujah," is used both in the Eucharistic rites and in the Daily Offices, as well as in other liturgies of *The Book of Common Prayer.*

1. The alleluia is appropriately used where indicated both at the Eucharist and the Daily Offices at any time, but it is omitted at all liturgies from the conclusion of Evening Prayer on the Tuesday before Ash Wednesday until the Great Vigil of Easter.

2. During the Fifty Days of Easter (from the Great Vigil of Easter through the Day of Pentecost), the alleluia is used in the Eucharist:

    a. at the opening acclamation *(Hymnal, S 78-79)*

    b. at the Breaking of the Bread *(Hymnal, S 151-152, S 154-155)*

    c. at the dismissal *(Hymnal, S 175-176)*

    The alleluia may also be added to the Peace and to the versicle and response of a stational collect in a solemn procession.

3. At the Daily Office, the alleluia is added:

    a. after the Gloria Patri before the Invitatory *(Hymnal, S 1, S 26, S 33, S 58)*

    b. at the conclusion of the Office (i.e. "Let us bless the Lord, alleluia, alleluia") during the Fifty Days of Easter *(Hymnal, S 25, S 32, S 55, S 66)*

4. The use of the alleluia at the Breaking of the Bread and the Commendation is appropriate at the Burial of the Dead and other Requiem Eucharists. (During Lent, see page 162.)

5. For the closure of the alleluia before Lent, see pages 96 and 152.

Commemoration of All Faithful Departed
(All Souls' Day, November 2)

Beginning in the tenth century, it became customary to set aside another day—as a sort of extension of All Saints—on which the Church remembered that vast body of the faithful who, though no less members of the company of the redeemed, are unknown in the wider fellowship of the Church. It was also a day for particular remembrance of family members and friends. Though the observance of this day was abolished at the Reformation because of abuses connected with Masses for the dead, a renewed understanding of its meaning has led to a widespread acceptance of this commemoration among Anglicans, and to its inclusion as an optional observance in the calendar of the Episcopal Church (LFF, 412). If this day falls on a Sunday, it is transferred to Monday.

1. The Eucharist may be celebrated as usual on this day, using the collect, lessons and psalm(s) appointed *(LFF, 413)* and the Preface of the Commemoration of the Dead *(BCP, 349 or 382)*.
2. The following Eucharistic Liturgy may be used, either said or sung.

The Entrance: The Burial Anthems *(BCP, 469 or 491-492)* (sung or recited by the officiant and people)

The Kyrie eleison or Trisagion (If the anthem on *BCP, 492*, is used the Kyrie eleison or Trisagion is omitted.)

The salutation and response (sung or said)

The Collect of the Day *(LFF, 364)*

The Word of God

Lesson: Wisdom 3:1-9 *or* Isaiah 25:6-9

Psalm: 130 *or* 116:10-17

Epistle: 1 Thessalonians 4:13-18 *or* 1 Corinthians 15:50-58

(Psalm: If Psalm 130 is used above, Psalm 116:10-17 is used; or a hymn is sung.)

Gospel: John 5:24-27

Sermon

The Prayers of the People: As at the Burial of the Dead *(BCP, 480-481 or 497-498)*

Note: The plural form should be used throughout.

If a list of names of those to be particularly prayed for is to be read, the deacon or celebrant or other person may read these prior to the beginning of the Prayers of the People.

The Peace

The Holy Communion
    Offertory: An appropriate hymn, psalm or anthem may be sung.
    The Great
    Thanksgiving: The Preface of the Commemoration of the Dead is used *(BCP, 349 or 382)*.
      Eucharistic Prayer D (without the proper Preface) is suitable for this day *(BCP, 372-375)*.
    The Breaking
    of the Bread: Christ our Passover

      and/or Agnus Dei

      or

      Anthem 6 *(BOS, 18-19)*

      (The above may be sung or said.)
    Communion: An appropriate hymn, psalm or anthem may be sung.
    Postcommunion: In place of the usual postcommunion prayer the proper postcommunion prayer may be said or sung *(BCP, 482 or 498)*.

The liturgy may conclude with the blessing and/or dismissal.

or

All stand after the postcommunion prayer and the *Contakion* ("Give rest, O Christ") is sung or said by all. If said, the italicized parts are recited by the people *(BCP, 482-483 or 499; for music, Hymnal, 355)*.
At the conclusion the celebrant sings or says:

    a. the concluding collect *(BCP, 483 or 499)*,
    b. one of the collects "For the Departed" *(BCP, 202 or 253)*,
    c. or some other suitable collect *(BCP, 486-489 or 503-505)*.

The following may be said or sung:

    V. Rest eternal grant to them, O Lord:
    R. *And let light perpetual shine upon them.*
    V. May their souls, and the souls of all the departed, through the mercy of God, rest in peace. *Amen.*

The priest may bless the people (using the blessing, *BCP, 486-487 or 503*, or the usual blessing), and the deacon (or celebrant) sings or says the dismissal, using one of the regular forms or that given for the Burial of the Dead *(BCP, 483 or 500)*.

A Eucharist for the Departed (Requiem Eucharist)

If a Eucharist is celebrated for a departed person or persons, the liturgy as suggested for All Souls' Day, November 2 (pages 160-161), may be used with the following variations:

Collect: *BCP, 202 or 253* or any of the collects appointed for use at the Burial of the Dead.

*Lesson: Isaiah 25:6-9 *or* Wisdom 3:1-9

 *Psalm: 116 *or* 103:13-22 *or* 130

*Epistle: 1 Corinthians 15:50-58 (*or* Revelation 7:9-17)

*Gospel: John 5:24-27 *or* John 6:37-40 *or* John 11:21-27

Homily:

Prayers of the People (see page 160) using either the singular or plural form.

Preface of the Commemoration of the Dead *(BCP, 349 or 382)*

Postcommunion prayer *(BCP, 482 or 498)*

Conclusion of the liturgy (as suggested, page 161) using either the singular or plural form.

---

*Any of the Psalms and Lessons appointed at the Burial of the Dead may be used instead (BCP, 928).

Concerning the Alleluia at the Burial of the Dead and Requiem Eucharists

The liturgy of *The Book of Common Prayer* (1979) for the Burial of the Dead or a Eucharist for the departed is intentionally a celebration of the Resurrection. The "Dies irae" character of former Western liturgies has been minimized and the true character is now found in the anthem at the Commendation: "yet even at the grave we make our song: Alleluia, alleluia, alleluia" *(BCP, 483, 499)*. Thus, the question arises as to the use of the alleluia during the season of Lent. Since the burial of the dead lies outside liturgical time, the use of the alleluia would seem appropriate and consistent with the whole tone of the liturgy for the dead. The following are suggested as guidelines during Lent:

1. The alleluia is used in the anthem at the Commendation.
2. Hymns that use the alleluia are appropriate.
3. The alleluia is omitted at the Breaking of the Bread.

The use of the Paschal Candle (see pages 241ff.) is appropriate at all times, even during Lent.

The Great Litany and The Supplication

The Great Litany *(BCP, 148-154; Hymnal, S 67)* is appropriate at times of special petition or supplication.

It may either be sung or said, kneeling or standing, in place or in procession. It is traditional that the Litany be sung in procession on the First Sunday (or all Sundays) of Advent, the First Sunday (or first five Sundays) in Lent, and on Rogation Sunday (the Sixth Sunday of Easter). At the Daily Office, it is traditional that the Great Litany be sung or said either within the Office or as a separate devotion on Wednesdays and Fridays from the Friday after Ash Wednesday through the Friday before Palm Sunday *(PBO, 166)*.

1. If the Litany is sung or said prior to the Eucharist:

   a. The ministers enter, and when they have reverenced the altar the person appointed begins the Litany.

   b. The Litany concludes with the Kyrie eleison *(BCP, 153)*.

   c. The Kyrie eleison may be sung to a different musical setting than that of the Litany, in which case the person chanting the Litany concludes with the petition "O Christ, hear us" *(BCP, 153)*.

   d. The celebrant continues with the salutation and the Collect of the Day, and the Eucharist continues as usual.

   e. When the Litany precedes the Eucharist, the Prayers of the People (see *note,* page 165) and the Confession of Sin should be omitted.

   f. On the First Sunday of Advent and the First Sunday in Lent and at other times the Litany may be preceded by the Penitential Order *(BCP, 319 or 351)*, in which case the Litany begins immediately after the absolution *(BCP, 321 or 353)*. It concludes as above (b, c and d), and the Prayers of the People may be omitted and the Confession of Sin (within the Eucharist) is omitted.

2. If the Litany is sung or said after Morning or Evening Prayer:

   a. After the collects *(BCP, 58, 71, or 101, 125)* the Litany begins. The prayers for mission are omitted as is the remainder of the Office (see *note,* pages 129 and 139). If desired, the Lord's Prayer may be omitted from the Office, since it is used at the conclusion of the Litany *(BCP, 153)*.

   b. After the Kyrie eleison (see 1.c above), the Lord's Prayer is sung (or said) followed by the versicle and response *(BCP, 153)*.

   c. The officiant concludes with the prayer *(BCP, 153)* or some other suitable collect. The Supplication *(BCP, 154-155)* may be added (see page 165). Other prayers may be added, concluding the Office with the Grace *(BCP, 154)*.

3. If the Litany is sung or said following An Order of Worship for the Evening:

    a. An Order of Worship for the Evening begins in the usual way (see pages 132-133; also, *BCP, 109-112*).

    b. The Litany begins either after the *Phos hilaron* (or some other hymn), or after the psalm, lesson and canticle.

    c. It continues and concludes as above (2.b and 2.c).

    d. The Lord's Prayer is not omitted at the conclusion of the Litany.

4. If the Litany is sung or said as a separate service:

    a. The Litany is sung or said throughout.

    b. The officiant concludes with suitable prayers and the Grace.

    c. The Supplication *(BCP, 154-155)* may be used in place of the versicle and collect which follows the Lord's Prayer. The Supplication may conclude with other prayers and the Grace, or with the collect alone *(BCP, 155)* or with a blessing.

5. When the Litany is sung in procession:

    a. The Litany in Procession may take place at any of the services as listed above (1-4).

    b. Incense is not ordinarily used when the Litany is sung in procession (except the Rogation Procession, see page 166).

    c. At the time of the Litany, the officiant and assisting ministers come before the altar and reverence it. (The officiant may be vested in a cope).

    d. A crucifer and acolytes (with lighted candles) may lead the procession.

    e. All remain facing the altar while the officiant sings the first four petitions, the people responding. After the Trinitarian supplication, "O holy, blessed, and glorious Trinity, one God, have mercy upon us" *(BCP, 148)*, all turn and the procession begins around the church.

    f. The route of the solemn procession is used (see page 169).

    g. A station is not normally made.

    h. The procession returns to the altar during the final petitions before "O Lamb of God" *(BCP, 152)*.

    i. The Litany concludes in one of the ways described above (1.b-d; 2.c; 3.c-d; 4.b-c).

    j. When the Litany is sung in procession, the people should stand.

The Supplication *(BCP, 154-155)* may be used at any time, but *especially in times of war, or of national anxiety, or of disaster (BCP, 154):*

   a. At the conclusion of the Great Litany, following the Lord's Prayer (see 4.c above).

   b. At the conclusion of Morning Prayer (see page 129) or Evening Prayer (see page 139).

   c. As a separate devotion.

   d. The Supplication may be either sung or said.

   e. Other appropriate collects may be added after the versicles and responses.

   f. Following the concluding collect *(BCP, 155)* a blessing and/or dismissal may be added.

   g. Music for The Supplication may be found in *HymAccEd, S 338-339).*

Notes Regarding The Great Litany

1. The Presiding Bishop and other bishops may be named in the sixteenth petition *(BCP, 150).*

2. The President of the United States and others in authority may be named in the twenty-second petition *(BCP, 150).*

3. Special intercessions for peace or social justice may be added to the twenty-third petition *(BCP, 151).*

4. The sick may be named in the twenty-ninth or thirtieth petition *(BCP, 151).*

5. The dead may be named in the thirty-fifth petition *(BCP, 152).*

6. The Blessed Virgin Mary and other saints may be named in the thirty-sixth petition *(BCP, 152).*

The Rogation Procession

A. This procession may take place on either the Sixth Sunday of Easter; on Monday, Tuesday and Wednesday before Ascension Day; or on other days, *depending on local conditions and the convenience of the congregation (BOS, 101).*

B. This procession may be a separate service; or follow the principal Eucharist of the Day; or follow one of the Offices; or precede a celebration of the Eucharist, but not the principal Eucharist of the Sunday.

C. When the Rogation Procession follows the Eucharist, it begins after the postcommunion prayer, before the blessing and/or dismissal.

D. It is not inappropriate to use incense in the Rogation Procession. If incense is used, the thurifer brings the thurible to the celebrant or officiant either before the ministers go to the altar or after they have reverenced the altar. The officiant fills the thurible (and blesses the incense). If the Great Litany *(BCP, 148; Hymnal, S 67)* is used, all remain in place until after the Trinitarian supplication. The thurifer leads the procession followed by the crucifer and acolytes, (choir), assisting ministers, and officiant. (In some places the celebrant and ministers follow immediately after the thurifer, crucifer and acolytes.) The people follow.

E. The Rogation Procession may take one of the following routes:

   1. From the altar, down the center aisle, out the doors of the church, to some suitable place (such as a parish garden or around a city block or the parish property). The procession may either conclude outdoors with suitable prayers, hymn, blessing and/or dismissal; or it may return to the church (if this is the case, the Great Litany is customarily begun as the procession enters the church).

   2. Within the church, following the route of a solemn procession (see page 169).

   3. From the altar to some other place, either by an outdoor or indoor route, with the procession ending either with the beginning of the Eucharist or with suitable prayers, hymn, blessing and/or dismissal.

F. If the Great Litany *(BCP, 148-154; Hymnal, S 67;* see also, pages 163-165) is used, the following *(BOS, 104)* may be inserted after the twenty-fifth petition (the third petition on *BCP, 151)*:

That it may please thee to bless the land and waters, and all who work upon them, to bring forth food and all things needful for thy people,
We beseech thee to hear us, good Lord.
That it may please thee to bless the lands and waters, and all who work upon them to bring forth food and all things needful for thy people,
We beseech thee to hear us, good Lord.
That it may please thee to look with favor upon all who care for the earth, the water, and the air, that the riches of thy creation may abound from age to age,
We beseech thee to hear us, good Lord.

G. Other hymns, psalms, canticles or anthems may be sung during the procession (see *BOS, 103* for suggestions). However, it is traditional to conclude the procession (when it reenters the church) with the Great Litany.

H. If other hymns, psalms, canticles, or anthems are sung during the procession, stations may be made at suitable places for appropriate Bible readings and prayers (see *BOS, 102)*. Again, the Great Litany should conclude the procession.
(For additional directions see *BOS, 103-105.)*

Solemn Processions

A solemn procession may take place prior to the Eucharist on Major Feast Days and other occasions. The sacred ministers and servers enter in the usual way. They reverence the altar. During the entrance, a psalm or anthem may be sung, or instrumental music may be played. The thurifer brings the thurible to the celebrant, who fills the thurible (and blesses the incense). The thurible is returned to the thurifer and when all are ready the deacon, other assisting minister or the celebrant turns and, facing the people, sings the bidding:

> V: Let us go forth in peace. (Alleluia)
> *R: In the Name of Christ. Amen. (Alleluia)*

The order for the procession is:

Thurifer
Acolyte   Crucifer   Acolyte
(Choir)
Assisting Ministers
(Subdeacon)
(Deacon)
(Subdeacon)   Celebrant   (Deacon)
(Bishop)

(*or* The celebrant and assisting ministers may lead the procession, walking directly after the thurifer, crucifer, and acolytes. Others follow, and the people may walk in the procession.)

The route of the solemn procession may vary, but the normal procedure is that it begins and ends at the altar. After the response to the bidding, the thurifer (or if incense is not used, the crucifer and acolytes) leads the procession down the center aisle, turns right, across to the "north aisle," turns right, up the aisle, turns right, across the front (the altar is not reverenced when passing in front of it) to the "south aisle," turns right, down the south aisle to the back, turns right to the center aisle, turns right and goes up the center aisle to the altar.

A station (that is, a stop for a versicle, response and collect, see pages 250-254) may be made at some appropriate place during the procession. Incense may be prepared and used at the station. After the collect the thurifer leads the procession along the route described above back to the altar. The Eucharist then continues with the song of praise and the Salutation and Collect of the Day. The altar may be censed during the song of praise.

The route of the solemn procession is:

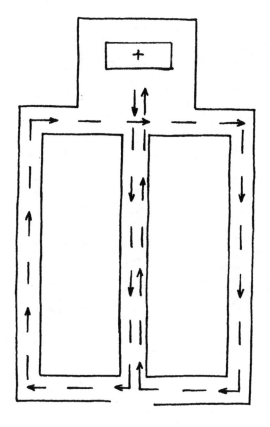

Holy Week

Holy Week

Introduction

The rites of Holy Week are ancient and by nature different from the liturgical celebrations of the rest of the Church Year. They are meant to be different in order to focus the attention of the people on the mysteries being celebrated in this sacred time.

Therefore, it is important that the priest and all who assist in the Holy Week rites be well prepared and familiar with what is happening. You cannot overplan for Holy Week. The extra time spent in preparation and the extra attention given to details will contribute substantially to a liturgical flow that will enable the people to participate fully in these rites and will also avoid confusion.

In the following pages, an introduction and a detailed outline for each service is given; a list of books and items needed at the beginning of each liturgy; basic liturgical matters along with movement and vestments; also some additional material, not given in *The Book of Common Prayer* but in accord with its rubrics, which may be used to heighten these liturgies.

If the time between Palm Sunday and Easter seems endless, it is meant to. Time is suspended as we ponder and celebrate the great mysteries of our redemption. A slow pace, reverence, and a continuity among services assist this contemplation.

The Sunday of the Passion: Palm Sunday

Introduction

The dual nature of the Liturgy for this Sunday is evident from the title. It begins with the pomp and glory of the triumphal entry into Jerusalem with shouts of "Hosanna" to our King. These hosannas soon change to "Crucify him, crucify him," as the Passion is narrated and dramatically proclaimed.

Regrettably, for some Christians, Holy Week consists solely of Palm Sunday and Easter Day. The rites of Maundy Thursday, Good Friday, and the Great Vigil of Easter are not observed or not attended. It is important, therefore, that the impact of the Passion and Death of our Lord be communicated on this day, so that the glory of the Resurrection may indeed be celebrated the following Sunday.

The Liturgy of the Palms must be in complete contrast to the Liturgy of the Passion and the celebration of the Eucharist on this day. As it begins in triumph it should end in silence. The Eucharist and conclusion should be in stark and vivid contrast to the beginning of the service.

The people should be given full opportunity to sing their praises at the procession and to cry their condemnation during the Passion. We are all part of this great drama, for it is the mystery of God's redemption of the world through his only-begotten Son. The strength of this day is in its "schizophrenic" nature. The truth of this day is that we all are responsible, through our sins, for the Passion and Death of our Lord. The glory of this day is that we know by faith the truth of the Resurrection and the promise of everlasting life "with him who suffered and died for us, and rose again."

Christ became obedient to the point of death—even death on a cross. Therefore God also highly exalted him and gave him the name that is above every name. (Philippians 2:8-9)

The Sunday of the Passion
Palm Sunday

Outline

I. The Liturgy of the Palms
   Entrance (psalm, anthem, antiphon)
   Acclamation and response
   Collect *(BCP, 270 or AB, 315)*
   Lesson (Gospel account of the entrance into Jerusalem)
   > Year A   Matthew 21:1-11
   > Year B   Mark 11:1-11a
   > Year C   Luke 19:29-40
   > (see *AB, 315-317*)
   The blessing of the branches *(BCP, 271 or AB, 318-319)*
   (Distribution of the branches)
   The Procession
   Station at the door of the church *(BCP, 272 or AB, 322)*
   Conclusion of the procession

II. The Word of God
   Salutation
   Collect of the Day *(BCP, 168 or 272; AB, 323)*
   Old Testament Lesson   Isaiah 45:21-25 *or* Isaiah 52:13—53:12
   Psalm 22:1-21 *or* 22:1-11
   Epistle   Philippians 2:5-11
   Psalm, tract, hymn or anthem
   Solemn reading of the Passion Gospel
   Sermon
   (Creed and Confession of Sin may be omitted)
   The Prayers of the People
   The Peace

III. The Holy Communion

   Preparation and Offering of Gifts
   The Great Thanksgiving with Preface of Holy Week
   The Breaking of the Bread
   Communion
   Conclusion of the liturgy

The Sunday of the Passion
Palm Sunday

Preparations

Vestments: Color: Passiontide red* or Lenten array.

Celebrant may wear a cope for the Liturgy of the Palms and change into chasuble for the Eucharist; or the cope may be worn for the Liturgy of the Word and the chasuble put on at the Offertory. Assisting ministers are vested according to their order.

Books: Altar Book (or other book) with the Liturgy of the Palms
Book for reading the Gospel at the Liturgy of the Palms *(Bible, AB, LT* or *ER, BOG* or *GR).*
Bible or *Lectionary* Texts for the lessons
Books for the participants in the solemn reading of the Passion
Parts for the congregation in the reading of the Passion
Altar Book for the Eucharist

Items: Palms
(or other green branches that may be locally available; the Russian Orthodox Church uses pussy willow):
1. on a table in full view of the people, to be distributed after the blessing
or
2. given to the people when they arrive

If holy water is used at the blessing of the palms, the aspergillum and bucket should be near the place of blessing, or a person should be assigned to carry them.

If incense is used, the thurible should be prepared ahead of time, and the thurifer well instructed as to duties.

For the
Eucharist: The usual setting of the credence and place from which the gifts of bread and wine will be brought at the Offertory procession.

---

*Passiontide red is a deep (dark) red with black orphreys.

The Liturgy of Palm Sunday

I. The Liturgy of the Palms

A. If possible the Liturgy of the Palms should take place in a location other than the church itself.

B. The palms or branches may either be distributed to the people as they arrive or placed on a table in the chancel for distribution after the blessing.

C. The celebrant and assisting ministers enter, during which a psalm, anthem, or the following is sung:

"Hosanna to the Son of David! Blessed is he who *comes* in the name of the Lord. Hosanna in the Highest."

D. The celebrant then sings (or says) the acclamation with the people responding (or this acclamation may be sung at the entrance) *(AB, 314; Hymnal, 153).*

Celebrant: Blessed is the King who *comes* in the name of the Lord.
People: Peace in heaven and glory in the highest.

E. With hands extended (orans position) the celebrant sings (or says) the collect *(BCP, 270; or AB, 315).*

F. The deacon, assisting priest, or the celebrant (a lay reader may read this lesson in the absence of the above assistants) then reads (or chants) the lesson from the Gospel. The Gospel is announced and concluded in the usual way, and the responses are made.

  1. If desired, incense may be used at the reading of this lesson and torches may be carried.

  2. All remain standing for the lesson.

Year A	Matthew 21:1-11	*(AB, 315-316; BOG, 36)*
Year B	Mark 11:1-11a	*(AB, 316; BOG, 119)*
Year C	Luke 19:29-40	*(AB, 317; BOG, 179-180)*

G. After the lesson, the celebrant and assisting ministers stand at the table on which the branches have been placed. It is appropriate that the celebrant and ministers face the people across the table. This blessing is not done at the altar.

  1. The table should have branches for the celebrant and assisting ministers. Also, if they have not been given to the people prior to the liturgy, those to be distributed to the people should be on this table.

  2. If incense is used, the thurible is filled (and the incense blessed). If holy water is to be used, a server with the aspergillum and bucket should stand near the celebrant and assisting ministers.

H. The celebrant greets the congregation with the salutation and bidding *(BCP, 271; Hymnal, 153)*. It is appropriate that this be sung to the tone of the Preface (see *AB, 318-319*).

Note: If palms are distributed to the people prior to the liturgy, the people should raise them during the blessing. Also, the palms distributed should be large enough to carry or wave, not small crosses.

1. After the salutation and bidding, the celebrant sings (or says) the blessing with hands extended (orans position). An assisting minister or server holds the book for the celebrant.
2. At the words "Let these branches be for us signs of his victory, and grant that we who bear them . . ." the celebrant may either make the sign of the cross over the branches or extend hands over them through the words "that leads to eternal life." Hands should then be joined for the concluding Doxology and Amen.
3. If incense is used, the branches are censed at the conclusion of the blessing.
4. If holy water is used, the branches are sprinkled at the conclusion of the blessing.

I. Distribution of the Branches

1. Immediately after the blessing (and censing and/or sprinkling) the palms are distributed to the assisting ministers and the people (unless they were distributed prior to the liturgy).
2. The celebrant gives branches to the assisting ministers and then representatives of the congregation come forward to receive branches and distribute them to the people.
3. During the distribution:
   a. the anthem
      "Blessed is he who *comes* in the name of the Lord. Hosanna in the highest" *(BCP, 271)* may be sung (see *AB, 320; Hymnal, 153*).
   b. *or* this anthem
      "The children of the Hebrews, bearing branches of olive, went out to meet the Lord, crying out and saying: 'Hosanna in the Highest.' "
   c. It is appropriate that Psalm 24:7-10 be sung with either of the above anthems.

J. The Procession

1. When all have received branches, preparations are made for the procession.

    a. If incense is used, the thurible is filled (and incense blessed) at this point and the thurifer moves into place to lead the procession.

    b. If the blessing of palms takes place in a location other than the church, the procession moves from that place to the church.

    c. If the blessing of palms takes place in the church, the route of a solemn procession (see page 169) is followed.

    d. It is appropriate that all present have the opportunity to walk in the procession. If there is a very large congregation and the procession takes place in the church proper, representatives may be appointed to participate in the procession.

2. When all is ready, the deacon (or celebrant or other assisting minister) sings (or says) the bidding *(BCP, 271; AB, 320; Hymnal, 153)* and the people respond.

    a. The procession then moves:

(Thurifer)

Candle Cross Candle

(Choir)

(Assisting Ministers)

(Subdeacon)

(Deacon)

(Subdeacon) Celebrant (Deacon)

(Choir)

People

    b. During the procession all carry branches, and suitable hymns, psalms or anthems are sung. The traditional hymn for this procession is "All glory, laud and honor" *(Hymnal, 154-155)* and *Psalm 118:19-29 (AB, 321-322; Hymnal, 157).*

3. At the door of the church or some other suitable place, the procession halts for a station. The celebrant sings (or says) the following:

V. Blessed is the King who *comes* in the name of the Lord.
R. *Peace in heaven and glory in the highest (AB, 314; Hymnal, 153).*

Let us pray (Collect, *BCP, 272; AB, 322*).

4. The procession then continues to the altar.

    a. During this second part of the procession, the hymn, "Ride on, ride on in majesty," *(Hymnal, 156)* may be sung. The collect at the station sets forth the change in emphasis at this point, with the focus now on the crucifixion and our walking in the way of the cross. A hymn or psalm that reflects this new theme will help underscore this dramatic shift.

   b. The choir, servers and assisting ministers go to their places; the people return to their places.

   c. The celebrant and assisting ministers go before the altar and face it.

II. The Word of God

At the conclusion of the hymn or psalm the celebrant turns and facing the people sings (or says) the salutation and then facing the altar sings (or says) the Collect of the Day *(BCP, 272 or 168 or 219)*. The people remain standing. At the conclusion of the collect, the celebrant and assisting ministers go to the sedilia.

   a. The reader goes to the lectern and reads the Lesson.

   b. The psalm is sung or said.

   c. The reader (or subdeacon) goes to the lectern and reads the Epistle.

   d. A psalm, hymn, or anthem is sung or said. The traditional anthem before the reading of the Passion:

   "Christ became obedient unto death, even the death of the cross. Wherefore God also *has* highly exalted him, and given him a name which is above every name."

Solemn Reading of the Passion Gospel

A. Incense or torches are not used at the reading of the Passion.

B. Three (or more) readers take their places facing the people during the hymn, psalm or anthem after the Epistle.

C. The placement and assignment of parts are:

   1. Deacon (or assisting minister) to the pulpit to read the part of the narrator.

   2. Celebrant to the center to read the part of Christ.

   3. Lay reader, subdeacon or other assisting minister to the lectern to read the remaining parts.

   4. Or, Priest and two lay persons may stand side by side at the head of the aisle or on a chancel step. The priest reads the part of Christ.

   5. If other readers are used they should be so located as not to detract from the focus on the narrator and the Christ.

   6. The people should have copies of the Passion with their parts clearly indicated so that they may fully participate in their role as the crowd. This is desirable whether the Passion is chanted or read.

D. The Passion, with parts assigned is found:

Year A Matthew	*(LTYA, 71-80)*	*(BOG, 37-47)*	*(GR, 29-38)*
Year B Mark	*(LTYB, 63-70)*	*(BOG, 120-127)*	*(GR, 107-114)*
Year C Luke	*(LTYC, 65-72)*	*(BOG, 181-188)*	*(GR, 164-171)*

E. The narrator announces the Passion Gospel *(BCP, 272)*.
No response is made and the narrator immediately begins reading the text.

F. Directly following the narration of the death of Jesus, it is customary for a period of silence to be kept, during which the people either kneel or bow. Those in the sanctuary and the readers do the same.

G. When the narrator continues after the silence, the people stand again.

H. No response is made at the conclusion of the Passion.

I. The readers return to their places and the person appointed to preach goes to the pulpit or other designated place for the sermon.

After the sermon:

1. The Nicene Creed may be omitted *(BCP, 273)*.
2. The Prayers of the People and the Peace follow.
3. The Confession of Sin may be omitted *(BCP, 273)*.

III. The Holy Communion

As usual, but note:

1. Choral music, anthems or hymns should not be of a "Palm Sunday" character but rather should focus on the Passion and Death of our Lord. The triumphal entry is celebrated in the Liturgy of the Palms only and not in the Eucharist.

2. The Preface of Holy Week is used.

3. At the conclusion of the Eucharist the tone should be somber, in marked contrast to the Liturgy of the Psalms. The hymn "Alone Thou goest forth, O Lord" *(Hymnal, 164, [68])* is suitable as a postcommunion hymn or before the dismissal.

4. The Prayer over the People *(BOS, 26)* may be used before the dismissal. The ministers and people leave in silence.

The Weekdays of Holy Week: Monday, Tuesday, Wednesday

At Celebrations of the Holy Eucharist

The proper color for vestments is Passiontide red.
The penitential opening acclamation is used on all three days *(BCP, 319, 323 or 351, 355)*.
Special collects are appointed for each day *(BCP, 168-169, or 220)*.
The lessons and psalm are the same for years A, B and C:

Monday	Lesson	Isaiah 42:1-9
	Psalm	36:5-10
	Epistle	Hebrews 11:39-12:3
	Gospel	John 12:1-11 *or* Mark 14:3-9
Tuesday	Lesson	Isaiah 49:1-6
	Psalm	71:1-12
	Epistle	1 Corinthians 1:18-31
	Gospel	John 12:37-38, 42-50 *or* Mark 11:15-19
Wednesday	Lesson	Isaiah 50:4-9a
	Psalm	69:7-15, 22-23
	Epistle	Hebrews 9:11-15, 24-28
	Gospel	John 13:21-35 *or* Matthew 26:1-5, 14-25

The Proper Preface of Holy Week is used on each day *(BCP 346 or 379)*. The optional solemn Prayer over the People may be used before the dismissal *(BOS, 26)*.

At Morning or Evening Prayer

The opening sentence is chosen from those appointed for Holy Week *(BCP, 39 or 76-77)*.
The alleluia is omitted after the Gloria Patri.
The full recitation of Psalm 95 as the Invitatory is appropriate at Morning Prayer *(BCP, 146 or 724-725; Hymnal, S 8 or S 34, S 36-40)*.
The Lenten Antiphon for use with the Invitatory is appropriate at Morning Prayer *(BCP, 43 or 81)*. At Evening Prayer the *Phos hilaron* is appropriately omitted during Holy Week.

The Lessons, Psalms and Canticles:

	Year One	*Year Two*
Monday		
Morning Prayer	Psalm 51:1-18 (19-20)	Psalm 51:1-18 (19-20)
	Jeremiah 12:1-16	Lamentations 1:1-2, 6-12
	Canticle 9 *(Ecce, Deus)*	Canticle 9 *(Ecce, Deus)*
	Philippians 3:1-14	Mark 11:12-25
	Canticle 4 or 16	Canticle 4 or 16
	(Benedictus)	(Benedictus)
Evening Prayer	Psalm 69:1-23	Psalm 69:1-23
	Lamentations 1:1-2, 6-12	Jeremiah 12:1-16
	Magnificat (or Canticle 14)	Magnificat (or Canticle 14)
	John 12:9-19	2 Corinthians 1:1-7
	Nunc dimittis (or Magnificat)	Nunc dimittis (or Magnificat)
Tuesday		
Morning Prayer	Psalms 6, 12	Psalms 6, 12
	Jeremiah 15:10-21	Lamentations 1:17-22
	Canticle 2 or 13	Canticle 2 or 13
	(Benedictus es)	(Benedictus es)
	Philippians 3:15-21	Mark 11:27-33
	Canticle 4 or 16	Canticle 4 or 16
	(Benedictus)	(Benedictus)
Evening Prayer	Psalm 94	Psalm 94
	Lamentations 1:17-22	Jeremiah 15:10-21
	Magnificat (or Canticle 14)	Magnificat (or Canticle 14)
	John 12:20-26	2 Corinthians 1:8-22
	Nunc dimittis (or Magnificat)	Nunc dimittis (or Magnificat)
Wednesday		
Morning Prayer	Psalm 55	Psalm 55
	Jeremiah 20:7-11	Lamentations 2:1-9
	Canticle 14	Canticle 14
	(Kyrie Pantokrator)	*(Kyrie Pantokrator)*
	Philippians 4:1-13	Mark 12:1-11
	Canticle 4 or 16 (Benedictus)	Canticle 4 or 16 (Benedictus)
Evening Prayer	Psalm 74	Psalm 74
	Lamentations 2:1-9	Jeremiah 17:5-10, 14-17
	Magnificat (or Canticle 14)	Magnificat (or Canticle 14)
	John 12:27-36	2 Corinthians 1:23-2:11
	Nunc dimittis (or Magnificat)	Nunc dimittis (or Magnificat)

Creed, Lord's Prayer and suffrages follow.

Collect of the Day *(BCP, 168-169, 220)* and/or Collect for Fridays on each of the days at either Morning Prayer or Evening Prayer *(BCP, 56, 69, 99, or 123).*

(If the Eucharist follows either Morning Prayer or Evening Prayer, the Collect of the Day is not used, and that for Fridays is suitable.)

(If the Eucharist does not follow, intercessions are offered or one of the prayers for mission is added.)

The Office is concluded in the usual way.

An Order of Service for Noonday

The Office begins in the usual way *(BCP, 103).*

A suitable hymn for Holy Week may be sung.

One or more of the suggested psalms is sung or said *(BCP, 103-105).*

The Short Lesson:	Monday	Romans 5:8
	Tuesday	Zechariah 12:10
	Wednesday	Hebrews 5:7-8

or those suggested *(BCP, 105-106).*

Kyrie, Lord's Prayer, versicle and response follow.

The Collect of the Day (see above) and/or the second collect *(BCP, 107)* is said. Intercessions are read and the Office is concluded *(BCP, 107).*

An Order of Worship for the Evening

This order is not appropriate for use on Monday, Tuesday, or Wednesday in Holy Week, or on Good Friday (BCP, 108).

Compline

The Office is read in the usual way *(BCP, 127-135).*

The lesson may be chosen from one of those given above for Morning or Evening Prayer.

The hymn after the lesson should be appropriate to Holy Week.

The Collect of the Day may be used after the Lord's Prayer, before one of the evening collects.

Tenebrae

The office of Tenebrae is appropriate on Wednesday evening of Holy Week. On Thursday and Friday the Proper Liturgies of the Day are the principal services and may be celebrated in the evening. A complete form for Tenebrae is found in *The Book of Occasional Services* beginning on page 73. Rubrics and ceremonial guides are given *(BOS, 74, 91-92).*

Maundy Thursday

Introduction

Ideally, there is only one celebration of the Holy Eucharist on this day and it should take place during the evening hours. For pastoral reasons a simple celebration may take place earlier in the day, but the washing of feet and the reservation of the Sacrament for the Good Friday Liturgy should not be part of this celebration. It has been and is the tradition of the Church that the Reserved Sacrament is consumed on Wednesday of Holy Week (keeping that which may be necessary for emergencies). Only that which is consecrated on Maundy Thursday is administered to the people, with a sufficient quantity consecrated for reservation for the Good Friday Liturgy.

A Seder in place of the Liturgy of Maundy Thursday is not in keeping with the emphasis of this day: a) the institution of the Holy Eucharist; b) the law of love, symbolized in the washing of feet; and c) the beginning of the celebration of the Passion and Death of our Lord Jesus Christ. For Christians, the Passover emphasis is in the Liturgy of the Great Vigil of Easter. The celebration of the Resurrection is our Passover. The parallel symbolism with the Jewish Passover is found in the Great Vigil and should be reserved for that celebration.

Likewise, restraint in the Liturgy of Maundy Thursday is preferable to the medieval and baroque practices adopted by many in the late nineteenth and early twentieth centuries. Passiontide red is more suitable than white as the color for vestments. The use of the Gloria in excelsis (or other festive songs of praise) and the ringing of bells should be reserved for the Great Vigil and the celebration of Easter. The liturgy of this evening should convey the strength of solemnity and restraint so that the actions may speak for themselves. For indeed, it is the beginning of the sacred three days of the celebration of the Passion and Death of our Lord Jesus Christ. It initiates a time of watching, waiting and contemplating, as we enter into the commemoration of the mystery of our redemption. The gift of love in the Sacrament of Christ's Body and Blood is the focus; the demonstration of self-giving in the washing of feet is a fitting symbol; the watch through the night and the continuation of this liturgy in that of Good Friday is the timelessness of silence, the silence of God. On this night we celebrate the Great Thanksgiving with the powerful knowledge that:

> *When the hour had come for him to be glorified by you, his heavenly Father, having loved his own who were in the world, he loved them to the end; at supper with them he took bread . . . After supper he took the cup of wine . . . Father, we now celebrate this memorial of our redemption (BCP, 374).*

Maundy Thursday

Outline

    I. Entrance Rite
        Acclamation
        Song of Praise
        Collect (*BCP, 169 or 274;* also *AB, 324*)
   II. The Word of God
        Lesson   Exodus 12:1-14a
        Psalm 78:14-20, 23-25
        Epistle   1 Corinthians 11:23-26 (27-32)
        Psalm, tract, hymn or anthem
        Gospel   John 13:1-15 *or* Luke 22:14-30
        Sermon (homily)
  III. The Washing of Feet
  IV. Prayers of the People and Confession of Sin
        The Peace
    V. The Holy Communion
        Reservation of the Sacrament
  VI. Stripping of the Altar
 VII. The Watch

Maundy Thursday

Preparations

Vestments: Color: Passiontide red (or in some places white)
Celebrant in chasuble and assisting ministers vested according to their order

Books: Altar Book for the Eucharist
Bible, *Lectionary Texts,* or *Eucharistic Readings* for the lessons
Gospel Book on the altar or carried in by the deacon
Altar Book (or other) for the Liturgy of the Word
Bible marked for the reading of the account of the Agony in the Garden (after the stripping of altars)

Items: At the place of the washing of feet:
(These may all be on a table in full sight of the congregation.)
    a basin
    a pitcher filled with water
    a sponge
    a towel

At the place of Reservation:
    a corporal, upon which the Sacrament will be placed
    a white cloth to cover the vessels containing the Sacrament
    an unlighted sanctuary lamp, to be lighted after the Sacrament is brought to the place of Reservation
    other candles (and flowers) according to custom

For the Eucharist: For the Reservation of the Sacrament:
a ciborium or other vessel with sufficient bread to be consecrated at this liturgy for distribution on Good Friday
a flagon filled with wine (and a little water) to be consecrated at this liturgy sufficient for distribution on Good Friday.

For the Offertory procession: bread and wine at the place from which the gifts will be brought to the altar.
The altar candles are lighted before the liturgy begins.

The Liturgy of Maundy Thursday

I. Entrance Rite

The celebrant and assisting ministers enter in the usual way. A hymn, psalm or anthem appropriate to the liturgy of the day may be sung.

All reverence the altar.

(If incense is used, the altar may be censed during the entrance song.)

Either "Blessed be God . . ." or the penitential acclamation may be sung or said.

The Kyrie eleison or Trisagion may follow the acclamation.

The greeting is said or sung by the celebrant (facing the people), followed by the Collect of the Day *(BCP, 274)*.

II. The Word of God

Lesson: Exodus 12:1-14a

Psalm: 78:14-20, 23-25. Suggested antiphon: "So they ate and were well filled, for he gave them what they craved" (Ps. 78:29) *or* "So mortals ate the bread of angels; he provided for them food enough" (Ps. 78:25)

Epistle: 1 Corinthians 11:23-26 (27-32)

Hymn: (See *Hymnal, 320, vv1-4, [193]*)
or
(Tract): ("O Savior of the world, who by *thy* Cross and Precious Blood *hast* redeemed us; save us, and help us, we humbly beseech *thee,* O Lord. Christ became obedient unto death, even the death of the Cross. Wherefore God also *hath* highly exalted him: and *hath* given him a Name which is above every name.")

Gospel: John 13:1-15 (The Washing of Feet)
or
Luke 22:14-30 (Institution narrative)
(If incense is used see page 80.)

Sermon: (Homily)

III. The Washing of Feet

Representatives of the congregation come forward to assigned places either in front of or in the midst of the congregation and sit. Chairs should be provided. Although in some places it is traditional to wash only one foot, the washing of both feet is preferable. The washing of hands in place of feet is not desirable. The celebrant may introduce the ceremony with a bidding *(BOS, 93)*. During the washing of feet, the celebrant should do the actual washing while assisting ministers pour the water and dry the feet. A sufficiently large basin, pitcher, towel (and sponge) should be ready for this action. During the footwashing, anthems *(BCP, 274-275;* also *HymAccEd, S 344-347)* are sung or said. It is traditional to conclude the ceremony with the singing (or saying) of the hymn *Ubi caritas* "Where charity and love prevail" *(Hymnal, 606, 576, 581;* see also page 255). It is desirable that the celebrant remove the chasuble or cope for the washing of feet.

IV. The Prayers of the People

The deacon or other assisting minister or person appointed leads the prayers. (*Note:* If Eucharistic Prayer D is to be used, the prayers may be omitted.)

Unless the liturgy has begun with the Penitential Order, a Confession of Sin and absolution follow the Prayers of the People.

The Peace

The celebrant greets the people with the Peace, and it is exchanged in the usual fashion. In some places those who have had their feet washed remain until this point and then return to their seats in the congregation.

V. The Holy Communion

The liturgy continues with the Offertory. The gifts are presented and offered. If incense is used, the gifts and the altar are censed (see pages 84-85). The Preface is that of Holy Week (unless Eucharistic Prayer D is used). Eucharistic Prayer D is especially suitable for the liturgy of this day. If Eucharistic Prayer D is used, the petitions are added in their proper place *(BCP, 375)*.

Communion is administered from the Bread and Wine consecrated at this liturgy. Enough is prepared and reserved for the Liturgy of Good Friday if Communion is to be administered on that day.

After Communion, ablutions are performed in the usual way (see page 73) and the postcommunion prayer is said.

The Sacrament to be reserved for Good Friday is left upon the altar (covered with a [fair linen] cloth). After the postcommunion prayer all kneel and sing the hymn *Pange Lingua* "Now my tongue the mystery telling" *(Hymnal, 329, [199-200]).* If incense is used, it is prepared and blessed, and the celebrant censes the Sacrament. Toward the end of the hymn (at verse 6) the Sacrament is taken to the place of Reservation by a simple and direct route. A solemn procession around the church is not in keeping with the spirit of the day.

When the Sacrament is to be reserved for administration on Good Friday, it should be kept in a separate chapel or other place apart from the main sanctuary of the church, in order that on Good Friday the attention of the congregation may be on the bare main Altar (BOS, 94). After the Sacrament is brought to the place of Reservation, it is reverently placed and covered. The celebrant and assisting ministers then return for the stripping of the altars.

Note on Reservation for the Good Friday Liturgy: The Sacrament may be reserved in both kinds, or the Bread only. If the Wine is reserved, it is fitting that a large flagon or cruet be used for this purpose, and not a chalice.

VI. The Stripping of the Altar

It is desirable that the congregation remain for the stripping of the altar(s). The celebrant and assisting ministers, having removed chasuble, dalmatic(s) and stole(s), come to the center and begin stripping the main altar. All movable hangings and ornaments are removed to the sacristy. *It may be done in silence; or it may be accompanied by the recitation of Psalm 22, which is said without Gloria Patri. The following antiphon may be said before and after the Psalm. "They divide my garments among them; they cast lots for my clothing" (BOS, 94).* Any crosses that cannot be removed are veiled (if possible) if this has not been done on Shrove Tuesday.

A final blessing and dismissal are omitted.

VII. The Watch

It is appropriate that a watch be kept throughout the night before the Reserved Sacrament. Thus, after the stripping of the altar(s)—except the altar where the Sacrament is reserved—the deacon or other appointed person may read the account of the Agony in the Garden (Matthew 26:30-46), after which the lights are extinguished (except at the place of Reservation). The celebrant, assisting ministers and the people depart in silence. Organ or other instrumental music is not appropriate.

If a common meal or Agapé is to follow the liturgy, the stripping of the altar(s) is deferred until after the meal (see *BOS, 95-96).*

Good Friday

Introduction

The Solemn Liturgy of the Passion and Death of Our Lord Jesus Christ should be celebrated in the afternoon or early evening hours. It is a continuation of the Maundy Thursday Liturgy and begins in silence as the night before ended in silence.

The Liturgy for Good Friday has four parts: 1) the Word of God (with the Passion according to John); 2) the Solemn Collects; 3) the bringing in of the Cross and Veneration; 4) Communion from the Reserved Sacrament.

In order that the solemnity of this day be maintained, careful planning and preparation are necessary. Nothing should detract from the total participation of all the people in the celebration of this liturgy.

Before the liturgy begins, the place of Reservation should be darkened so that all attention may be focused on the action in the sanctuary. A single lamp should be kept burning, signifying the sacramental presence, but all other candles should be extinguished.

The main altar is bare, without linens or frontals. There are no candles. If possible, all crosses should be removed until the third part of the liturgy.

Outline

I. Word of God
   Entrance (in silence)
   Acclamation
   Collect   *(BCP, 169 or 276;* also *AB, 327)*
   Lesson   Isaiah 52:13-53:12, *or* Genesis
            22:1-18, *or* Wisdom 2:1, 12-24
   Psalm   22:1-11 (12-21), *or* 40:1-14, *or* 69:1-23
   Epistle   Hebrews 10:1-25
   (Psalm, see list above)
   Solemn reading of the Passion Gospel
   Sermon

II. The Solemn Collects

III. The Bringing in of the Cross
   Veneration of the Cross
   Anthems 1, 2 and 3
   (Reproaches)
   Hymn "Sing my tongue, the glorious battle"

IV. Communion from the Reserved Sacrament
   Sacrament is brought to the altar
   A Confession of Sin
   The Lord's Prayer
   Communion
   Concluding Collect

Good Friday

Preparations

Vestments: Color: Passiontide red (see Note on Vestments below)
Note on Vestments: Those seeking simplicity may wish to celebrate the entire Good Friday Liturgy in alb and Passiontide red stoles. Others will want to be vested in chasuble for the entire Liturgy. Those who seek to retain the chasuble for the Communion may wish to use all or part of the following, adapted from traditional Western use. At the beginning of the liturgy the celebrant and assisting ministers may be vested in albs and stoles. After the reading of the Passion (and sermon) the celebrant may put on a Passiontide red cope for the Solemn Collects and the Veneration of the Cross. Likewise, the deacon (and other assisting ministers) may put on red dalmatics or tunicles. After the Veneration of the Cross the celebrant may put on a Passiontide red chasuble for the Communion and the remainder of the liturgy.

Books: Altar Book (or other book with the Liturgy of Good Friday)
Bible, *Lectionary Texts,* or *Eucharistic Readings* for the readings
Books for the participants in the reading of the Passion
Parts for the congregation in the reading of the Passion

Items: In the sacristy (or other designated place):
A plain wooden crucifix or cross for the Veneration
Two torches or candles to be carried in with the cross
On the credence:
(altar cloth)
Corporal
Chalice(s) for administration of Communion
Cruet of water (and wine) for ablutions
Lavabo bowl for ablutions
Purificator(s) for the chalice(s)
Altar Book (with stand)

Note: The altar is bare at the beginning of the liturgy, without cross, candles, or vestings. Candles are not lighted.

The Liturgy of Good Friday

I. The Word of God

Entrance: The celebrant and assisting ministers enter the church in silence. Processional cross, torches, or incense are not carried. Prior to the entrance, there should be no instrumental music. A solemn and dignified procession from the back of the church up the center aisle is very effective in silence. When the celebrant and assistants reach the sanctuary, all reverence the altar with a solemn bow. All kneel (or prostrate themselves) for silent prayer *(BCP, 276)*.

Acclamation and
Collect: After a substantial period of silence, the celebrant alone stands and sings or says the acclamation *(BCP, 276 or AB, 326)*, followed immediately by the collect. There is no salutation before the collect. If the acclamation and collect are sung, this may be done on one note without inflection (or sung as in *AB, 326* and Collect Tone I *AB, 374*). At the conclusion of the collect, the assisting ministers stand and they and the celebrant go to the sedilia and sit for the lessons and psalms.

Lesson: Isaiah 52:13-53:12, *or* Genesis 22:1-18, *or* Wisdom 2:1, 12-24

Psalm: 22:1-11 (12-21), *or* 40:1-14, *or* 69:1-23

Epistle: Hebrews 10:1-25

(Psalm):   One of those listed above or the Tract suggested for Maundy Thursday (see page 187).

Solemn Reading of the Passion Gospel

A. Incense or torches are not used at the reading of the Passion.
B. Three (or more) readers take their places facing the people during the hymn, psalm or anthem after the Epistle.
C. The placement and assignment of parts are:

    1. Deacon (or assisting minister) to the pulpit to read the part of the narrator.
    2. Celebrant to the center to read the part of Christ.
    3. Lay reader, subdeacon or other assisting minister to the lectern to read the remaining parts.
    4. If other readers are used they should be so located as not to detract from the focus on the narrator and the Christ.

5. The people should have copies of the Passion with their parts clearly indicated so that they may fully participate in their role as the crowd. This is desirable whether the Passion is chanted or read.

D. Always John 18:1-19:37 (for text see: *LTYA, 99-107; LTYB, 88-96; LTYC, 90-98; ER, 92-99; BOG, 54-62; GR, 45-52).*

E. The narrator announces "The Passion of our Lord Jesus Christ according to John."
   No response is made and the narrator immediately begins reading the text.

F. Directly following the narration of the death of Jesus, it is customary for a period of silence to be kept, during which the people either kneel or bow. Those in the sanctuary and the readers do the same.

G. When the narrator continues after the silence, the people stand again.

H. No response is made at the conclusion of the Passion.

I. The readers return to their places and the person appointed to preach goes to the pulpit or other designated place for the sermon.

J. The sermon

K. A hymn may be sung *(Hymnal, 168, [75], or 169)*

II. The Solemn Collects

After the sermon, a hymn may be sung *(BCP, 277).*

The celebrant and assisting ministers stand and the prayers are sung or said in one of the following ways:

A. The celebrant and assisting ministers come to the center, reverence the altar with a solemn bow, and turn and face the people.
   The deacon (or celebrant) reads the bidding *("Dear People of God . . ." BCP, 277* or if sung, *AB, 332).*
   After *"We pray, therefore, for people everywhere according to their needs,"* the celebrant and assisting ministers turn and face the altar; the deacon (or other person appointed) remains facing the people.
   The deacon (or other person appointed) then begins the solemn biddings (which may be sung, *AB, 332ff)* in the following way:

   1. Each of the five sets of biddings is read or sung facing the people.
   2. The deacon may direct the people to kneel for the period of silence *(BCP, 277; AB, 333).* The deacon turns and faces the altar and all kneel. After the silence, the deacon directs all to stand for the collect.
   3. All stand for the collect, which is sung or said by the celebrant (if sung, *AB, 333-338).*
   4. After the Amen, the deacon again turns to the people for the bidding, and so forth as above until the conclusion of the final collect *(BCP, 280).*

B. The celebrant and other assisting ministers remain at the sedilia. The deacon (or other person appointed) comes to the center alone.

1. The deacon faces the people for the biddings. (The deacon may also bid them kneel for the silences, see A. 2 above.)
2. The deacon may turn and face the altar while the celebrant sings or says the collect.
3. After the collect, the deacon again turns to the people for the bidding and so on until the conclusion of the final collect *(BCP, 280)*.

C. The celebrant, deacon, and other assisting ministers may remain at the sedilia for the entire singing or reading of the Solemn Collects.

Again the deacon or other person appointed reads the biddings and the celebrant the collects.

Note: It is not permissable to omit any of the five sets of petitions. However, *the indented portions may be adapted by addition or omission, as appropriate, at the discretion of the Celebrant (BCP, 277).* Additional collects are not added.

The service may be concluded here with the singing of a hymn or anthem, the Lord's Prayer, and the final prayer on page 282 (BCP, 280).

III. The Bringing in of the Cross and Veneration

At the conclusion of the Solemn Collects, the deacon (or other assisting minister, or the celebrant) goes to the sacristy to prepare for the bringing in of the cross or crucifix.

During this period silence may be kept, or an appropriate hymn or anthem sung.

A wooden cross is brought into the church in one of the following ways:

Form A.   1. The minister carrying the cross enters at the doors of the church accompanied by two acolytes with candles lighted.

Bringing in of Cross

2. Three stations are made (at the same places "The Light of Christ" will be proclaimed at the Easter

Vigil). The deacon (or other person) stops, and facing the people, may say or sing (each time at a higher pitch):

"Behold the wood of the Cross,
on which was hung the world's salvation"
and the people respond:
"Come, let us adore him."

(The people may kneel for each of the stations, standing after the response.)

3. The deacon moves up the aisle from station to station until the final station before the altar. After this third station the Veneration follows (see below).

Form B. 1. The minister carrying the cross enters at the doors or from the sacristy accompanied by two acolytes with candles lighted.

2. The cross is carried to the altar while one or more of the anthems *(BCP, 281-282;* for music see *HymAccEd, S 349-351)* is sung or said. It is appropriate for the people to respond with the italicized portions of these anthems.

3. When the minister carrying the cross has reached the altar, the Veneration follows (see below).

Form C. 1. The cross is brought to the altar in silence. The minister carrying the cross may be accompanied by two acolytes with lighted candles.

2. When the minister carrying the cross has reached the altar, the Veneration follows (see below).

Note: It is not appropriate for instrumental music to accompany the bringing in of the cross or crucifix.

The Veneration of the Cross

Appropriate devotions may follow, which may include any or all of the following, or other suitable anthems (BCP, 281).

The Veneration may be done in one of the following ways:

Form A. 1. Upon reaching the altar, the deacon or other minister places the cross in a stand on the altar and the candles are placed on either side of it.

2. The celebrant and other assisting ministers come to the center and kneel before the altar for the Veneration.

3. During the Veneration the people kneel.

4. The anthems *(BCP, 281-282;* for music see *HymAccEd, S 349-351)* may be said or sung, as may the traditional *Improperia* (Reproaches) (see pages 256-257).

5. The Veneration concludes with the hymn "Sing, my tongue, the glorious battle." *(Hymnal, 166, [66] or 165)* or some other hymn extolling the glory of the cross *(BCP, 282)*. All remain kneeling for this hymn.

Form B.

1. Upon reaching the altar, the minister carrying the cross (assisted by others) holds the cross. The acolytes may put their candles on the altar or hold them on either side of the cross.

2. The celebrant and other assisting ministers come forward, kneel and kiss the foot of the cross. A genuflection or a solemn bow may be made on approaching the cross (this may be done three times).

3. After those in the sanctuary have venerated the cross, the Veneration may continue as in A. 2-5 above, or the people may be invited to come forward and venerate the cross individually.

4. During the Veneration, the anthems *(BCP, 281-282;* for music see *HymAccEd, S 349-351)* are said or sung, as may be the traditional *Improperia* (Reproaches) (see pages 256-257).

5. The hymn "Sing, my tongue, the glorious battle" *(Hymnal, 166 or 165)* or some other hymn extolling the glory of the cross *(BCP, 282)* is sung as the Veneration concludes.

6. The cross is placed in a holder on the altar as are the candles if this has not been done previously.

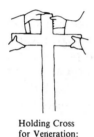

Holding Cross
for Veneration:
Form B.

A Note on the Veneration

Simple dignity is in order so that the solemnity of the action may be focal. Form A above is preferable and likely to be less distracting for the people.

Concerning music or recited texts during the Veneration

1. After the anthems *(BCP, 281-282;* for music, see *HymAccEd, S 349-351)* are sung or said, silence may be kept while the Veneration continues.

2. Silence may be kept throughout the entire Veneration, with only the hymn sung at the conclusion.

3. The traditional *Improperia* (Reproaches) have been criticized for having anti-Semitic overtones. However, it is appropriate to use these, especially with the response of the Trisagion, as long as the people understand that the texts are directed to all of humanity, and that we all, through our sins, are brought to the judgment of the cross, and there are forgiven and saved through Jesus Christ. (The texts for the *Improperia* are found on pages 256-257).

4. The hymn "Sing, my tongue, the glorious battle" *(Hymnal, 166, [66], or 165)* is the ancient hymn before the Cross which concludes the Veneration.

After the Veneration is completed, *The service may be concluded here with the Lord's Prayer and the final prayer (BCP, 282).*
In the absence of a bishop or priest, all that precedes may be led by a deacon or lay reader (BCP, 282).

IV. Communion from the Reserved Sacrament

Note: The Sacrament is not to be consecrated on this day.

A. An acolyte or assisting minister brings a corporal to the altar and spreads it. (In some places a full altar cloth is spread.) If the Sacrament has been reserved in both kinds a chalice (or chalices) for administration is brought to the altar and placed upon the corporal.

B. During the conclusion of the hymn at the end of the Veneration, or after the hymn is completed, the deacon (or celebrant, or other assisting minister) goes to the place of Reservation and brings the Sacrament to the altar. Acolytes with lighted candles may precede the deacon.

C. When the deacon arrives at the altar the Sacrament is placed upon the corporal (and the chalices filled from the flagon or cruet).

D. The acolytes place their candles at either end of the altar if they have carried them before the Sacrament (or the candles are still in place on the altar from the time of the Veneration).

E. During the above, silence may be kept, or one of the anthems *(BCP, 281-282)* may be sung, or the conclusion of the hymn "Sing, my tongue, the glorious battle."

F. When all is ready, the deacon (or celebrant) bids the people to make the Confession of Sin. After the confession the celebrant pronounces the absolution.

G. The Lord's Prayer is said, and the celebrant invites the people to receive Communion ("The Gifts of God . . ."). It is fitting that the full form of the invitation be used.

H. Communion is administered in the usual way. Hymns, psalms or anthems appropriate to the day may be sung or silence may be kept.

I. After all have received, the consecrated elements are consumed. (A small amount may be reserved in a private place for emergencies.) The vessels are cleansed in the usual way.

J. A postcommunion hymn extolling the glory of Christ is suitable *(Hymnal, 494, [322], or 450, 451, [355]).*

K. The celebrant then sings or says the concluding prayer *(BCP, 282; AB, 344* for music).

L. No blessing or dismissal is added. All leave in silence. No closing hymn or instrumental music should be used.

The cross (with lighted candles) may be left upon the altar for those who wish to remain for silent prayer and veneration.

Concerning the "Three Hours"

If a three-hour service, with preaching, is desired, the proper Liturgy of Good Friday should take the main part of this time.
A suggested pattern for the three hours might be:
1. Hymn, collect, lesson, sermon, followed by silence.
2. The Good Friday Liturgy (with the second sermon coming after the reading of the Passion).
3. Silence following the Liturgy; then hymn, sermon, collect (hymn).

or

The Liturgy, with appropriate periods of silence can extend the entire three hours. (Sermons may be preached before the Passion, before the Solemn Collects, before the bringing in of the Cross, and before Communion.)

Good Friday Evening

If the Liturgy of the Day takes place during the afternoon hours, a service at the end of the day may be pastorally desirable. Either Evening Prayer or the following may be used. Either may be preceded by the Veneration of the Cross (using Form A, page 195).

Stations of the Cross (see pages 156-157) would also be appropriate for the evening and may be followed by the Commemoration.

The Commemoration of the Burial of Our Lord Jesus Christ

(To be used on the evening of Good Friday, when the Liturgy has taken place at an earlier hour.)

The ministers enter in silence.

All kneel in silence before the altar (with the cross and two lighted candles upon it).

The anthems *(BCP, 281-282;* for music see *HymAccEd, S 349-351),* the *Improperia* (Reproaches) (pages 256-257), or other devotions may be said or sung.

The hymn "Sing, my tongue, the glorious battle" *(Hymnal, 166, [66], or 165)* may be sung.

The celebrant then says or sings the Collect for Holy Saturday *(BCP, 283).*

Then follows: Lesson: Job 14:1-14
                    Psalm: 130, *or* 31:1-5
                    Epistle: 1 Peter 4:1-8
                    (Psalm): (130, *or* 31:1-5, whichever was not used earlier)
                    Gospel: John 19:38-42, *or* Matthew 27:57-66
                    (Homily)

The anthem "In the midst of life" *(BCP, 484 or 492)* is sung or said (for music, see *HymAccEd, S 379 or S 382).*

The Lord's Prayer

(The Grace or Anthem 2, *BCP, 281-282* may be said or sung.)

The hymn "O Sorrow Deep" *(Hymnal, 173, [83])* may be sung.

All depart in silence.

Note: Communion from the Reserved Sacrament is not administered at this service.

Holy Saturday

There is no celebration of the Eucharist on this day (BCP, 283).
The Liturgy of the Word *(BCP, 283)* may be used with the given conclusion. This liturgy may be celebrated on Good Friday evening (see page 198) or on Holy Saturday in the morning or at noon. The altar remains stripped. The wooden cross from the Good Friday Liturgy is on the altar, without candles.
The celebrant and assisting ministers are vested in Passiontide red.
Incense, torches or processional cross are not used.
At the entrance, the celebrant is preceded by the servers and other assisting ministers. After reverencing the altar, all kneel for silent prayer. As at the Solemn Collects on Good Friday (see *AB, 333*), the deacon or other assisting minister may bid the people to kneel after the celebrant sings or says "Let us pray." Likewise, the deacon or other assisting minister bids the people to stand at the end of the period of silence before the Collect of the Day *(BCP, 170, 221 or 283)*. All then sit for the reading of the lessons.

> Lesson: Job 14:1-14
> Psalm: 130, *or* 31:1-5
> Epistle: 1 Peter 4:1-8

One of the Good Friday anthems *(BCP, 281-282; HymAccEd, S 349-351)* or the hymn "O Sorrow Deep" *(Hymnal, 173, [83])* may be said or sung before the Gospel.

> Gospel: Matthew 27:57-66, *or* John 19:38-42

It is suitable that the Gospel be announced in the following manner:
"The Conclusion of the Passion of our Lord Jesus Christ according to Matthew (John)."
The customary responses before and after the Gospel are omitted *(PBO, 110)*.
A homily may be preached.
In place of the Prayers of the People the anthem "In the midst of life" *(BCP, 484 or 492)* is sung or said (for music, see *HymAccEd, S 379 or S 382)*. The service then concludes with the Lord's Prayer and the Grace. After reverencing the altar, the celebrant, assisting ministers and servers leave in silence. The people leave in silence.

Note: At Evening Prayer on this day the hymn *Phos hilaron* is omitted.

The Great Vigil of Easter

Introduction

The Great Vigil of Easter is the culmination of the sacred celebration of Holy Week and the beginning of the celebration of the Lord's Resurrection. It is the climax of the Christian Year and unfolds in Scripture, psalm, Sacrament and liturgy the story of redemption. It begins in darkness and proceeds to a joyous burst of light. It begins in silence and proceeds to the glorious proclamation of the Paschal Alleluia.

It is the Christian Passover, for it celebrates the passing from death to life, from sin to grace. The story of the Exodus is central to the Liturgy of the Word; Baptism is the means of the full realization of redemption; Holy Communion is the promise of the glory that shall be ours with our Risen Lord.

This liturgy moves with austere solemnity from one part to the next, as we watch and wait for the Lord's Resurrection. It is not to be rushed through, for time is suspended as we recount the story of creation, celebrate the glory of the New Creation in the waters of Baptism, and profess our faith in the perfection of all creation in the fullness of time, in the glory of God.

Of all the celebrations of the Church Year, the Great Vigil of Easter is pre-eminent, for it alone vividly and dramatically portrays all that was, that is, and that ever shall be in the drama of our redemption:

Christ yesterday and today, the Beginning and the End, the Alpha and Omega. His are the times and ages and to him be glory and dominion through all ages of eternity. Amen.

The Great Vigil of Easter

Outline

I. The Service of Light
   The kindling and blessing of the New Fire
   The inscription of the Paschal Candle
   The lighting of the Paschal Candle
   The procession into the church
   The Exsultet

II. The Liturgy of the Word
   Lessons, Canticles or Psalms, and Collects

III. The Baptismal Liturgy
   The blessing of Baptismal Water
   (Holy Baptism)
   The Renewal of Baptismal Vows
   (The Great Litany or other appropriate Litany)

IV. The First Eucharist of Easter
   The Easter Proclamation
   Canticle: Song of Praise
   Collect: *(BCP, 170 or 295; AB, 60 or 210)*
   Epistle: Romans 6:3-11
   The Great Alleluia and Psalm 114
   The Holy Gospel: Matthew 28:1-10
   Sermon
   (The Prayers of the People)
   The Peace
   Preparation and offering of Gifts
   The Eucharistic Prayer with Preface of Easter
   The Breaking of the Bread
   Conclusion of Liturgy with Easter Dismissal

Preparations

Vestments: Color: White
             Celebrant in cope (or alb and stole) changing to chasuble for the Eucharist; other assisting ministers are vested according to order.

Books: Altar Book for Eucharist
         Altar Book or other book for the Vigil
         Bible, *Lectionary Texts,* or *Eucharistic Readings*
         Gospel Book on altar
         Altar Book or other book for the Baptismal liturgy
         Altar Book or other book on lectern for the Exsultet

Items: At the entrance to the church, unlighted candles to be given to the people

At the place of the kindling of the New Fire:
a grate or basin with kindling
charcoal (if incense is used)
the Paschal Candle
a stylus if the Candle is to be inscribed
grains of incense if they are to be put into the Candle
a taper to light the Candle
a lighter or other device to light the New Fire
(a small pocket flashlight)
(a fire extinguisher near at hand, for use in emergency)

In the chancel:
the stand to hold the Paschal Candle
a lectern (with the Exsultet text) before the Paschal Candle stand
(a light for the lectern so that the text may be seen)
a Bible or *Lectionary Texts* marked for the lessons
(a light for the reading of the lessons)

At the font or place of the Blessing of Water (and Baptisms):
a flagon filled with water
a purificator or other towel

If there is to be a Baptism:
a shell or other device to pour the water
container with chrism
candles to be presented to each of those baptized
cotton to cleanse the celebrant's fingers

If the people are to be sprinkled with Baptismal water after the Renewal of Vows:
an aspergillum and bucket, to be filled after the water is blessed

At the altar:
altar vested in white
Gospel Book

At the credence:
the usual items for the Eucharist

At the place from which the gifts are brought:
bread and wine

The candles are not lighted before the Liturgy, and the altar candles are left unlighted throughout the Vigil until the beginning of the Eucharist (*BCP, 294;* also, page 209).

The Liturgy of The Great Vigil of Easter

The Great Vigil, when observed, is the first service of Easter Day. It is celebrated at a convenient time between sunset on Holy Saturday and sunrise on Easter Morning (BCP, 284).

I. The Service of Light

A. The Kindling of the New Fire

The celebrant, concelebrants and assisting ministers are vested in white.
The church is in total darkness.
Outside the church door or in the narthex, the New Fire is kindled in a convenient and safe container. (Traditionally the New Fire is kindled with flint.)
The celebrant may address the congregation with the bidding *(BCP, 285)* or similar words.
The celebrant then sings or says the blessing of the New Fire *(BCP, 285)*.
If incense is used, coals are lighted from the New Fire. They are then placed in the thurible and the celebrant puts incense on the coals (and blesses the incense) and then censes the New Fire.

B. The Blessing of the Paschal Candle

At the discretion of the celebrant this form for the inscription of the Paschal Candle may be used:

The celebrant traces the cross, Alpha and Omega, and year into the Paschal Candle using a stylus, saying:

tracing the cross	"Christ yesterday and today, the Beginning and the End."
tracing the Alpha and Omega	"Alpha and Omega"
tracing the year	"His are the times and ages. To him be glory and dominion through all ages of eternity. Amen."

The celebrant then places five grains of incense, one each into the four points and center of the traced cross on the Candle, saying:

Preparation
of the Paschal Candle

"Through his holy and glorious wounds may Christ the Lord guard and preserve us."

A taper is lighted from the New Fire and the celebrant lights the Paschal Candle, saying:

"May the light of Christ gloriously rising dispel the darkness of our hearts and minds."

or

The celebrant lights the Paschal Candle from the New Fire immediately after the blessing of the fire.

C. The Procession into the Church

If incense is used, the thurible is filled (and the incense blessed).
The procession forms as follows:

(thurifer), the deacon carrying the lighted Paschal Candle, assisting ministers, celebrant (and the people).

If there is no deacon or assisting minister, the celebrant carries the Paschal Candle.
All carry unlighted candles.

The procession pauses at the door of the church and the deacon (or other minister carrying the Paschal Candle) sings, each time at a higher pitch (for music see *AB, 348,* or *Hymnal, S 68),* or says

"The light of Christ."

The people respond

"Thanks be to God."

The celebrant and other assisting ministers light their candles.

The procession moves to the middle of the church and, pausing again, the deacon sings or says as above, the people responding.
The candles of all those in the procession are lighted.

The procession moves to the entrance of the chancel and, pausing again, the deacon sings or says as above, the people responding.
All other candles are lighted (except those on or near the altar).

The Paschal Candle is placed in its stand near the pulpit or altar. The deacon stands before the Candle, with the book containing the Exsultet on a lectern.

If incense is used, the thurifer brings the thurible and boat to the celebrant, who fills the thurible with incense (and blesses it). The thurifer brings the thurible to the deacon, who censes the Candle and then returns the thurible to the thurifer.

D. The Exsultet

The deacon (or person appointed) sings or says the Exsultet *(BCP, 286-287;* for music, *AB, 351-356;* responses, *Hymnal, S 69).* All remain standing.
When the Exsultet is completed, the deacon returns to the sedilia and all sit.

II. The Liturgy of the Word

(The people extinguish their candles.)

The celebrant may introduce the lessons with the bidding *(BCP, 288)* or similar words.

At least two of the following Lessons are read, of which one is always the Lesson from Exodus. After each Lesson, the Psalm or Canticle listed, or some other suitable psalm, canticle, or hymn may be sung. A period of silence may be kept; and the Collect provided, or some other suitable Collect, may be said (or sung) (BCP, 288; AB, 356-360).

The ministers and people sit for the lessons, psalms and canticles and stand for the collects.

Lay persons read the Lessons and the Epistle . . . It is desirable that each Lesson be read by a different reader (BCP, 284).

A homily may be preached after any of the preceding Readings (BCP, 292).

When the service of lessons is completed, preparations are made for the Baptismal Liturgy.

III. The Baptismal Liturgy

(If the Baptismal Liturgy is to follow the Gospel, continue with IV., see page 209.) If the people have extinguished their candles for the service of lessons, they light them again at this point, or before the Prayers for the Candidates. An assisting minister may bring the light from the Paschal Candle.

A. 1.   If there are candidates for Holy Baptism, they are presented to the celebrant *(BCP, 301)* and the questions are asked.

2.   In place of the bidding to the people *(BCP, 303)*, the following adaptation of the bidding *(BCP, 292)* may be used:

> Through the Paschal mystery, dear friends, we are buried with Christ by Baptism into his death, and raised with him to newness of life. I call upon you, therefore, now that our Lenten observance is ended to renew with *these persons* about to be baptized the solemn promises and vows of Holy Baptism, by which we renounce Satan and all his works, and promise to serve God faithfully in his holy Catholic Church.

The first question then addressed to the people is:

> Do you reaffirm your renunciation of evil and renew your commitment to Jesus Christ?

The people answer: *I do.*

3.   The celebrant then continues with the Baptismal Covenant *(BCP, 304-305).*

4. The procession to the font then forms, during which either the Prayers for the Candidates are sung *(BCP, 305-306; AB, 361)* or Psalm 42:1-7. The concluding collect is sung by the celebrant *(BCP, 306; AB, 362* for music).

   The procession is led by the deacon, carrying the Paschal Candle, followed by the candidates, sponsors, godparents, parents, other assisting ministers and the celebrant.

5. The liturgy continues with the Thanksgiving over the Water *(BCP, 306-307; AB, 362-364)*, followed by Holy Baptism, anointing with Chrism, giving of the candle and welcome (see pages 215-216 and *BCP, 307-308)*. The bishop, if present, may consecrate Chrism, placing a hand on the vessel of oil, and saying or singing the blessing *(BCP, 307; AB, 365)*. The procession returns to the altar.

B. 1. If there are no candidates for Holy Baptism, the Baptismal Liturgy begins with this litany, in the following or similar form:

> On this most Holy Night, let us pray for all those who will receive the Sacrament of new birth and for ourselves as we prepare to renew our own Baptismal vows, saying, "Lord, hear our prayer."
>
> Deliver us, O Lord, from the way of sin and death.
> > *Lord, hear our prayer.*
>
> Open our hearts to *your* grace and truth.
> > *Lord, hear our prayer.*
>
> Fill us with *your* holy and life-giving Spirit.
> > *Lord, hear our prayer.*
>
> Keep us in the faith and communion of *your* holy Church.
> > *Lord, hear our prayer.*
>
> Teach us to love others in the power of the Spirit.
> > *Lord, hear our prayer.*
>
> Send us into the world in witness to *your* love.
> > *Lord, hear our prayer.*
>
> Bring us to the fulness of *your* peace and glory.
> > *Lord, hear our prayer.*
>
> Grant that we may find our inheritance with the Blessed Virgin Mary, with patriarchs, prophets, apostles and martyrs and all the saints; and we pray that, encouraged by their examples, aided by their prayers, and strengthened by their fellowship, we also may be partakers of the eternal life of the saints in light, through the merits of *your* Son Jesus Christ our Lord. *Amen.*

(The pointing of this litany and response is that found in *AB, 361*.)

2. The liturgy continues with the procession to the font (see A.4. above), the Blessing of the Baptismal water, and Renewal of Baptismal Vows *(BCP, 292-294).*
or
The liturgy may continue with the Renewal of Baptismal Vows *(BCP, 292)*, omitting the litany, the Blessing of water and the procession.

C. The Blessing of Baptismal Water

When the procession arrives at the font, the deacon pours water into the font. If incense is used it is prepared at this point.

1. The celebrant sings or says the Thanksgiving over the Water *(BCP, 306-307; AB, 362-364).*
2. The celebrant may follow the suggested rubric:

Where it is desired to follow the custom of touching the water by dipping the Paschal Candle into the font, it is done in the following manner. The Celebrant takes the Candle, lowers the base of it into the water, and sings on a comfortably low pitch to the melody given above (AB, 364):

Now sanctify this water, we pray *you,*
by the power of *your* Holy Spirit,

then raises the Candle out of the water, lowers it again, and sings the same words on a higher pitch; then raises the Candle, lowers it a third time and sings the same words on a still higher pitch. The Celebrant then continues the prayer to the end, after which the Candle is removed from the font (AB, 364).

Lowering Paschal Candle
into Water

3. After the Blessing of the water, the font is censed by the celebrant.
4. If there are candidates for Holy Baptism, they are baptized with the prescribed ceremonies (*BCP, 307-308,* and pages 215-216).

5. If there are no candidates for Baptism, the Renewal of Baptismal Vows follows *(BCP, 292-294)*.

6. If there are no candidates for Holy Baptism, the newly blessed Baptismal water may be poured into a container (bucket), and the celebrant may sprinkle the people using the aspergillum as the procession returns. (The asperging of the people may be done even if there are candidates for Holy Baptism.)

7. The procession returns.

During this procession the antiphon *Vidi Aquam* may be sung or said:

I saw water proceeding out of the temple, from the right side thereof; and all they to whom that water came shall be saved.

When the procession has reached the chancel, the candidates, sponsors, parents and godparents return to their places.

IV. The First Eucharist of Easter

The celebrant and ministers go either to the sedilia or to the sacristy or to the altar:

a. At this point the Great Litany *(BCP, 148-153,* concluding with the Kyrie) may be sung or said.

b. The celebrant (and concelebrants) put on white chasuble(s) (see page 78).

c. The candles on the altar and other altars are lighted.

If the Great Litany is sung, the ministers enter during the singing of the Kyrie eleison. The Litany concludes with the Kyrie.

The Easter Proclamation *(BCP, 294)* is sung or said. At the conclusion, the Gloria in excelsis (or Te Deum or Pascha Nostrum, see *BCP, 294*) is sung. Bells are rung and the organ is played. During the canticle the altar is censed (if incense is used).

When the canticle is concluded, the celebrant greets the people and sings or says one of the collects *(BCP, 295)*. (The second collect is especially appropriate for the Vigil.)

Epistle	Romans 6:3-11
The Great Alleluia	(for music see *AB, 369;* *Hymnal, S 70)*

Psalm 114 or some other psalm or a hymn may be sung *(BCP, 295)*.

The Holy Gospel	Matthew 28:1-10
Sermon or homily	(unless preached earlier, see *BCP, 292*)

The Nicene Creed is omitted *(BCP, 295)*.

(If they have not occurred earlier in the Vigil, *Holy Baptism, Confirmation, or the Renewal of Baptismal Vows may take place here (BCP, 295;* also page 206).

(The Prayers of the People are omitted if the Great Litany or some other litany was used prior to the Eucharistic Liturgy.)

The Eucharist continues, with the proper Preface of Easter at the Eucharistic Prayer. The dismissal at the end of the liturgy is that of Easter with the alleluias added (sung or said, see *AB, 390-391; Hymnal, S 175 or S 176)*.

Note: The Paschal Candle is lighted for all services throughout the Fifty Days of Easter, i.e., from the Great Vigil through the Day of Pentecost.

"Alleluia. Christ is Risen" *(Hymnal, S 78-79)* is the opening acclamation at the Eucharist. The Easter dismissal with "alleluia, alleluia" is used until after the Day of Pentecost *(Hymnal, S 175 or S 176)*. At the Daily Office the alleluias are added to the concluding versicle and response *(Hymnal, S 32 or S 66)*.

Holy Baptism, Other Sacraments and Pastoral Offices

Holy Baptism

Baptism is appropriately administered within the Eucharist as the chief service on a Sunday or other feast (BCP, 298). Holy Baptism is especially appropriate at the Easter Vigil, on the Day of Pentecost, on All Saints' Day or the Sunday after All Saints' Day, and on the Feast of the Baptism of our Lord (The First Sunday after the Epiphany) (BCP, 312).

Outline

    I. The Word of God
        The entrance (with hymn, psalm or anthem)
        Acclamation *(BCP, 299; Hymnal, S 71-73)*
        Versicles and responses *(BCP, 299; Hymnal, S 74).*
        (Gloria in excelsis) *(BCP, 312)*
        Salutation and Collect of the Day
        Lesson
        Psalm, hymn or anthem
        Epistle
        Psalm, hymn or anthem
        Gospel
        Sermon
   II. The Baptismal Liturgy
        Presentation and Examination of the Candidates *(BCP, 301-303)*
        The Baptismal Covenant *(BCP, 304-305)*
        Prayers for the Candidates *(BCP, 305-306; Hymnal, S 75)*
        (Procession to the font, with Psalm 42 or other suitable psalm, hymn or anthem *(BCP, 312)*
        Thanksgiving over the Water *(BCP, 306-307 or AB, 362-364;* responses, *Hymnal, S 75)*
        (Consecration of Chrism, if the bishop is present, *BCP, 307)*
        The Baptism *(BCP, 307)*
        (Procession to front of church, with Psalm 23 or other psalm, hymn, or anthem, *BCP, 313*)
        Prayer over the newly baptized *(BCP, 308)*
        Signing with the sign of the cross (and Chrism) *(BCP, 308)*
        (Presentation of chrysom [white garment])
        (Presentation of a lighted candle)
        Welcome and reception
        The Peace
        (Prayers of the People)
  III. The Holy Communion
        Preface of the Feast
            If not a principal feast (see *BCP, 15*), the Proper Preface of Baptism may be used *(BCP, 310).*

Note: The formal Preparation of Adults for Holy Baptism (the Catechumenate) is found in *The Book of Occasional Services (BOS, 117-130)*. A Vigil on the Eve of Baptism is also provided for *(BOS, 131-135)*.

I. The Word of God

The Entrance

The celebrant and assisting ministers enter in the usual way (see page 32). A hymn, psalm or anthem may be sung during the entrance. All reverence the altar. (If incense is used, the altar may be censed during the entrance song.)

Acclamation

The celebrant says or sings the appropriate initial acclamation *(BCP, 299; Hymnal, S 71-73)* and then continues with the Baptismal versicles and responses *(BCP, 299; Hymnal, S 74)*

Prior to the salutation ("The Lord be with you"), the Gloria in excelsis may be sung *(BCP, 312)* and is proper on principal feast days. (If incense is used, the altar is censed during the Gloria in excelsis if it has not been censed during the entrance song.)

The celebrant greets the people and sings or says the collect.

At the principal service on a Sunday or other feast, the Collect and Lessons are properly those of the Day. On other occasions they are selected from "At Baptism" (BCP, 300). (Collects for "At Baptism": *BCP, 203 or 254.)*

The Lessons

The lessons, psalm and Gospel are properly those of the day *(BCP, 300)*. However, on other occasions those appointed for use at Baptism may be substituted for one or more of the lessons of the day.

"At Baptism" *(BCP, 928):*

*Lesson:	Ezekiel 36:24-28 (*or* any other Old Testament lesson for the Easter Vigil; *or BCP, 288-291; or* "At Baptism," *928)*
Psalm:	15, 23, 27, 42:1-7; 84 *or* Canticle 9 (Ecce, Deus, *BCP, 86)*
*Epistle:	Romans 6:3-5; Romans 8:14-17; *or* 2 Corinthians 5:17-20
	Alleluia verse, hymn, psalm or anthem
Gospel:	Mark 1:9-11; Mark 10:13-16; *or* John 3:1-6
	(If incense is used, see page 80.)

The Sermon

(or the Sermon may be preached after the Peace, BCP, 301)

---

*It is fitting that these be read by the sponsors, godparents or parents. The Gospel is always read by an ordained person.

II. The Baptismal Liturgy

Presentation and Examination of the Candidates

Note: The candidates, sponsors, godparents and parents should be instructed prior to the service concerning all that follows.
The celebrant initiates the presentation *(BCP, 301):*

For adults and older children, after presentation they answer for themselves.

For infants and younger children, the candidates are presented by the parents and godparents, who answer for them.

The renunciations and affirmations follow *(BCP, 302-303).*

After the final affirmation *(BCP, 303)*, before the question addressed to the congregation, the celebrant may anoint the candidate (if *he* has not been prepared through the period of the catechumenate, *BOS, 117ff)*, with the Oil of Catechumens using the following words:

I anoint you with the oil of salvation, in the name of Christ Jesus our Lord. May he strengthen you with his power, who lives and reigns forever and ever. *Amen.*
or
May Almighty God, our heavenly Father, who has put the desire into your heart to seek the grace of our Lord Jesus Christ, grant you the power of the Holy Spirit to persevere in this intention and to grow in faith and understanding. *Amen. (BOS, 118).*
or
Drive out of this catechumen, Lord God, every trace of wickedness. Protect *him* from the Evil One. Bring *him* to the saving waters of Baptism, and make *him* yours for ever; through Jesus Christ our Lord. *Amen (BOS, 121).*

The celebrant continues with the question and bidding *(BCP, 303).*

The Baptismal Covenant

The celebrant addresses the questions to the people *(BCP, 304-305).*

Prayers for the Candidate(s)

If the Presentation of the Candidates does not take place at the font, then before or during the petitions [BCP, 305], the ministers, candidates and sponsors go to the font for the Thanksgiving over the Water (BCP, 312).
If the movement to the font is a formal procession, a suitable psalm, such as Psalm 42, or a hymn or anthem, may be sung (BCP, 312).

1. If the prayers are sung or said as the procession moves to the font, the deacon or other person appointed leads the petition *(BCP, 305-306;* for music, *AB, 361; Hymnal, S 75).*

2. If the prayers are sung or said from the midst of the people or facing the altar, the deacon or other person appointed leads the petitions *(BCP, 305-306;* for music, *AB, 361; Hymnal, S 75).*

The celebrant always sings or says the concluding collect *(BCP, 306; AB, 362).*

(The procession to the font may take place at this point with the singing or saying of Psalm 42 or some other suitable psalm, hymn or anthem.)

Thanksgiving over the Water

Where practicable, the font is to be filled with clean water immediately before the Thanksgiving over the Water (BCP, 313).

At the Thanksgiving over the Water, and at the administration of Baptism, the celebrant, whenever possible, should face the people across the font, and the sponsors should be so grouped that the people may have a clear view of the action (BCP, 313).

The celebrant blesses the water, either singing or saying the Thanksgiving (for music, see *AB, 362-364; Hymnal, S 75).* The orans position for the hands of the celebrant is appropriate.

At the words "Now sanctify this water," the celebrant touches the water (or makes the sign of the cross in the water) *(BCP, 307).* (If incense is used, the water may be censed after the Thanksgiving.) Chrism may be consecrated by the bishop at this point *(BCP, 307 or AB, 365),* or previously consecrated Chrism may be used by bishop or priest at the signing (see below).

If a priest uses Chrism in signing the newly baptized, it must have been previously consecrated by the bishop (BCP, 298).

The Baptism

Each candidate is presented by name to the celebrant, or to an assisting priest or deacon, who then immerses, or pours water upon the candidate, saying . . . (BCP, 307).

After the Baptism of the candidates, the procession may return to the front of the church for the prayer "Heavenly father, we thank you that by water and the Holy Spirit," and the ceremonies that follow it. *A suitable psalm, such as Psalm 23, or a hymn or anthem, may be sung during the procession (BCP, 313).*

The bishop or priest then says the prayer over the newly baptized *(BCP, 308),* or this prayer may follow the signing with the cross (and chrismation) if desired.

At the signing and chrismation, the sign of the cross is marked on the forehead of the newly baptized (with Chrism if desired) *(BCP, 308).*

The chrysom (white garment) may be put upon the newly baptized at this point, with the following declaration:

N., you have become a new creation and have clothed yourself in Christ. Take this white garment and bring it unstained to the judgment seat of our Lord Jesus Christ so that you may have everlasting life. *Amen.*

or

N., you have become a new creation and have clothed yourself in Christ. See in this white garment the outward sign of your Christian dignity. With your family and friends to help you by word and example, bring that dignity unstained into the everlasting life of heaven. *Amen.*

A candle (which may be lighted from the Paschal Candle) may be given to each of the newly baptized or to a godparent *(BCP, 313),* using these or similar words:

Receive the light of Christ as a sign that you have passed from darkness into light. Shine as his light in the world to the glory of God the Father.

or

Receive the light of Christ, that when the bridegroom comes you may go forth with all the saints to meet him; and see that you keep the grace of your Baptism. *Amen.*

or

N., receive the light of Christ, a sign of the new life enkindled within you.

The celebrant may bless the family (see *BCP, 445*).

If the procession has not returned to the front of the church earlier it does so at this point. *A suitable psalm, such as Psalm 23, or a hymn or anthem, may be sung during the procession (BCP, 313).*

The celebrant and people then welcome the newly baptized *(BCP, 308).*
The Peace is exchanged.

(If Confirmation, Reception, or Reaffirmation follows, the Peace is exchanged after all of this is completed, see page 222.)

III. The Holy Communion

The Eucharist continues with the Prayers of the People or the Offertory. The bishop, when present, is the principal celebrant *(BCP, 310). The oblations of bread and wine at the baptismal Eucharist may be presented by the newly baptized or their godparents (BCP, 313).*

If incense is used, the oblations are censed at the Offertory (see pages 84-85).

Except on Principal Feasts, the Proper Preface of Baptism may be used (BCP, 310).

It is fitting that the newly baptized receive the Body and Blood of our Lord in the Sacrament of the Eucharist at this celebration.

(If there is no celebration of the Eucharist, see *BCP, 311.*)

Emergency Baptism

In case of emergency, any baptized person may administer Baptism . . . using the given name of the one to be baptized (if known), pour water on him or her, saying

I baptize you in the Name of the Father, and of the Son, and of the Holy Spirit *(BCP, 313).*

The Lord's Prayer and other prayers may follow (see *BCP, 314).*

If a priest or deacon has administered the Baptism of an infant in emergency circumstances, see below for a public thanksgiving if the baptized person recovers.

The person who administers emergency Baptism should inform the priest of the appropriate parish, so that the fact can be properly registered (BCP, 314).

If the baptized person recovers, the Baptism should be recognized at a public celebration of the Sacrament with a bishop or priest presiding, and the person baptized under emergency conditions, together with sponsors or godparents, taking part in everything except the administration of the water (BCP, 314).

For an Infant Baptized
under Emergency Circumstances

The following form of thanksgiving is appropriate if the full baptismal rite took place and a priest (or deacon) administered the Sacrament. (For rubrics dealing with different circumstances of emergency Baptism, see *BCP, 313-314.*)

After the Prayers of the People at the Eucharist (or at one of the Offices following the collects) the celebrant addresses the people with the form "For the Birth of a Child" *(BCP, 440).*

The celebrant then continues with the bidding to the Act of Thanksgiving *(BCP, 441),* and the Magnificat and/or psalm(s) follow *(BCP, 441-443).*

The celebrant then says the collect *(BCP, 443).*

The prayer "For a child already baptized" *(BCP, 444)* follows and the prayer "For the parents" *(BCP, 444)* may follow.

If the child has not been signed (and chrismated) the celebrant does so (and a candle may be given, see page 216).

The celebrant and people then welcome the infant, saying,

We receive you into the household of God. Confess the faith of Christ crucified, proclaim his resurrection, and share with us in his eternal priesthood *(BCP, 308).*

The celebrant may then bless the family *(BCP, 445),* after which the Peace is exchanged and the Eucharist (or Office) continues.

A Thanksgiving for the Birth or Adoption of a Child

As soon as convenient after the birth of a child, or after receiving a child by adoption, the parents, with other members of the family, should come to the church to be welcomed by the congregation and to give thanks to Almighty God (BCP, 439).

This thanksgiving is especially appropriate on a Sunday, or at some other time when the congregation is present. It may take place:

1. During the celebration of the Eucharist, following the Prayers of the People and before the Peace.
2. At Morning or Evening Prayer, following the collects, where authorized intercessions and thanksgivings are indicated.
3. If used as a service in itself, a passage from Scripture (either Luke 2:41-51 *or* Luke 18:15-17 is appropriate) should be read after the bidding *(BCP, 440-441)* followed by the Magnificat and/or one or more of the psalms given *(BCP, 441-443)*. After the collect *(BCP, 443)*, the Lord's Prayer and other suitable prayers are added and the celebrant concludes with the blessing of the family *(BCP, 445)* and a dismissal.

A briefer form of this service, especially for use in the hospital or at home, is provided *(BCP, 439):*

1. The celebrant begins with the Act of Thanksgiving (canticle or psalm); a passage from Scripture may first be read (see 3. above).
2. The celebrant may begin with the collect *(BCP, 443)*.

Appropriate prayers are found as follows:

1. "For the Gift of a Child" *(BCP, 841)*
2. "For Families" *(BCP, 828)*
3. "A General Thanksgiving" *(BCP, 836)*

Confirmation with Forms for Reception
and for the Reaffirmation of Baptismal Vows

In the course of their Christian development, those baptized at an early age are expected, when they are ready and have been duly prepared, to make a mature public affirmation of their faith and commitment to the responsibilities of their Baptism and to receive the laying on of hands by the bishop (BCP, 412).

Although Confirmation is technically an episcopal function, *The Book of Common Prayer* gives it as the first of the Pastoral Offices. Unlike the other episcopal services *(BCP, 510-579),* which are not covered in this handbook, Confirmation involves the responsibility of the parish priest, who would normally prepare the candidates.

The liturgy given in the Prayer Book is for use outside of the Baptismal Liturgy.

It is intended for use within the Holy Eucharist but may be used by itself.

The Entrance

A hymn, psalm or anthem may be sung. The bishop sings or says the proper acclamation *(BCP, 413)* and then continues with the Baptismal acclamation. Before the salutation and collect, the Gloria in excelsis or other song of praise may be sung.

The Collect of the Day

At the principal service on a Sunday or other feast, the Collect and Lessons are properly those of the Day. At the discretion of the bishop, however, the Collect (BCP, 203 or 254) and one or more of the Lessons provided "At Confirmation" (BCP, 929) may be substituted (BCP, 414).

The Lessons

The lesson(s) are read as at the Eucharist, as are the psalm and Gospel. A deacon or priest reads the Gospel and lay persons may read the lesson(s). The sermon follows the Gospel. It is customary that the bishop preach.

The Creed is not recited.

A chair may be placed in the center near the people, and the bishop sits for the Presentation and the Examination, facing the people.

Presentation and Examination of the Candidates

The candidates are presented using the forms provided *(BCP, 415)*.
The candidates stand with their presenters before the bishop and respond to the questions addressed to them *(BCP, 415)*. These questions are answered in unison by all of the candidates.
The bishop addresses the congregation *(BCP, 416)* and then (standing) bids the people to join in the renewal of the Baptismal Covenant.

The Baptismal Covenant

The bishop asks the questions, and all present answer *(BCP, 416-417)*.

Prayers for the Candidates

The bishop bids the people pray for the candidates *(BCP, 417)*.
The prayers are in one of the following forms:

a. As at Baptism *(BCP, 305-306)*.
b. One of the forms of the Prayers of the People with special intentions for the Candidates.
c. Other authorized prayers or litany.

After a period of silence, the bishop concludes the prayers with the collect *(BCP, 418)*.

For Confirmation

The bishop is seated in a chair. The candidates come before the bishop individually (and kneel). The bishop lays hands upon each one and says one of the given prayers *(BCP, 418)*. (If desired, the bishop may anoint each candidate for Confirmation with Chrism.) An assisting minister should be with the bishop to give the names of those being presented and to assist with the book (and Chrism if used). (If Chrism is used, the bishop's hands are cleansed after the candidates for Confirmation have all been confirmed.)

Note: The use of Chrism at Confirmation does not imply a completion of the Baptismal Sealing. Western use has established this custom at the discretion of the bishop. The details described above are solely for the purpose that all may be done with decency and order.

For Reception and/or Reaffirmation

The bishop may stand for the Receptions and Reaffirmations *(BCP, 418-419).*

The candidate may stand or kneel.

The bishop may take the right hand of each candidate while saying the form for Reception or Reaffirmation. The bishop may also make the sign of the cross over the person (and lay a hand upon the person's head) during or after the sentence.

When all have been confirmed, received and reaffirmations have been made, the bishop says the concluding prayer *(BCP, 419).* The bishop may extend hands over all the candidates during this prayer. The bishop stands for this prayer.

The Peace is exchanged *(BCP, 419),* and the newly confirmed, or received, or those who have reaffirmed their vows, return to their places.

The service then continues with the Prayers of the People [these may be omitted if used earlier at the Prayers for the candidates] or the Offertory of the Eucharist, at which the bishop should be the principal celebrant (BCP, 419).

It is appropriate that the oblations of bread and wine be presented by persons newly confirmed (BCP, 412).

If there is no celebration of the Eucharist, the service continues with the Lord's Prayer and such other devotions as the bishop may direct (BCP, 419).

The Proper Preface is that of the feast or season or that of Baptism or Pentecost, depending on the direction of the bishop. It is fitting that those newly confirmed or received or who have reaffirmed their vows receive Holy Communion first, after the bishop and other ministers. The service concludes as usual, but the bishop may use the Pontifical Blessing (see *BCP, 523 or AB, 388*).

If incense is used it is customary that the bishop prepare (and bless) the incense, even if the bishop is not the principal celebrant at the Eucharist.

After the Peace, before the Offertory, *the bishop may consecrate oil of Chrism for use at Baptism, using the prayer on page 307 (BCP, 419).* (Or, if Chrism is to be used at Confirmation and the bishop blesses it at this service, the prayer *[BCP, 307]* for the consecration of Chrism is said after the Gospel or after the sermon, prior to the presentation and examination of the candidates.)

Concerning Holy Baptism when a Bishop is present
and Confirmation, Reception, or Reaffirmation, is to follow

In order to avoid cluttering the liturgy with unnecessary repetition and also to retain the fullness of the Baptismal rite, the following is suggested:

1. After the sermon, the bishop is seated and all of the candidates and their presenters come forward. They are presented to the bishop using the forms for those to be baptized *(BCP, 301-302)* and then the forms for the others *(BCP, 303)*.

2. The Baptismal Covenant and the prayers for the candidates follow *(BCP, 304-306)*.

3. The bishop and the candidate(s) for Baptism and the presenter(s) then go to the font (see page 215). The other candidates remain in place.

4. The Baptism follows (see page 216), through the welcoming of the newly baptized *(BCP, 308)*.

5. The bishop then returns to the chair and bids the people to pray *(BCP, 309)*. Confirmation, Reception and Reaffirmation follow *(BCP, 309-310; see also pages 220-221)*.

6. After the concluding collect ("Almighty and everliving God . . .", *BCP, 310*) the bishop exchanges the Peace with the newly baptized, those who have been confirmed, received or who have reaffirmed their vows.

7. The bishop then goes to the altar for the Eucharist, and those who have been baptized, confirmed, received, or have reaffirmed their vows return to their places with their presenters.

8. Any or all of the above persons may present the gifts at the Offertory *(BCP, 313)*.

A Form of Commitment to Christian Service

This pastoral office [BCP, 420-421] may be used when a person wishes to make or renew a commitment to the service of Christ in the world, either in general terms, or upon undertaking some special responsibility (BCP, 420).

In addition to the provision in this general form intended for secular vocations, and the rubrics in *The Book of Common Prayer,* special ecclesiastical circumstances and occasions are noted in *The Book of Occasional Services.*

These forms are used following the homily (and Creed or Reaffirmation of Baptismal Vows, *BCP, 292-294*); or after the Prayers of the People; at the conclusion of the collects (at the time of the hymn) at Morning or Evening Prayer; or as a separate service. When used as a separate service, a Scripture reading *(BOS, 176)* (and a homily) follows the Examination.

Each of the following begins with the Examination *(BOS, 161-162)*. Note that within each commissioning, appropriate symbols of the ministry being blessed may be given to the candidates as they are commissioned.

1. Wardens and Members of the Vestry	*(BOS, 178)*
2. Deputies to the General Convention or Delegates to Diocesan Convention	*(BOS, 178)*
3. Servers at the Altar	*(BOS, 179)*
4. Altar Guild Members and Sacristans	*(BOS, 180)*
5. Catechists or Teachers	*(BOS, 181)*
6. Evangelists	*(BOS, 182)*
7. Singers	*(BOS, 183)*
8 Directors of Music, Organists, and other Musicians	*(BOS, 184)*
9. Lectors (Lay Readers)	*(BOS, 184)*
10. Those Licensed to Administer the Chalice	*(BOS, 185)*
11. Licensed Lay Readers (see also No. 9 above)	*(BOS, 186)*
12. Parish Visitors	*(BOS, 187)*
13. Members of Prayer Groups	*(BOS, 187)*
14. Parish Canvassers	*(BOS, 188)*
15. Officers of Church Organizations	*(BOS, 189)*
16. Other Lay Ministries	*(BOS, 190)*

When used with the Eucharist, the service continues with (the Prayers of the People and) the exchange of the Peace (BOS, 175).

Concerning the symbols presented at the above commissionings, discretion must be exercised. A chalice is not appropriate as a symbol to those licensed to administer the chalice (No. 10), since this is traditionally reserved for presentation to a priest at ordination; likewise, presenting the organ to the director of music or the organist (No. 8) is impractical; but the presentation of a copy of the parish constitution and bylaws to a warden or member of the vestry (No. 1), or the presentation of a Bible to lectors (No. 9) or licensed lay readers (No. 11) is fitting. Selection of objects for presentation requires careful consideration.

Setting Apart for a Special Vocation

This form of commitment to Christian service *(BOS, 264-268)* is intended to be made directly to the bishop of the diocese. *The order which follows is not intended to supplant forms in use for admitting members to religious communities (BOS, 264).*

The rite implies testing, acceptance of a rule of life, and commitment to that rule for a period of time, or after a specified time, for life.

This is basically an episcopal service, since it involves the presence of the bishop, but, like Confirmation, preparation for it may involve the direction of the parish priest. The rubrics should be read carefully and the form of the service (within the guidelines of the rubrics) planned by both the parish priest and the candidate.

If this form of commitment to Christian service is used in a parish setting, the priest should be sure that the congregation is aware of the implications of the rite and the call to a special vocation. This requires both prior teaching and homiletical material within the service. Above all, it must be made clear that this is a normal part of the life of the Church and thus needs the support and prayers of the people of God. A special vocation is not an individual matter, but involves parish, bishop, diocese, family and friends. They should be made aware of the gravity of this vocation and their part in it.

The Celebration and Blessing of a Marriage
Introduction

The celebrant and assisting ministers are vested in white. If the celebrant is going to bind the hands of the couple with the stole (see below), a cope (with stole) is preferable for the first part of the liturgy and then a chasuble from the Offertory on.

If holy water is used, a container and the aspergillum should be placed near the altar, or a person appointed should carry it. If incense is used the thurifer should be well instructed as to which points of the liturgy will require incense.

Note: The Celebration and Blessing of a Marriage may be used with either the Rite I or Rite II Eucharist.

If Banns are to be published, the form is given *(BCP, 437). A priest or a bishop normally presides at the Celebration and Blessing of a Marriage, because such ministers alone have the functions of pronouncing the nuptial blessing and of celebrating the Holy Eucharist (BCP, 422).*

The Celebration and Blessing of a Marriage

The Liturgy for Holy Matrimony as given in *The Book of Common Prayer* is intended to be celebrated with the Holy Eucharist. Thus, the first act of the newly married couple is to receive the Body and Blood of our Lord.

The Entrance

The persons to be married, with their witnesses, enter the church according to local custom. (In some places, the celebrant and assisting ministers also enter either with this procession or from the sacristy at the same time.) Incense, cross and candles may precede either procession. *During the entrance, a hymn, psalm or anthem may be sung, or instrumental music may be played (BCP, 423).*

The Opening Exhortation

After reverencing the altar, the celebrant faces the people and the persons to be married, with the woman to the officiant's right and the man to the left.

The celebrant reads the bidding ("Dearly beloved: . . .").

In the third paragraph the full names of the persons to be married are declared. Subsequently, only their Christian names are used *(BCP, 422)*.

A deacon, or an assisting priest, may deliver the charge and ask for the Declaration of Consent *(BCP, 422)*.

The Declaration of Consent

The celebrant asks the questions of the persons to be married *(BCP, 424)* and then addresses the congregation *(BCP, 425)*.

If there is to be a presentation or a giving in marriage, the celebrant asks,

Who gives (presents) this woman to be married to this man?

or the following

Who presents this woman and this man to be married to each other?

To either question, the appropriate answer is, "I do." If more than one person responds, they do so together (BCP, 437).

The Ministry of the Word

A hymn, psalm or anthem may follow. The Gloria in excelsis or other song of praise may be sung. If incense is used, the altar may be censed after the celebrant fills the thurible (and blesses the incense) during this singing.

The celebrant then sings or says the salutation and the collect *(BCP, 425)*. After the collect, the celebrant and other assisting ministers go to the sedilia.

For the Ministry of the Word it is fitting that the man and woman to be married remain where they may conveniently hear the reading of Scripture (BCP, 437).

The lesson, psalm and Epistle are chosen from those listed *(BCP, 426)*. *If there is to be a Communion, a passage from the Gospel always concludes the Readings (BCP, 426). It is desirable that the Lessons from the Old Testament and the Epistles be read by a lay person (BCP, 422).* At the reading of the Gospel, the deacon or assisting priest announces the reading in the usual way.

If incense is used, the celebrant fills the thurible (and blesses the incense) prior to the reading of the Gospel. The Gospel procession is done in the usual way (see page 37) with torches and incense carried. After the announcement of the Gospel, the deacon (or other minister) censes the Gospel Book.

A hymn, psalm or anthem may precede the reading of the Gospel. *A homily or other response to the Readings may follow (BCP, 426). The Apostles' Creed may be recited after the Lessons, or after the homily . . . (BCP, 437).*

The Marriage

After the homily (if there is one) or immediately after the proclamation of the Gospel, the persons to be married come to the altar and stand facing the celebrant. The witnesses may accompany them to the altar. During this time a hymn, psalm or anthem may be sung or instrumental music may be played.

or

The movement to the altar may take place after the vows and before the Prayers, or after the Prayers and before the Blessing of the Marriage.

The man and woman exchange their vows *(BCP, 427).*

The celebrant blesses the ring(s), using the form given *(BCP, 427).*

(If holy water is used, the celebrant may sprinkle the rings after this blessing.)

The rings are then given *(BCP, 427).*

When desired, some other suitable symbol of the vows may be used in place of the ring (BCP, 437).

During the pronouncement and proclamation of the marriage *(BCP, 428),* the celebrant may bind the right hands of the couple together using the ends of the stole.

The Prayers

All remain standing. If the Eucharist does not follow, the Lord's Prayer is said. The deacon or other person appointed then reads the Prayers *(BCP, 429-430),* and the people respond "Amen." (The petition with the vertical margin line may be omitted, or *If there is not be be a Communion, one or more of the prayers may be omitted [BCP, 429].*)

The Blessing of the Marriage

The husband and wife kneel. The priest says one of the prayers *(BCP, 430-431).* It is suitable during these prayers for the priest to extend hands over the heads of the husband and wife (a server or other assisting minister holds the book).

The concluding blessing *(God the Father, God the Son, God the Holy Spirit, bless . . . BCP, 431)* is not an option but is the nuptial blessing.

If holy water is used the priest may sprinkle the husband and wife at the conclusion of the blessing. The priest may make the sign of the cross over the husband and wife during the blessing.

Note: Where it is permitted by civil law that deacons may perform marriages, and no priest or bishop is available, a deacon may use the service . . . omitting the nuptial blessing which follows the Lord's Prayer (BCP, 422).

The celebrant may greet the people with the Peace. *The newly married couple then greet each other, after which greetings may be exchanged throughout the congregation (BCP, 431).*

When Communion is not to follow, the wedding party leaves the church. A hymn, psalm or anthem may be sung, or instrumental music may be played (BCP, 431).

At the Eucharist

At the Offertory, it is desirable that the bread and wine be presented to the ministers by the newly married persons. They may then remain [standing or kneeling] before the Lord's Table and receive Holy Communion before other members of the congregation (BCP, 438).

If incense is used, the celebrant fills the thurible (and blesses the incense) after the gifts are prepared. It is fitting that the couple be censed either by the celebrant during the censing of the altar, or by the deacon or other assisting minister after the altar has been censed (see pages 80-85).

The Proper Preface of Marriage is sung or said *(BCP, 349 or 381; AB, 119, 139 or 269, 289).*

Any of the approved Eucharistic Prayers may be used (Rite I *or* Rite II).

At the Communion, it is appropriate that the newly married couple receive Communion first, after the ministers (BCP, 432).

After all have received communion (the people should be encouraged by the priest to do so), the ablutions are done in the usual way.

In place of the usual postcommunion prayer, a proper postcommunion is given *(BCP, 432; AB, 45 or 195).*

The celebrant may bless the people and the deacon or other assisting minister dismisses them.

As the wedding party leaves the church, a hymn, psalm, or anthem may be sung; or instrumental music may be played (BCP, 432).

The Blessing of a Civil Marriage

The rubrics *(BCP, 433)* presume that this Rite will take place in the context of the celebration of the Eucharist. The collect and lessons are those appointed in the marriage service *(BCP, 425-426;* see also page 226).

After the Gospel (or after the homily) the celebrant addresses the couple in the words of the bidding *(BCP, 433)* or in similar words. The celebrant then asks for the affirmation of vows, and each of the persons responds *(BCP, 433)*. The congregation is asked for their affirmation and promise, and they respond *(BCP, 434)*.

The ring(s) may be blessed (see page 227) using the form given *(BCP, 434)*. After the blessing of the ring(s) the celebrant may bind the right hands of the couple (see page 227) during the declaration of the marriage *(BCP, 434)*.

The Prayers

The people stand. (If the Eucharist does not follow, the Lord's Prayer is said.) The deacon or other person appointed then reads the Prayers *(BCP, 429-430)*, and the people respond "Amen." The petition with the line in the margin may be omitted, or *If there is not to be a Communion, one or more of the prayers may be omitted (BCP, 429)*.

The service continues with the Blessing of the Marriage *(BCP, 430-431;* also page 227) and the Peace.

When Communion is not to follow, the wedding party leaves the church. A hymn, psalm, or anthem may be sung, or instrumental music may be played (BCP, 431).

The Eucharist continues (see page 228); the Proper Preface of Marriage is used *(BCP, 349 or 381);* the couple receive Communion first, after the ministers *(BCP, 432);* and the proper postcommunion is used *(BCP, 432; AB, 45 or 195)*.

As the wedding party leaves the church, a hymn, psalm, or anthem may be sung; or instrumental music may be played (BCP, 432).

Anniversary of a Marriage

When two people wish to celebrate and give thanks for their years of married life together, this form *(BOS, 163-165)* is appropriate. At a principal service on a Sunday or Major Holy Day, the Proper of the Day is used; at other times those given for the Celebration and Blessing of a Marriage are used *(BCP, 426)* and the collect is taken from *BOS, 163-164.*

After the sermon (or creed, if appointed), the husband and wife stand before the celebrant and the renewal of the promises of Holy Matrimony begins *(BOS, 164-165).*

After the renewal of vows the couple says together the thanksgiving *(BOS, 165),* and the celebrant says the blessing (holy water may be used). *The service continues with the Peace, or, at a principal service, with the Prayers of the People (BOS, 165).*

It is appropriate that the husband and wife present the bread and wine at the Offertory.

If there is not to be a Communion, the service concludes with the Lord's Prayer and the Peace (BOS, 165). However... *this form is intended for use in the context of a celebration of the Holy Eucharist (BOS, 163).*

The Exhortation

The "long" exhortation may be used at any time, and may be read by a priest, deacon or lay person *(BCP, 316-317).*
The exhortation is appropriate on the following occasions:

> The First Sunday of Advent
> The day before Ash Wednesday (Shrove Tuesday)
> The First Sunday in Lent
> Wednesday in Holy Week
> The Sunday before Holy Cross Day (September 14)

It is suitable for use on other occasions at the discretion of the priest.
In the liturgy, it may be used in the following ways:

1. In the Penitential Order *(BCP, 319 or 351);* it may be followed by the Decalogue *(BCP, 317 or 350).*
2. In the Penitential Order *(BCP, 319 or 351),* followed by the Confession of Sin and absolution *(BCP, 320-321 or 352-353).* Here it is used in place of the invitation to confession *(BCP, 320 or 352).* In this case, the bracketed words concluding the exhortation ["and humbly confess our sins to Almighty God"] *(BCP, 317)* are said and may be followed with "devoutly kneeling."
3. At the Holy Eucharist:
   a. After the Gospel, as a homiletic reading, in which case the bracketed words are omitted.
   b. As the invitation to confession *(BCP, 330 or 360),* in which case the bracketed words are used and the phrase "devoutly kneeling" may be added.
   The Confession of Sin and absolution follow *(BCP, 331-332 or 360).*
4. At Morning or Evening Prayer:
   a. As the invitation to confession *(BCP, 41 or 62),* in which case the bracketed words are used and the phrase "devoutly kneeling" may be added.
   The Confession of Sin and absolution follow *(BCP, 41-42 or 62-63).*
   b. As a reading from "non-biblical Christian literature" which may follow the biblical readings *(BCP, 142).*
   c. As a homiletic reading either at the conclusion of the Office, after the readings, or (at the time of the hymn or anthem) after the collects *(BCP, 142).*
   Note: In "b" or "c" above the Confession of Sin and absolution may follow.
5. As a reading prior to the Reconciliation of a Penitent. If a public service of preparation is used, see page 248.
6. Before, during, or after An Order of Service for Noonday or Compline.

The Reconciliation of a Penitent

The introductory material *(BCP, 446)* is important to this rite, especially the rubric concerning the hearing of a confession by one who is not a priest and the final paragraph concerning the secrecy of a confession.

The priest is normally vested in cassock, surplice and (violet) stole; or cassock-alb and (violet) stole; or alb and (violet) stole.

The confessor may sit inside the altar rails or in a place set aside to give greater privacy, and the penitent kneels nearby. If preferred, the confessor and penitent may sit face to face for a spiritual conference leading to absolution or a declaration of forgiveness (BCP, 446).

Form One

The priest may make the sign of the cross over the penitent at the initial blessing. After the confession, *the Priest may offer counsel, direction, and comfort (BCP, 447). Before giving absolution, the priest may assign to the penitent a psalm, prayer or hymn to be said, or something to be done, as a sign of penitence and act of thanksgiving (BCP, 446).* One of the two forms of absolution is used *(BCP, 448).*

During the absolution the priest may either extend a hand over the penitent, lay a hand upon the penitent's head, make the sign of the cross over the penitent, or place the stole over the penitent's shoulder. The rite concludes with a dismissal *(BCP, 448).*

Form Two

The verses from Psalm 51 are recited by the priest and penitent together as is the concluding Trisagion. The priest may make the sign of the cross over the penitent at the blessing ("May God in his love enlighten . . ."). The priest may then say one or more of the sentences of Scripture given *(BCP 449-450),* or read some other appropriate passage of Scripture. After the Confession of Sin, *the Priest may then offer words of comfort or counsel (BCP, 450)* and *assign a psalm, prayer or hymn to be said, or something to be done as a sign of penitence and act of thanksgiving (BCP, 446),* after which the two questions are asked of the penitent and the prayer said. One of the two forms of absolution is used *(BCP, 451).*

During the absolution the priest may either extend a hand over the penitent, lay a hand upon the penitent's head, make the sign of the cross over the penitent, or place the stole over the penitent's shoulder. The rite concludes with a dismissal *(BCP, 451).*

Note: For the Declaration of Forgiveness to be used by a deacon or lay person, see *BCP, 448 or 452.*

Ministration to the Sick

The service of the Ministration to the Sick may be celebrated either privately (as in a home or hospital) or publicly (as a regular or special liturgy in the church).

Private Ministration to the Sick

The priest should take:

1. the Reserved Sacrament (Bread, and if convenient, Wine) if the Eucharist is not to be celebrated in the presence of the sick person
2. Oil of the Sick (OI) which has been previously blessed or oil to be blessed during the rite *(BCP, 455)*
3. cotton, to cleanse the fingers after anointing
4. a purificator and either a second purificator or small corporal on which to place bread and wine or the Reserved Sacrament
5. a Prayer Book and Bible (or a volume containing the Ministration to the Sick, prayers for the sick, and suitable passages of Scripture)
6. a stole

At the home, or at the hospital bedside there should be:

1. a table near the sick person
2. a glass of water (and if needed, a straw)
3. a spoon

Note: The priest should check, if possible, with the nursing staff or some other responsible person to ascertain whether there is any problem about the sick person receiving the consecrated Bread or Wine.

When the priest enters the house (or hospital room) the Peace is pronounced *(BCP, 453)*.

Ministry of the Word

A. Any of the opening parts of the Word of God in the Eucharist may be used, (acclamation, Collect for Purity, Summary of the Law, Kyrie eleison or Trisagion) depending on pastoral need.

B. The greeting ("The Lord be with you") and response may be used.

C. A collect may be read (either 20. "For the Sick," *BCP, 208 or 260;* some other appropriate prayer, *BCP 458-460;* or a seasonal, Sunday or Feast Day collect).

D. A passage or passages from Scripture are read *(BCP, 453-454)* with an appropriate psalm. (If Communion is to follow, one of the passages should be from the Gospels.) *After any Reading, the Celebrant may comment on it briefly (BCP, 454).*

E. Prayers may be offered according to the occasion, or the Litany of Healing *(BOS, 167-168)* may be used.

F. The person may wish to make a private confession *(BCP, 447-452),* or one of the general confessions from the Eucharistic liturgies may be used, or that provided *(BCP, 454-455).* The priest gives the absolution. A deacon or lay person follows the rubrics *(BCP, 455)* or uses the Declaration of Forgiveness *(BCP, 448 or 452).*

Laying on of Hands and Anointing

A. If oil is to be blessed the form *(BCP, 455)* is used.

B. If the blessed Oil of the Sick has been brought, the priest continues with the anthem "Savior of the world . . ." *(BCP, 455).*

C. The priest lays hands upon the sick person (usually on the head; see *Note* in D. below) and says one of the prayers *(BCP, 456).*

D. If the person is to be anointed, the priest dips a thumb in the oil and makes the sign of the cross on the sick person's forehead, saying the sentence (and adding the prayer if desired, *BCP, 456*).

Note: If because of the nature of the illness or surgical dressings or any other reason, the person's head or forehead cannot be touched, the priest may lay hands on the person's shoulders or hands (and anoint them). If the body cannot be touched, the priest may extend a hand over the person and say the prayer *(BCP, 456).*

E. If Communion is not to follow, the Lord's Prayer is said and the concluding collect *(BCP, 456-457).*

F. If Communion follows, this collect may still be used.

Note: In cases of necessity, a deacon or lay person may perform the anointing, using oil blessed by a bishop or priest (BCP, 456).

Holy Communion

A. If the Eucharist is to be celebrated:

1. The Peace may follow the laying on of hands or anointing.
2. The small corporal or purificator is spread upon the table.
3. The bread and the vessel which contains wine (mixed with a little water) are placed upon the cloth.
4. Any of the Eucharistic Prayers may be used.
5. The Lord's Prayer and Breaking of the Bread follow.
6. The Agnus Dei and the Prayer of Humble Access may follow.
7. The invitation to Communion is said.
8. The priest receives first and then communicates the sick person (in one or both kinds) and then any others who may be present and desirous of receiving Communion.
9. The priest consumes what remains of the consecrated elements.
10. One of the usual postcommunion prayers is said or the proper postcommunion (BCP, 457).
11. The priest may say a blessing and/or a form of the dismissal ("Let us bless the Lord" or "Abide in Peace" with the response "Thanks be to God").

B. If Communion is to be administered from the Reserved Sacrament:

1. The Peace may follow the laying on of hands or anointing.
2. The small corporal or purificator is spread upon the table.
3. The consecrated Bread and Wine are placed upon the cloth. (The Wine should be in a vessel suitable for drinking, being poured from a cruet with a stopper or other appropriate bottle in which it was brought.)
4. The Lord's Prayer is said.
5. The Agnus Dei and/or the Prayer of Humble Access may be said.
6. The invitation to Communion is said.
7. The priest then communicates the sick person (in one or both kinds) and any others who may be present and desirous of receiving Communion.
8. The priest consumes what remains of the consecrated elements.
9. One of the usual postcommunion prayers is said or the proper postcommunion (BCP, 457).
10. The priest may say a blessing and/or a form of the dismissal ("Let us bless the Lord" or "Abide in Peace" with the response "Thanks be to God").

Notes:

1. It is appropriate that members of the family and friends be present for the Ministration to the Sick (and receive Holy Communion if they desire to).

2. Only a small particle of the Bread (dipped in the Wine) is suggested for the sick person, especially if the person is lying down. Water should be offered the person after receiving to prevent choking or difficulty in swallowing the Bread.

3. If the sick person can receive only the consecrated Bread or only the Wine, *it is suitable to administer the Sacrament in one kind only (BCP, 457).* The Bread may be placed upon a spoon filled with water to ease swallowing.

4. *If a person desires to receive the Sacrament, but, by reason of extreme sickness or physical disability, is unable to eat and drink the Bread and Wine, the Celebrant is to assure that person that all the benefits of Communion are received, even though the Sacrament is not received with the mouth (BCP, 457).*

5. Care should be taken to cleanse properly all of the vessels used in Communion of the sick.

6. Additional prayers for the sick *(BCP, 458-460)* may be used:
   a. after the reading(s) from Scripture
   b. after the Litany of Healing
   c. after the Laying on of Hands (and anointing) before the Peace
   d. after the postcommunion prayer before the blessing (and/ or dismissal)

7. It is pastorally desirable that familiar forms be used in the prayers so that the sick person may participate even without a Prayer Book. Also, the officiant must use discretion to keep the service from being burdensome or too long.

8. The person should be made aware of the Prayers for use by a Sick Person *(BCP, 461).*

9. If it is doubtful that the person understands the rite of anointing with oil, the priest should say a few words of explanation prior to this rite.

10. If the person is not familiar with Communion from the Reserved Sacrament, this also should be explained briefly, so that he or she may be assured of the true presence of Christ in the Bread and Wine.

Public Ministration to the Sick
(A Public Service of Healing)

When the Laying on of Hands or Anointing takes place at a public celebration of the Eucharist, it is desirable that it precede the distribution of Holy Communion, and it is recommended that it take place immediately before the exchange of the Peace (BCP, 453). This suggests that a public service of healing will take place in the context of the Eucharist. However, *BOS, 171* states, *If there is not to be a Communion, the service concludes with the Lord's Prayer and the prayer and blessing . . .* Given the *BCP* rubric, one can assume that the normal celebration of this rite is within the context of the Eucharistic Liturgy.

A full service with detailed rubrics is given *(BOS, 166-173).*

The Word of God

A. The Entrance (A hymn, psalm, or anthem may be sung or said.)
   The Penitential Order *(BCP, 319 or 351)*

   or

   The greeting ("Grace and peace be with you...") *(BOS, 166)*

   or

   Acclamation, Collect for Purity, (Summary of the Law), Kyrie eleison or Trisagion *(BCP, 323 or 355)*
B. The Salutation and Collect No. 20. "For the Sick" *(BCP, 208 or 260)*; the collect given *(BOS, 166)*; or a seasonal, Sunday, or Feast Day collect
C. The Lessons
   One or two lessons are read before the Gospel, and between the lessons a hymn, psalm or anthem may be sung or said. If the Proper of the Day is not used, the lessons, psalm, and Gospel are selected from those suggested *(BCP, 453-454; or BOS, 171-173).*
D. A homily or sermon may follow the Gospel.
E. The Creed may be said.
F. The Prayers of the People, using one of the six forms *(BCP, 383-393)*, and an appropriate concluding collect, such as No. 1 or No. 5 *(BCP, 394-395)*, or one of the Prayers *(BCP, 458-460)*

   or

   The Litany of Healing (BOS, 167-168) and one of the concluding collects *(BOS, 169,* or those listed above)
G. Confession of Sin and absolution (unless the liturgy began with the Penitential Order)

The Laying on of Hands and Anointing

A. The celebrant invites those who wish to receive the laying on of hands (and anointing) to come forward.

If oil has not been previously blessed, it is blessed at this point, *(BCP, 455)*.

B. The anthem "Savior of the world..." *(BCP, 455; BOS, 169)* is sung or said.

The celebrant says the blessing over those who have come forward *(BOS, 170)*.

C. The Laying on of Hands (and anointing), using one of the prescribed forms *(BCP, 456 or BOS, 170), or prayer may be offered for each person individually according to that person's need, with laying on of hands (and anointing) (BOS, 170).*

Lay persons with a gift of healing may join the celebrant in the laying on of hands (BOS, 170).

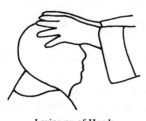

Laying on of Hands

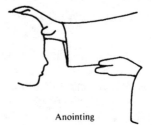

Anointing

D. The prayer after the anointing *(BCP, 456)* may be said by the celebrant after all have been anointed. The celebrant may extend hands over the people during this prayer.

E. The Peace is exchanged and those who have come forward return to their places.

The Holy Communion

A. The liturgy continues with the Offertory. (A hymn, psalm or anthem may be sung.)
B. If a Proper Preface is appointed for the feast or the season, it is used.
C. Any of the Eucharistic Prayers may be used.
D. Lord's Prayer, Breaking of the Bread, Communion
E. In place of the usual postcommunion prayer, one of the following may be said:
   1. "Gracious Father, we give you praise and thanks . . . " *(BCP, 457;* also, *AB, 46 or 196)*
   2. "Almighty and eternal God, so draw our hearts..." *(BOS, 171)*
F. The usual blessing may be given or the special blessing *(BOS, 171).*
G. The deacon, assisting minister, or celebrant dismisses the people.

Note on anointing: In many places people come forward at the Laying on of Hands to receive this prayer on behalf of another person. Traditionally, the Laying on of Hands has not been viewed as a vicarious or surrogate sacramental. In any case the anointing with oil is always reserved for those who are sick and present at the service.

Ministration at the Time of Death

When a person is near death, the Minister of the Congregation should be notified, in order that the ministrations of the Church may be provided (BCP, 462).

If the person is able to receive Holy Communion, and desires to do so, the priest brings the Reserved Sacrament or celebrates the Eucharist at the person's bedside (see page 235).

If for pastoral reasons an anointing is desired, the priest may anoint the sick person during the opening prayer *(BCP, 462)*. The Oil of the Sick (OI) should be used. If the person wishes (and is able) to make a private confession, this is done prior to the anointing and prayer above.

Note: The Ministration at the Time of Death may take place after the absolution or after Communion is administered.
If Communion is to be administered the order is:

Confession of Sin (either private or general)
Absolution (A deacon or lay person uses the Declaration of Forgiveness
     BCP, 448 or 452.)
The Lord's Prayer
Communion from the Reserved Sacrament

(For Communion of the Sick, see pages 233-236.)

The Litany at the Time of Death *(BCP, 462)* is appropriately said in the company of family and friends of the sick person.

The Commendation *(BCP, 464)* is said by the priest, if present at the time of death, as is the Commendatory Prayer *(BCP, 465)*.

If the priest arrives after the person has died, the Commendation and Commendatory Prayer are still said.

The Litany, Commendation and Commendatory Prayer may be said by a lay person present at the time of death.

The priest may add the prayer for those who mourn *(BCP, 467)* and other suitable prayers *(BCP, 487-489 or 503-505)* at discretion.

The Burial of the Dead

Prayers for a Vigil

It is appropriate that the family and friends come together for prayers prior to the funeral. Suitable Psalms, Lessons and Collects (such as those in the Burial service) may be used. The Litany at the Time of Death may be said (BCP, 465).

This vigil may be held in the home or in the place where the body is kept until the burial. The Prayers for a Vigil may be led by a priest, deacon or lay person.

If the body is brought to the church before the time of burial, the form for the Reception of the Body *(BCP, 466-467)* is used, and then the Prayers for a Vigil and other prayers added.

Reception of the Body

It is appropriate that the Burial Service begin at the door of the church with this form of reception. If the body has already been cremated, the opening words can be changed to "With faith in Jesus Christ, we receive the ashes of . . ." The use of holy water is appropriate at this reception. Either after the initial paragraph *(BCP, 466)* or after "Deliver your servant . . ." the coffin or urn of ashes may be sprinkled. It is then covered with a pall. A vigil may follow (see *BCP, 467*), or the Order for the Burial of the Dead may begin immediately.

The Entrance

An acolyte or some other person leads the procession carrying the lighted Paschal Candle. If cross and torches are used, they are carried after the Paschal Candle. The celebrant follows (with assisting ministers).

1. If there is a coffin, it is covered with a white or violet pall; it is carried behind the celebrant and placed before the altar. The foot of the coffin faces the altar.

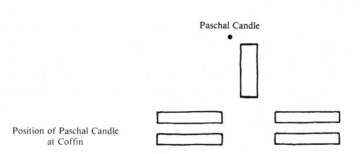

Paschal Candle

Position of Paschal Candle
at Coffin

2. If there is an urn of ashes, it is appropriate to have the celebrant carry it. The urn is veiled with a white or violet cloth (a chalice veil works well for this). The urn is placed on a table before the altar.
3. The urn may be on a table and veiled (see above) before the people gather.

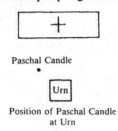

Paschal Candle
•
Urn

Position of Paschal Candle
at Urn

Members of the family may follow the coffin or the celebrant. The anthems *(BCP, 469 or 491-492;* also, *HymAccEd, S 375-378 or S 380-382)* are sung or said during this procession, or a hymn or psalm may be sung. In the latter case, when the celebrant reaches the altar, the anthems may then be read either by the celebrant, some other person, or by the congregation. The Kyrie eleison or Trisagion may follow the anthems, before the collect. If incense is used, it would be appropriate to cense the altar during the Kyrie or Trisagion. The celebrant then sings (or says) the salutation and sings (or says) the appropriate collect *(BCP, 470 or 493-494).*

Note: After the coffin is covered with a pall it is not to be opened again.

The Liturgy of the Word

One or more lessons are read with suitable psalms, canticles or hymns between them (see *BCP 470-480 or 494-495).* If there is to be a Eucharist, a passage from the Gospel must be used *(BCP, 480 or 495).* Incense may be used at the Gospel (see page 80). A homily may be preached after the proclamation of the Gospel. The Apostles' Creed may be said after the homily. (If there is no celebration of the Eucharist, the Lord's Prayer is said here, then the prayer of intercession or other suitable prayers followed by the Commendation [and Committal]).

The Prayers

The deacon, other assisting minister, lay reader, or the officiant sings or says the prayers *(BCP, 480, or 497),* the people responding with either "Amen" (Rite I) or "Hear us, Lord" (Rite II). It is appropriate that the final paragraph *(BCP, 481)* (Rite I) be sung or said by the celebrant, and in Rite II the concluding collect *(BCP, 498)* is sung or said by the celebrant. Other prayers may be used.

The Peace follows the prayers. The celebrant may greet members of the family and the people.

The Offertory

It is appropriate that the gifts of bread and wine be presented to the celebrant by members of the family. If incense is used, the celebrant may cense the coffin or urn after censing the gifts.

1. At a freestanding altar, the celebrant turns right and censes that side and front of the altar; then, after censing the cross, the celebrant bows to the cross, goes to the coffin or urn and walks around it, beginning at the right side, and censes it. The celebrant then returns to the altar, bows and continues censing it.

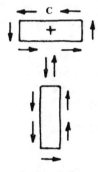

Censing of Altar
and Coffin or Urn

2. If the altar is affixed to the wall, the celebrant censes the altar in the usual fashion (see page 83) and then censes the coffin or urn. After this the celebrant returns to the center of the altar.

   Note: The coffin or urn may be censed at this time or at the Commendation.

(The thurible is given to the deacon or thurifer, who may then cense those in the sanctuary and the people.)

The celebrant proceeds with the lavabo.

The Great Thanksgiving

The salutation is sung or said and followed by the Preface of the Commemoration of the Dead *(BCP, 349 or 382)* or the Preface of Easter *(BCP, 346 or 379)*. If Eucharistic Prayer D is used, there is no Proper Preface.

After the Sanctus and Benedictus qui venit the celebrant continues with the Eucharistic Prayer.

The Lord's Prayer and the Breaking of the Bread follow. (*Note:* The Alleluia is appropriate in the versicle and response, except during Lent.)

Communion is administered.

During the administration of Communion a hymn, psalm, or anthem may be sung. The hymn "Jesus, Son of Mary" *(Hymnal, 357, [223])* is fitting. A proper postcommunion prayer is provided *(BCP, 482 or 498; AB, 46 or 196)* and is used in place of, not in addition to, the usual prayer of thanksgiving. The people may join the celebrant in the recitation of the postcommunion prayer. (After the postcommunion prayer, the celebrant may change from the chasuble into a cope or remain in chasuble.)

Note: Concerning the use of the alleluia at the Burial of the Dead, see page 162.

The Commendation

After the postcommunion prayer the celebrant and assistants take their places at the coffin or urn, facing it and the people for the Commendation *(BCP, 482 or 499)*. If holy water and/or incense are used, the person with the aspergillum and bucket stands near to the celebrant as does the thurifer. The anthem "Give rest, O Christ . . ." *(Hymnal, 355 or 358;* also, *HymAccEd, S 383)* or some other suitable anthem is then sung (or said).

1. If holy water is used, the celebrant sprinkles the coffin (or urn).
2. During this anthem the celebrant may fill the thurible (bless the incense), and walking around the coffin cense it (or cense the urn).

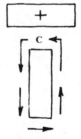

Censing of Coffin

Note: If the coffin or urn has been censed at the Offertory (see above), it should not be censed again at this point.

At the conclusion of the anthem, the celebrant sings or says the prayer of Commendation *(BCP, 483 or 499)*. A blessing of the people may follow, and the deacon or other minister dismisses the congregation with "Let us go forth in peace." A hymn or one or more of the anthems *(BCP, 483-484 or 500;* for music see *HymAccEd, S 384-388)* may be sung while the coffin or urn is carried from the church. The anthem "In paradisum" *(Hymnal, 354 or 356)* is traditional. Also, one of the three canticles cited below (A.3) may be sung or said.

Again, it is appropriate that the Paschal Candle be carried at the head of the procession.

If there is an urn, again it is appropriate for the celebrant to carry the urn out of the church.

The Committal

The Committal is used either at the place of burial or crematorium; or if the priest is not present for the burial or cremation, the Committal follows the postcommunion prayer; or, if there is no Eucharist, the Committal follows the Prayers *(BCP, 481 or 498)*.

A. If the Committal takes place in the church:

The anthems are sung or said *(BCP, 484 or 501;* also *491-492;* for music see *HymAccEd, S 379 or S 389)*.

The celebrant stands at the foot of the coffin (or at the urn) facing the people. If cross and torches are used, those carrying them stand at the opposite end of the coffin facing the celebrant (or to the celebrant's left facing the urn).

During the anthems, the priest may cense the coffin or urn and sprinkle it with holy water (see page 244).

After the anthems, the priest may pour a small amount of earth on the coffin or simply lay a hand upon the coffin (or urn).

The commendation is sung or said by the priest *(BCP, 485 or 501)* and the sign of the cross made over the coffin or urn at the words, "The Lord bless *him* and keep *him* . . ."

The celebrant sings or says the salutation and bidding, and the Lord's Prayer is said or sung *(BCP, 485-486 or 501-502)*.

Other prayers may be said *(BCP, 487-489 or 503-505)*.

The versicle and response may be added at the conclusion of the prayer(s): "Rest eternal grant . . ." *(BCP, 486 or 502)*.

The celebrant dismisses the people with the prayer *(BCP, 486-487 or 503)* or with the Resurrection proclamation and dismissal *(BCP, 502)*.

As the body or urn is borne from the church:

1. A hymn may be sung.
2. One or more of the anthems may be sung or said *(BCP, 483-484 or 500)*.

3. One of these canticles may be sung or said:
   a. The Song of Zechariah, Benedictus *(BCP, 50 or 92)*
   b. The Song of Simeon, Nunc dimittis *(BCP, 51 or 93)*
   c. Christ our Passover, Pascha nostrum *(BCP, 46 or 83)*

B. If the Committal is at the place of burial (or cremation):
The anthems are said by the celebrant or sung *(BCP, 484 or 501; also, 491-492)*.
During the anthems the celebrant (standing at the head of the coffin) may sprinkle the coffin or urn with holy water.
After the anthems, the celebrant says the Commendation *(BCP, 485 or 501)* either:

1. while earth is cast upon the coffin
2. while the urn is placed in the earth
3. while the body is lowered into the water
4. while the coffin or urn is put into a vault
5. or if the body is to be cremated, the celebrant lays a hand upon the coffin during the Commendation

The sign of the cross may be made over the coffin or urn at the words, "The Lord bless *him* and keep *him* . . ."
The celebrant says the salutation and bidding, and the Lord's Prayer is said *(BCP, 485-486 or 501-502)*.
Other prayers may be said *(BCP, 487-489 or 503-505)*.
The versicle and response may be added at the conclusion of the prayer(s): "Rest eternal grant . . ." *(BCP, 486 or 502)*.
The celebrant dismisses the people with the prayer *(BCP, 486-487 or 503)* or with the Resurrection proclamation and dismissal *(BCP, 502)*.

The Consecration of a Grave

If the grave is in a place that has not previously been set apart for Christian burial, the Priest may use the following prayer, either before the service of Committal or at some other convenient time (BCP, 487 or 503).

1. If holy water is used, the grave is sprinkled after this prayer.
2. A sign of the cross may be made over the grave at the words "Bless, we pray, this grave . . ." *(BCP, 487 or 503)*.

An Order For Burial

This form is to be followed *when, for pastoral considerations, neither of the burial rites in this book is deemed appropriate (BCP, 506)*. This order may be used when the 1928 Prayer Book Burial Office is pastorally desirable.

Burial of One Who Does Not Profess the Christian Faith

If a priest or lay person is called upon to officiate at the burial of a person who is not a Christian, this form may be used *(BOS, 156-159)*.

Appendix

A Public Service of Penitence

On occasion, it may be desirable to have a public service of penitence leading to private confessions (Reconciliation of a Penitent) or general confession and absolution.

1. A Penitential Order *(BCP, 319 or BCP, 351)* may be used:
   Hymn, psalm or anthem (Psalm 51 is appropriate)
   Proper acclamation *(BCP, 319 or 351)*
   Exhortation *(BCP, 316;* see also page 231) *or* Homily
   Decalogue *(BCP, 317-318 or 350)*
   Reading of Scripture (either *BCP, 319-320 or 351-352;* or other suitable passage)
   Invitation to Confession (A period of silence follows.)
      a. Private confessions using the Reconciliation of a Penitent *(BCP, 447-452).* (See *Note* below.)
      b. General confession and absolution *(BCP, 320-321 or 352-353)*
      c. Litany of Penitence *(BCP, 267-269)*
   The Lord's Prayer
   Other suitable prayers may be added.
   (A hymn, psalm or anthem may follow.)
   The Grace or a blessing (See below for suggested blessing.)

2. The following may be used:
   Hymn, psalm or anthem
   Acclamation:
      V: Bless the Lord who forgives (forgiveth) all our sins;
      R: His mercy endures (endureth) for ever.
   A reading from Scripture
   Homily
   Psalm 51 (or other suitable penitential psalm)
   (If "a" below is used, the Exhortation follows here.)
   Litany of Penitence *(BCP, 267-269)*
      a. If the initial confession is used, then the absolution *(BCP, 269)* follows.
      b. The initial confession may be omitted (if either private confession or a general confession is to follow) in which case the absolution *(BCP, 269)* is omitted.
   Exhortation *(BCP, 316)* concluding with the invitation to confession (see page 231)
   Confession of Sin:
      a. Private confessions using the Reconciliation of a Penitent *(BCP, 447-452),* and absolution
      b. General confession and absolution *(BCP, 320-321 or 352-353)*

The Lord's Prayer
Other suitable prayers may be added.
The General Thanksgiving *(BCP, 58-59, 71-72, or 101, 125)*
A hymn or psalm of thanksgiving
The Grace or a blessing
The following blessing is appropriate:

The God of peace, who brought again from the dead our Lord Jesus Christ, the great Shepherd of the sheep, through the blood of the everlasting covenant: Make you perfect in every good work to do his will, working in you that which is well pleasing in his sight; and the blessing of God Almighty, the Father, the Son, and the Holy Spirit, be among you, and remain with you always, *Amen. (BOS, 27 or BCP, 486-487 or 503)*

Note: If either of these forms is used with private confessions, one or more priests should be available to hear confessions. They are seated in an appropriate place that will ensure privacy for the penitent. The priest(s) are vested in cassock and surplice, or cassock-alb and (violet) stole. The people come individually to the priest after the invitation, make their confession, receive absolution and return to their places. During this time silence may be kept, or a hymn, psalm or anthem sung.

Hymns, Versicles, Responses and Collects for use in Solemn Processions

Note: The number is a hymn in *The Hymnal 1982.*

Note: In the collects suggested below, the tradition of omitting the Trinitarian ending and substituting "through (the same) Jesus Christ our Lord" may be observed.

After the versicle and response, before the collect, the celebrant sings or says, "Let us pray."

Christmas   *(Hymnal, 83)*   Station at the Creche

V. The word was made flesh and dwelt among us:
R. *And we beheld his glory.*
or
V. The glory of the Lord has been revealed:
R. *And all flesh shall see the salvation of our God.*

Collect: *(BCP, 160-161 or 212-213)*
Note: The second alternative is appropriate as the collect for the Midnight Eucharist. If the procession precedes this Eucharist, one of the other two collects is used at the Station. (A form for the Blessing of the Creche is found on page 269.)

Epiphany   *(January 6)*   Station at the Creche
(Hymnal, 109 or 119)

V. The Lord has manifested forth his glory:
R. *And all the peoples shall bow before him.*
or
V. The kings of Tarshish and the isles shall pay tribute:
R. *The kings of Arabia and Saba shall offer gifts.*

Collect: Christmas I *(BCP, 161 or 213)*
or Christmas II *(BCP, 162 or 214)*
or the following:

O God the Son, highest and holiest, who *didst* humble *thyself* to share our birth and our death: Bring us with the shepherds and wise men to kneel before *thy* lowly cradle, that we may come to sing with *thine* angels *thy* glorious praises in heaven; where *thou livest* and *reignest,* world without end. *Amen.*

The First Sunday after Epiphany: Station at the Font
The Baptism of Our Lord   *(Hymnal, 120)*

> V. The voice of the Lord is upon the waters:
> R. *The voice of the Lord is upon many waters.*

Collect: 10. "At Baptism" *(BCP, 203 or 254)*

The Presentation of Our Lord in the Temple
Candlemas   *(February 2) (Hymnal, 259)*

> V. We have waited in silence on *your* loving-kindness, O Lord:
> R. *In the midst of your temple.*
> *or*
> V. Behold, the Lord and Ruler has come to his temple:
> R. *Rejoice and be glad in meeting* thy *God, O Zion.*

Collect: O God, you have made this day holy by the presentation of
your Son in the Temple, and by the purification of the Blessed
Virgin Mary: Mercifully grant that we, who delight in her
humble readiness to be the birth-giver of the Only-begotten,
may rejoice for ever in our adoption as his sisters and brothers;
through Jesus Christ our Lord. *Amen.*

> *or*

O God, who didst make this day holy by the presentation of
thy Son in the Temple, and by the purification of the Blessed
Virgin Mary; Mercifully grant that we, who delight in her
humble readiness to be the bearer of the Only-begotten, may
rejoice for ever in our adoption as children of God; through
Jesus Christ our Lord. *Amen.*

The Last Sunday after the Epiphany
[The Transfiguration]   *(Hymnal, 137)*

> V. All the ends of the earth shall see:
> R. *The salvation of our God.*

Collect: The Transfiguration *(August 6) (BCP, 191 or 243)*

The Sunday of the Passion: Station at the Door
Palm Sunday   (see page 178)   of the Church

> V. Blessed is he that cometh in the Name of the Lord:
> R. *Hosanna in the highest.*

Collect: Monday in Holy Week *(BCP, 168)*

> *or*
> V. Blessed is he who comes in the name of the Lord:
> R. *Hosanna in the highest.*

Collect: Palm Sunday Procession *(BCP, 272* top)

Easter Day *(Hymnal, 175)* Station at the Creche

> V. This is the day which the Lord *hath* made, alleluia:
> R. *Let us rejoice and be glad in it, alleluia.*

Collect: Easter Day (first collect, *BCP, 170 or 222*)

> *Note:* The third collect is used at the Eucharist.

Ascension Day *(Hymnal, 216)* Station at the Door
of the Church

> V. God *has* gone up with a shout, alleluia:
> R. *The Lord with the sound of the ram's horn, alleluia.*
> *or*
> V. When Christ ascended up on high, alleluia:
> R. *He led captivity captive, alleluia.*

Collect: Ascension Day (first collect, *BCP, 174 or 226*)

> *Note:* The second collect is used at the Eucharist.

The Day of Pentecost: *(Hymnal, 225)* Station at the Font
Whitsunday

> V. The Spirit of the Lord now fills the whole world, alleluia:
> R. *The Spirit who searches even the depths of God, alleluia.*
> *or*
> V. The apostles spoke in other tongues, alleluia:
> R. *The wonderful works of God, alleluia.*

Collect: The Day of Pentecost (first collect, *BCP, 175 or 227*)

> *Note:* The second collect is used at the Eucharist.

The First Sunday After Pentecost: Station at the Door
Trinity Sunday *(Hymnal, 370)* of the Church

> V. Let us glorify the Lord: Father, Son, and Holy Spirit:
> R. *Praise him and highly exalt him for ever.*

Collect: 1. "Of the Holy Trinity" *(BCP, 199 or 251)*

The Last Sunday After Pentecost: Station at the Door
[Christ the King] *(Hymnal, 495)* of the Church

> V. Be still, then, and know that I am God:
> R. *I will be exalted among the nations.*
> *or*
> V. The Lord is in his holy temple:
> R. *Let all the earth keep silence before him.*

Collect: Proper 24 *(BCP, 183 or 235)*
> *or*
> Proper 3 *(BCP, 177 or 229)*

Transfiguration *(August 6)*
(Hymnal, 137)

Station at the Door
of the Church

> V. All the ends of the earth shall see:
> R. *The salvation of our God.*

Collect: Last Sunday after Epiphany *(BCP, 165 or 217)*

Holy Cross Day *(September 14)*
(Hymnal, 473)

Station at the Door
of the Church
(or at the Rood)

> V. When I am lifted up:
> R. *I will draw the whole world to myself.*
> *or*
> V. and R. given above for the Transfiguration

Collect: 6. "Of the Holy Cross" *(BCP, 201 or 252)*

All Saints' Day *(November 1)*
(Hymnal, 287)

Station at the Font

> V. Let the righteous rejoice in the presence of God:
> R. *Let them be merry and joyful.*
> *or*
> V. Be glad, O *ye* righteous, and rejoice in the Lord:
> R. *And be joyful, all* ye *that are true of heart.*

Collect: No. 8 *(BCP, 395)*
          or
          Second collect *(BCP, 489 or 504):* "O God the King of Saints . . ."

Saints' Days   *(Hymnal, 231-287)*

> As on All Saints' Day above

Apostles and Evangelists   *(Hymnal, 233-234, 235)*

> V. Their sound has gone out into all lands:
> R. *And their words to the ends of the world.*

Collect for Feasts of Apostles: Proper 8 *(BCP, 178 or 230)*
Collect for Feasts of Evangelists: Proper 28 *(BCP, 184 or 236)*

Feasts of the Incarnation   *(Hymnal, 82)*

> V. The Word was made flesh and dwelt among us:
> R. *And we beheld his glory.*

Collect: 4. "Of the Incarnation" *(BCP, 200 or 252)*

Feasts of the Blessed Virgin Mary
(Hymnal, 268-269, 277-278)

> V. Behold the handmaid of the Lord:
> R. *Be it unto me according to* thy *word.*

Collect: The Visitation *(BCP, 189 or 240-241)*
or
O God, who *didst* endue with singular grace the Blessed Virgin Mary, the Mother of our God and Savior Jesus Christ; grant us to follow her example of humility and purity; through the same Christ our Lord. *Amen.*

St. Michael and All Angels *(September 29)*   *(Hymnal, 283)*

> V. O *ye* angels of the Lord, bless the Lord:
> R. *Praise him and magnify him for ever.*

Collect: O Lord our God, who *orderest* all things in heaven and earth; look upon us, we beseech *thee,* and mercifully vouchsafe to refresh us by the protection and ministry of *thy* holy Angels; through Jesus Christ our Lord. *Amen.*

The Dedication of a Church   *(Hymnal, 360-361)*

> V. How dear to me is *your* dwelling, O Lord of hosts:
> R. *My soul has a desire and longing for the courts of the Lord.*
> *or*
> V. Happy are they who dwell in *your* house:
> R. *They will always be praising* you.

Collect: 7. "For the Church" *(BCP, 816)* or 11. "For the Parish" *(BCP, 817)*

The Patronal Festival   *(Hymn appropriate to the Feast)*

The appropriate versicle, response and collect given above for feast days and holy days.
A second station may be made with the following:

> V. Happy are they who dwell in *your* house:
> R. *They will always be praising* you.

Collect: 11. "For the Parish" *(BCP, 817)*

The Conclusion of the Maundy: *Ubi Caritas*

Various translations and settings are found in The Hymnal, 1982 (Hymnal, 576, 581, 606) or the following may be used:

Antiphon: Where charity and love prevail, there our God is found.
We have been gathered together by the love of Christ.
Let us rejoice and be glad now in Christ our God.
Let us fear and let us all love the living God.
Repeat Antiphon.
Therefore when we are assembled, let us be as one;
not to be divided in mind let us take care.
Let there be an end to quarrels, an end to strife.
And may he appear in our midst, our Christ and God.
Repeat Antiphon.
And together with the blessed may we behold the glory of thy countenance,
O Christ our God,
which shall be for us our chief joy, pure unbounded,
for ever and for evermore, world without end.
Repeat Antiphon.

Note: The following may be added to the anthem at the washing of feet *(BCP, 274-275)*, before the singing or saying of the *Ubi Caritas.*
Let these three, faith, hope, and love remain in you;
but the greatest of these is love.
Peace is my last gift to you, my own peace I now leave with you;
peace which the world cannot give, I give to you.

Anthem at the Veneration of the Cross on Good Friday

Note: See page 196

Improperia *(The Reproaches)**

Is it nothing to you, all you who pass by?
Look and see if there is any sorrow like my sorrow
which was brought upon me,
which the Lord inflicted on the day of his fierce anger.
Holy God, holy and mighty,
Holy immortal One, have mercy upon us.

O my people, O my Church,
What have I done to you,
or in what have I offended you?
Testify against me.
I led you forth from the land of Egypt,
and delivered you by the waters of Baptism,
but you have prepared a cross for your Saviour.
Holy God, holy and mighty,
Holy immortal One, have mercy upon us.

I led you through the desert forty years,
and fed you with manna,
I brought you through tribulation and penitence,
and gave you my body, the bread of heaven,
but you have prepared a cross for your Saviour.
Holy God, holy and mighty,
Holy immortal One, have mercy upon us.

What more could I have done for you
that I have not done?
I planted you, my chosen and fairest vineyard,
I made you the branches of my vine;
but when I was thirsty, you gave me vinegar to drink,
and pierced with a spear the side of your Saviour.
Holy God, holy and mighty,
Holy immortal One, have mercy upon us.

I went before you in a pillar of cloud,
and you have led me to the judgment hall of Pilate.
I scourged your enemies and brought you
to a land of freedom,
but you have scourged, mocked, and beaten me.
I gave you the water of salvation from the rock,
but you have given me gall and left me to thirst.

Holy God, holy and mighty,
Holy immortal One, have mercy upon us.

I gave you a royal scepter,
and bestowed the keys to the kingdom,
but you have given me a crown of thorns.
I raised you on high with great power,
but you have hanged me on the cross.
Holy God, holy and mighty,
Holy immortal One, have mercy upon us.

My peace I gave, which the world cannot give,
and washed your feet as a sign of my love,
but you draw the sword to strike in my name,
and seek high places in my kingdom.
I offered you my body and blood,
but you scatter and deny and abandon me.
Holy God, holy and mighty,
Holy immortal One, have mercy upon us.

I sent the Spirit of truth to guide you,
and you close your hearts to the Counselor.
I pray that all may be as one in the Father and me,
but you continue to quarrel and divide.
I call you to go and bring forth fruit,
but you cast lots for my clothing.
Holy God, holy and mighty,
Holy immortal One, have mercy upon us.

I grafted you into the tree of my chosen Israel,
and you turned on them with persecution
and mass murder.
I made you joint heirs with them of my covenants,
but you made them scapegoats for your own guilt.
Holy God, holy and mighty,
Holy immortal One, have mercy upon us.

I came to you as the least of your brothers and sisters;
I was hungry and you gave me no food,
I was thirsty and you gave me no drink,
I was a stranger and you did not welcome me,
naked and you did not clothe me,
sick and in prison and you did not visit me.
Holy God, holy and mighty,
Holy immortal One, have mercy upon us.

*From *Ashes to Fire*, Supplemental Worship Resource 8. Copyright © 1979 by Abingdon. Used by permission.

Propers for Various Occasions
approved by General Convention, 1979

World Hunger

Collect

I.   O Loving God, who openest thy hand to fill all things living with plenteousness: Break down, we beseech thee, the barriers of ignorance, indifference, and greed, that the multitudes that hunger may share thy bounty; through Jesus Christ or Savior, who liveth and reigneth with thee and the Holy Spirit, one God, for ever and ever. *Amen.*

II.   Loving God, whose hand is open to satisfy the needs of every living creature: Break down the barriers of ignorance, indifference, and greed, we pray, that the multitudes that hunger may share your bounty; through Jesus Christ our Savior, who lives and reigns with you and the Holy Spirit, one God, for ever and ever. *Amen.*

Psalm—146:4-9
Lessons—Isaiah 58:6-11; James 2:14-17; Matthew 25:31-46
Preface of Baptism

Human Rights

Collect

I.   O holy God, who lovest righteousness and hatest iniquity: Strengthen, we beseech thee, the hands of all who strive for justice throughout the world, and seeing that all human beings are thine offspring, move us to share the pain of those who are oppressed, and to promote the dignity and freedom of every person; through Jesus Christ the Liberator, who liveth and reigneth with thee and the Holy Spirit, one God, for ever and ever. *Amen.*

II.   O holy God, you love righteousness and hate iniquity: Strengthen, we pray, the hands of all who strive for justice throughout the world, and seeing that all human beings are your offspring, move us to share the pain of those who are oppressed, and to promote the dignity and freedom of every person; through Jesus Christ the Liberator, who lives and reigns with you and the Holy Spirit, one God, for ever and ever. *Amen.*

Psalm—85:7-13
Lessons—Isaiah 63:11b-13a, 15-16; I John 4:16b-21; Matthew 22:35-40
Preface of Apostles

Oppression

Collect

I.   O righteous God, who didst send thy Christ to establish the reign of justice, on earth as it is in heaven: Prosper every effort, we beseech thee, to root out arrogance, intolerance, and prejudice, and to eliminate all forms of discrimination, degradation, and oppression; through him who died at the oppressor's hands, Jesus Christ our Redeemer, who liveth and reigneth with thee and the Holy Spirit, one God, now and for ever. *Amen.*

II.   O righteous God, you sent your Christ to establish the reign of justice, on earth as in heaven: Prosper every effort to root out arrogance, intolerance, and prejudice, and to eliminate all forms of discrimination, degradation, and oppression; through him who died at the oppressor's hands, Jesus Christ our Redeemer, who lives and reigns with you and the Holy Spirit, one God, now and for ever. *Amen.*

Psalm—23
Lessons—Micah 2:1-4, 12; Philippians 2:1-5 (6-11); Luke 1:49-53
Preface of Baptism

Propers for Commemorations not in the Calendar

The Feast of Corpus Christi

The Thursday or Sunday after Trinity Sunday

Collect   (BCP, 201 or 252)

I.   God our Father, whose Son our Lord Jesus Christ in a wonderful Sacrament hath left unto us a memorial of his passion: Grant us so to venerate the sacred mysteries of his Body and Blood, that we may ever perceive within ourselves the fruit of his redemption; who liveth and reigneth with thee and the Holy Spirit, one God, for ever and ever. *Amen.*

II.   God our Father, whose Son our Lord Jesus Christ in a wonderful Sacrament has left us a memorial of his passion: Grant us so to venerate the sacred mysteries of his Body and Blood, that we may ever perceive within ourselves the fruit of his redemption; who lives and reigns with you and the Holy Spirit, one God, for ever and ever. *Amen.*

Psalm—116:10-17 *or* 34:1-8
Lessons—Deuteronomy 8:2-3; 1 Corinthians 11:23-29; John 6:47-58
Preface of the Epiphany

Charles Stuart

King of England and Scotland, Martyr
January 30

Collect

I.   O sovereign God, who didst grace thy servant Charles Stuart with nobility and fortitude, so that he was content to forfeit his throne, and life itself, for the cause of apostolic order in the Church: Bestow on us, we beseech thee, the like grace, that we, being steadfast in all adversity, may persevere unto the end, and attain with him the crown of everlasting life; through Jesus Christ the faithful witness, who with thee and the Holy Spirit liveth and reigneth, one God, for ever and ever. *Amen.*

II.   O sovereign God, who graced your servant Charles Stuart with nobility and fortitude, so that he was content to forfeit his throne, and life itself, for the cause of apostolic order in the Church: Bestow on us, we pray, the like grace, that we, being steadfast in all adversity, may persevere to the end, and attain with him the crown of everlasting life; through Jesus Christ the faithful witness, who lives and reigns with you and the Holy Spirit, one God, for ever and ever. *Amen.*

Psalm—143:1-9 *or* 124
Lessons—1 Timothy 6:12-16; Matthew 10:34-39
Preface of Baptism

Devotions Before the Blessed Sacrament

This extra-liturgical devotion of hymns, Scripture readings, silence and meditation may be used as a service in itself, or in those places in the Prayer Book where the rubrics permit an office to conclude with a "suitable devotion." The form may be adapted to local pastoral and devotional needs.

The officiant is vested in cassock, surplice and white stole or cassock-alb and white stole. A white cope may be worn.

If incense is used, the thurifer leads the officiant to the altar (two acolytes with lighted torches may walk ahead of the priest).

At the entrance, the officiant makes the appropriate reverence at the altar.

At the beginning of the devotions one of the following may be done:

1. The officiant may put the reserved Sacrament on the altar. It may be placed on a corporal, and the container(s) may be covered with a white cloth.
2. The officiant may open the door of the aumbry or tabernacle and leave the reserved Sacrament inside.
3. The officiant may put the Host in a container (monstrance) and place it on the altar.
4. The Sacrament may remain inside the aumbry or tabernacle with the door closed.

All kneel for a period of silent prayer.

A hymn in honor of the Blessed Sacrament or some other suitable hymn may be sung. The traditional hymn is *O Salutaris Hostia* ("O Saving Victim"; *Hymnal, 310-311).*

One or more of the following, or some other suitable passage of Scripture may be read:

> John 6:27-35
> John 15:4-17
> John 6:47-58
> 1 Corinthians 10:1-4, 16-17
> 1 Corinthians 11:23-29
> Revelation 19:1-2a, 4-9

A hymn, psalm (34 or 116:10-17), or anthem may follow.

A homily or meditation may be given.

Other prayers or litanies may be added.

All kneeling, the hymn *Tantum ergo, Sacramentum* ("Therefore, we before him bending"; *Hymnal, 330-331).* If incense is used, the Sacrament may be censed during the hymn.

When the hymn is concluded, the following versicle and response may be sung or said before the collect. The officiant stands.

V. Thou gavest them Bread from heaven (Alleluia):
R. *Containing within itself all sweetness (Alleluia).*

or

V. You gave them Bread from heaven (Alleluia):
R. *Containing in itself all sweetness (Alleluia).*

This collect is sung or said (the officiant remains standing):

Let us pray. God our Father, whose Son our Lord Jesus Christ in a wonderful Sacrament hath left unto us a memorial of his passion: Grant us so to venerate the sacred mysteries of his Body and Blood, that we may ever perceive within ourselves the fruit of his redemption; who liveth and reigneth with thee and the Holy Spirit, one God, for ever and ever. *Amen. (BPC, 201)*

or

Let us pray. God our Father, whose Son our Lord Jesus Christ in a wonderful Sacrament has left us a memorial of his passion: Grant us so to venerate the sacred mysteries of his Body and Blood, that we may ever perceive within ourselves the fruit of his redemption; who lives and reigns with you and the Holy Spirit, one God, for ever and ever. *Amen. (BCP, 252)*

After the collect, one of the following may be done:

1. Silent devotion while all remain kneeling.
2. The officiant may take the Sacrament from inside the tabernacle or aumbry, and turning toward the people make the sign of the cross with the Sacrament over the people.
3. The officiant may pick up the Sacrament from the altar, and turning toward the people make the sign of the cross with the Sacrament over the people.
4. The officiant may pick up the monstrance from the altar, and turning toward the people make the sign of the cross with the Sacrament over the people.

   Note: In some place it is traditional for the officiant to pick up the Sacrament using the ends of a white veil (humeral veil) which is worn over the shoulders.

The officiant kneels and appropriate prayers may follow.
A hymn, psalm or anthem is sung while the officiant returns the Sacrament to the tabernacle or aumbry, or when the doors are closed.
All stand for this hymn, psalm or anthem.*
The officiant and servers return to the sacristy.

---

*Psalm 117 is traditionally sung at the conclusion of the devotions. This antiphon may be sung before the psalm and after the Gloria Patri: "Let us forever adore the most holy Sacrament. (Alleluia.)"

Dedication (and Blessing) of Church Furnishings and Ornaments

The Book of Occasional Services provides a rite of dedication (blessing) for the following objects. *The form may be used after the sermon (and Creed) at the Eucharist, or at the Daily Office at the time of the hymn or anthem following the collects (BOS, 177-178).* Other rubrics are found on *BOS, 178.* The "reservations," as found in *BOS*, are also listed below.

1. An Altar	*Reserved to the Bishop*	*(BOS, 197)*
2. A Font	*Reserved to the Bishop*	*(BOS, 198)*
3. Chalices and Patens	*Reserved to the Bishop*	*(BOS, 200)*
4. A Bell	*Traditionally reserved to the Bishop*	*(BOS, 201)*
5. A Cross		*(BOS, 201)*
6. Candlesticks and Lamps		*(BOS, 202)*
7. Altar Cloths and Hangings	*(BOS, 202)*	
8. A Service (Altar) Book		*(BOS, 203)*
9. A Bible, Lectionary, or Gospel Book		*(BOS, 203)*
10. A Repository for the Scriptures		*(BOS, 204)*
11. An Aumbry or Tabernacle for the Sacrament		*(BOS, 205)*
12. An Aumbry for the Oils		*(BOS, 205)*
13. An Ambo (or Lectern, or Pulpit)		*(BOS, 206)*
14. Chairs, Benches and Prayer Desks		*(BOS, 206)*
15. A Stained Glass Window		*(BOS, 207)*
16. Pictures and Statues		*(BOS, 207)*
17. An Organ or Other Musical Instrument		*(BOS, 208)*
18. A Vessel for Incense		*(BOS, 209)*
19. Surplices and Albs		*(BOS, 209)*
20. Vestments for the Liturgy		*(BOS, 210)*
21. A Funeral Pall		*(BOS, 210)*
22. Any Church Ornament		*(BOS, 211)*

Notes:

1. When the object to be dedicated is fixed, a procession is made to that place.
2. When the object is movable, it is brought to the altar and presented to the celebrant.
3. A longer form of dedication is given with prayers for the benefactor(s) and, if a memorial, a commemoration *(BOS, 212-213).*
4. If holy water is used, the object is sprinkled after the collect.
5. If incense is used, the object is censed after the collect.
6. The appointed antiphons may be read or sung by all, or by the celebrant, or by the choir (and cantor).
7. The following forms of blessing may be added to the dedications (with a sign of the cross) by the celebrant over the object:

1. An Altar	Collect reads: "Sanctify *and* + *bless* this Table..." *(BOS, 198)*
2. A Font	Collect reads: "We *bless* + and dedicate this Font..." *(BOS, 199)*
3. Chalices and Patens	No addition to the collect but a sign of the cross at the words "which we now consecrate for use in your Church..." *(BOS, 200)*
4. A Bell	No addition to the collect but a sign of the cross at the words "which we consecrate" *(BOS, 201)*
5. A Cross	Collect reads: "...and we pray *your* + *blessing* that this cross may draw our hearts to him..." *(BOS, 202)*
6. Candlesticks and Lamps	Collect reads: "...before your throne: + *Bless these lights (lamps),* and grant that they be kindled for your glory..." *(BOS, 202)*
7. Altar Cloths and Hangings	Collect reads: "...your perfect beauty: + *Bless and* accept our offering..." *(BOS, 202)*
8. A Service (Altar) Book	Collect reads: "Bless us, O Lord of hosts, + *and this* _____ which we dedicate and use to your service..." *(BOS, 203)*
9. A Bible, Lectionary, or Gospel Book	Collect reads: "Accept *and* + *bless* this _____ which we dedicate here today..." *(BOS, 203)*
10. A Repository for the Scriptures	Collect reads: "+ *Bless and* accept, we pray, this repository for the..." *(BOS, 204)*
11. An Aumbry or Tabernacle for the Sacrament	Collect reads: "...Grant that in this aumbry (tabernacle) which we + *bless* and set apart today..." *(BOS, 205)*
12. An Aumbry for the Oils	Collect reads: "...We here offer to you for your + *blessing* this aumbry..." *(BOS, 205-206)*
13. An Ambo (or Lectern or Pulpit)	Collect reads: "and proclaim your holy Word from this *ambo* which we + *bless and* dedicate today..." *(BOS, 206)*
14. Chairs, Benches and Prayer Desks	Collect reads: "O Lord God Almighty, you disclosed in a vision the elders seated around your throne: + *Bless this chair* for the use..." *(BOS, 206)*
15. A Stained Glass Window	Collect reads: "...with the radiance of your glory: + *Bless the* offering of this window..." *(BOS, 207)*

16. Pictures and Statues	Collect reads: "...and visible to be a means to percieve realities unseen: + *Bless*, we pray this representation of _____; and grant..."	*(BOS, 207-208)*
17. An Organ or other Musical Instrument	Collect reads: "...+ *Bless this* organ for the worship of your temple..."	*(BOS, 208)*
18. A Vessel for Incense	Collect reads: "...foretold by the prophet: We + *bless and* dedicate to your worship *this vessel...*"	*(BOS, 209)*
19. Surplices and Albs	Collect reads: "...clothed in white robes: + *Bless* this _____ which we dedicate..."	*(BOS, 209)*
20. Vestments for the Liturgy	Collect reads: "...in majesty and glory: + *Bless* this _____ for the use of ..."	*(BOS, 210)*
21. A Funeral Pall	Collect reads: "...and all to be honored: + *Bless and* make this pall to be a sign of our common..."	*(BOS, 210-211)*
22. Any Church Ornament	Collect reads: "...the use of material things: + *Bless and receive this* _____, which we offer..."	*(BOS, 211)*

Note: The addition of a specific blessing to the above dedications does not presume a departure from the understanding that objects are set aside and made holy by use. The above are given as a pastoral aid for those who need a full blessing to assist their understanding of sanctification.

Blessing of the Creche at Christmas

V. Behold, the dwelling of God is with creation.
R. *He will dwell with us and we shall be his people.*
V. God himself is with us. Alleluia.
R. *Come let us adore him. Alleluia.*

Eternal Father, *you* sent *your* only-begotten Son to take our human nature upon him, and to be born (this day) of a pure virgin: [+ Bless, we pray, this Creche that it may be a sign of his humble birth; and] grant that we who joyfully behold his appearing may be strengthened to greet him when he comes again in glory; even the same Jesus Christ Our Lord and Redeemer, who *lives* and *reigns* with *you* and the Holy Spirit, one God, in glory everlasting. *Amen.*

Forms for the Blessing of Incense during the Liturgy

To be said privately by the celebrant or officiant:

Let my prayer be set forth in *your* sight as incense.

or

Receive, O Father, this gift of incense. Grant that our prayers may ascend in *your* sight, and the pure oblation of *your* Son be proclaimed. Amen.

or

May this offering of incense be a sign unto us, O Lord, of our prayers ascending in *your* sight.

or

Bless, O Lord, this incense. Grant that it may be a sign of the prayers we offer; through Jesus Christ our Lord. Amen.

or this traditional blessing of the incense at the Offertory:

By the intercession of Blessed Michael the Archangel, who stands at the right hand of the altar of incense, and of all the Saints, may the Lord bless this incense and accept it as a pure oblation; through Christ our Lord. Amen.

A Form for Blessing Holy Water

(Water is poured into a container and, traditionally, a little salt is added to it.)

The priest says:

Almighty God, who through the water of baptism *has* raised us from sin into new life, and by the power of *your* life-giving Spirit ever cleanses and sanctifies *your* people: + Bless, we pray *you*, this water for the service of *your* holy Church; and grant that it may be a sign of the cleansing and refreshment of *your* grace; through Jesus Christ our Lord. *Amen.*

This Antiphon may be added:

Cleanse me from my sin, and I shall be pure; wash me, and I shall be clean indeed.

During the Fifty Days of Easter, in place of the above antiphon, this may be added:

I saw water proceeding out of the temple, from the right side it flowed; and all those to whom that water came shall be saved. Alleluia.

Parts of the Eucharist
Traditionally Sung by the Celebrant or Other Minister

Acclamation	*(AB, 372)*	*Celebrant*
Salutation	*(AB, 373)*	*Celebrant*
Collect of the Day	*(AB, 374-376)*	*Celebrant*
Lesson	*(AB, 377)*	*Reader*
Epistle	*(AB, 377)*	*Reader*
Gospel	*(AB, 378-381)*	*Deacon or Priest*
The Prayers of the People	(see page 44-45)	*Deacon or Leader*
Concluding Collect	*(AB, 375-376;* Form V, *384-385)*	*Celebrant*
The Peace	*(AB, 386)*	*Celebrant*
Sursum Corda	*(AB, 21 or 157)**	*Celebrant*
Proper Preface	*(AB, 102-140* *or 252-290)**	*Celebrant*
Conclusion of Eucharistic Prayer and Amen	*(AB, 34, 40, 169, 174,* *180, 190)**	*Celebrant*
Introduction to the Lord's Prayer	*(AB, 34, 40, 170, 174,* *180, 190)*	*Celebrant*
Fraction Anthem		*Celebrant or all*
Invitation to Communion	*(AB, 387)*	*Celebrant*
Blessing	*(AB, 387-389)*	*Celebrant*
Dismissal	*(AB, 390-391)*	*Deacon or Priest*

Also, the intonation of the Gloria in excelsis and the Creed (if appropriate to the musical setting).

---

*Eucharistic Prayer D is noted for the Mozarabic Tone, both for the Preface and the Conclusion *(AB, 184-185 and 190)*.

Parts of the Eucharist
Traditionally Sung by the People and/or the Choir (or Cantor)

The Entrance	Hymn, psalm or anthem	
Acclamation	Response to celebrant	*(AB, 372)*
Song(s) of Praise	(Kyrie eleison, Gloria in excelsis, Trisagion or other Song of Praise)	
Salutation	Response to celebrant	*(AB, 373)*
Collect of the Day	"Amen" at conclusion	*(AB, 374-376)*
Lesson	Response at the conclusion	*(AB, 377)*
Psalm	Appointed for the day	
Epistle or Lesson	Response at the conclusion	*(AB, 377)*
Alleluia or Tract	Proper to the day (psalm or anthem)	
Sequence Hymn	Appropriate to the day	
Gospel	Responses at announcement and conclusion	*(AB, 378-381)*
Nicene Creed		
The Prayers of the People:	Responses	(see page 44-45)
Concluding Collect	"Amen" at conclusion	
The Peace	Response	*(AB, 386)*
Offertory	Hymn, psalm or anthem	
Sursum Corda	Responses	*(AB, 21 or 157)*
Sanctus and Benedictus qui venit		
(Memorial) Acclamation		(see page 56)
Conclusion of Eucharistic Prayer	"Amen" at conclusion	(see page 56)
The Lord's Prayer		
Fraction Anthem and/or other anthem at the Breaking of the Bread	Response or full throughout	(see page 71)
		(BOS, 17-21)
Ministration of Communion	Hymn, psalm or anthem	
Blessing	"Amen" at conclusion	*(AB, 387-389)*
Dismissal	Response	*(AB, 390-391)*

Private Prayers for the Priest

Before Celebrating the Eucharist

Purify our consciences, we beseech thee, Almighty God, that we may worthily hear and receive thy Holy Word, magnify thy Holy Name, and offer unto thee the spotless sacrifice of thy Son, even Jesus Christ our Lord. Amen.

or

Cleanse our consciences, we beseech thee, O God, by thy visitation, that thy Son our Lord Jesus Christ, when he cometh, may find in us a dwelling place made ready for himself; who liveth and reigneth with thee and the Holy Spirit, ever one God, world without end. Amen.

or

Be present, be present, O Jesus, our great High Priest, as *you were* present with *your* disciples, and be known to us in the breaking of bread; who lives and reigns with the Father and the Holy Spirit, now and for ever. Amen.

After Celebrating the Eucharist

Blessed, praised, worshipped, hallowed and adored be Jesus Christ on his throne of glory in heaven, in the most holy Sacrament of the altar, and in the hearts of his faithful people (and may the souls of the faithful departed, through the mercy of God, rest in peace). Amen.

or

By the power of the Holy Spirit may I be a reasonable, holy, and living sacrifice to *you* all the days of my life, O Lord. Amen.

or

O Lord Jesus Christ, who in a wonderful Sacrament hast left unto us a memorial of thy passion: Grant us, we beseech thee, so to venerate the sacred mysteries of thy Body and Blood, that we may ever perceive within ourselves the fruit of thy redemption; who livest and reignest with the Father and the Holy Spirit, one God, for ever and ever. Amen.

Prayers for use at the Offertory

Offering of the Bread

Blessed *are you*, Lord God of all creation; through *your* goodness we have this bread to offer, which earth has given and human hands have made.
It will become for us the Bread of Heaven.

Response: *Blessed be God forever.*

Preparation of the Cup

By the Mystery of this water and wine may we come to share in the divinity of Christ, who humbled himself to share in our humanity.

Offering of the Cup

Blessed *are you,* Lord God of all creation; through *your* goodness we have this wine to offer, fruit of the vine and work of human hands.
It will become for us the Cup of Salvation.

Response: *Blessed be God forever.*

Of the Alms: Receive, O Lord, these gifts presented by *your* people for the work of *your* Church.

At the Lavabo: Create in me a clean heart, O God,
and renew a right spirit within me.
or
Lord, wash away my iniquity and cleanse me from my sin.
or
I will wash my hands among the innocent, Lord,
and walk around your altar, that I may tell of your wondrous deeds.

The First Eucharist of a newly Ordained Priest

In the new ordination rites, the first celebration of the Eucharist by a newly ordained priest is that of the ordination, when the priest concelebrates with the bishop. However, a festive celebration with the newly ordained priest as the celebrant is traditionally held soon after the ordination. Several ceremonies may accompany this celebration.

1. Before the Eucharist, in the sacristy, the priest and other assisting ministers sing or say the hymn *Veni Creator Spiritus (Hymnal, 502-504).* The priest then sings or says the following, with those present responding.

    V. Send forth *thy* Spirit and they shall be made new:
    R. *And* thou shalt *renew the face of the earth.*
    V. O Lord hear my prayer:
    R. *And let my cry come unto* thee.
    V. The Lord be with you:
    R. *And* with thy spirit.

    Let us pray. O God, who *didst* teach the hearts of *thy* faithful people, by sending to them the light of the Holy Spirit; Grant us by the same Spirit to have a right judgment in all things, and evermore to rejoice in his holy comfort; through the merits of Christ Jesus our Savior, who *liveth* and *reigneth* with *thee*, in the unity of the same Spirit, one God, world without end. *Amen.*

2. The recitation of Psalm 43 may follow, with this antiphon said or sung before the psalm and after the Gloria Patri:
    I will go to the altar of God, to the God of my joy and gladness.

3. This prayer of preparation may then be said by the priest:
    Take away from us our iniquities, we beseech *thee,* O Lord, that we may be worthy to enter with pure minds into the Holy of Holies; and grant that we may worthily praise and magnify *thy* Holy Name through the sacrifice we are to offer *thee;* through Christ our Lord. *Amen.*
    or
    one of the prayers given on page 271.

4. The Eucharist then begins in the usual way with the entrance.

5. Other priests present may concelebrate with the newly ordained priest (see page 78).

6. An "assisting priest" may be assigned to stand next to the celebrant and assist with the celebration. It is also appropriate that this assisting priest concelebrate. (The assisting priest may be vested in a cope.)

7. At the conclusion of the Eucharist, after the postcommunion prayer and before the blessing and dismissal, the Te Deum may be sung (see page 145).

8. The newly ordained priest gives the final blessing (after the versicles and responses following the Te Deum).

The Burial of a Priest

Various traditions accompany the preparation of the body of a priest prior to burial. These are set forth here for those who may wish to use them.

1. The absolution of the body

    In the presence of other priests (vested in surplice with violet or white stoles), the officiant begins with the Litany at the Time of Death *(BCP, 462-464)* and continues with the Kyrie and Lord's Prayer.

    The officiant then says the prayer "Deliver *your* servant . . ." *BCP, 464)*, after which the body may be sprinkled with holy water.

2. The vesting of the body

    The priests appointed begin the vesting of the body while the others present begin the recitation of the Psalter, starting with Psalm 1 and continuing without Gloria Patri.

    Traditionally the body is vested in cassock, amice, alb, cincture (or cassock-alb) and Eucharistic vestments. (The color may be violet, green or white.) When the vesting is completed, the recitation of the Psalter concludes with the versicle and response "Rest eternal . . ." *(BCP, 486 or 502)*. The officiant then says the Commendatory Prayer *(BCP, 465 or 483)*.

3. The sealing of the coffin

    Those present then begin with Psalm 147 and continue the recitation through Psalm 150. During this recitation the coffin is closed and sealed.

4. The taking of the body to the church

    The priests carry the coffin to the church, during which the anthems are recited (*BCP, 483-484, or 500;* or one of the canticles suggested).

5. The reception and vigil

    The body is received (see page 241) and placed before the altar (with the head at the altar end and the feet facing the door). A vigil is then kept until the Requiem Eucharist and Burial (see page 241).

    It is not proper for the coffin to be opened again after being sealed (see 3 above).

The Vigil of Pentecost

I. Service of Light

The Entrance
*The church is in darkness except for the lighted Paschal Candle.
The people are given unlighted candles when they arrive.
The ministers enter in silence, reverence the altar, and take their
places near the candle. (See page 132)*

Easter Acclamation *(BCP, 109; Hymnal, S 78-79)*

Prayer for Light *(BCP, 111, "Easter Season")*
*The Short Lesson is omitted and the celebrant sings (or says) the
Prayer for Light.*

Hymn
*An appropriate hymn or the proper Lucernarium (BOS, 12) may
be sung while the altar candles (and the candles of the people) are
lighted.*

Gloria in excelsis
*This song of praise is sung in place of the Phos hilaron. During
the Gloria the celebrant may cense the Paschal Candle and altar.
It is appropriate for bells to be rung.*

Salutation and Collect of the Day *(BCP, 175 or 277)*
*The first alternative is appropriate for the Vigil. (After the collect
the people extinguish their candles.)*

II. The Liturgy of the Word

The Lessons
*Three or more of the appointed lessons are read before the Gospel,
each followed by an appropriate psalm, canticle, or hymn (BCP,
896, 906, 917).*

Sequence Hymn *(Hymnal, 226)*
*(The people may light their candles for the proclamation of the
Gospel. These candles are extinguished for the sermon.)*

The Holy Gospel   *John 7:37-39a*
*It is appropriate that the Gospel be read (or chanted) several times,
each time in a different language.*

Sermon

III. The Baptismal Liturgy
(The people may light their candles.)

The Nicene Creed is omitted.

Holy Baptism and/or Confirmation with the Renewal of Baptismal
Vows
*This begins with the Presentation of the Candidates (BCP, 301-310
or 415-419; also pages 214-220).*

or if there are no candidates

The Renewal of Baptismal Vows *(BCP, 292-294;* also pages 206-209).
   *The celebrant may introduce the Renewal of Baptismal Vows with
   the bidding (BCP, 292). If this is used, the words "now that our
   Lenten observance is ended" are omitted.
   (The people extinguish their candles.)*
The Prayers of the People
The Confession of Sin is omitted.
The Peace

IV. The Holy Communion

   The Offertory
   Preface of Pentecost
   The Breaking of the Bread
      Alleluias are added.
   Pentecost Blessing *(BOS, 25)*
   Easter Dismissal
      Alleluias are added.

*Note: The Paschal Candle is lighted for all services from the Great Vigil of
Easter through the final service on the Day of Pentecost.*

Epilogue

In our lives as priests, too often we forget the obligation to our people and to ourselves for rest, relaxation and reflection. There are many examples from the past and the present of holy men and women who died of exhaustion. As surprise is not a legitimate element of liturgy, so also exhaustion is not a necessary element of ministry.

Upon completion of this book, a time and place for rest, relaxation and reflection was graciously offered by the Reverend and Mrs. John McLaughlin and the people of the Church of St. Mary of the Harbor. In the spirit of grateful appreciation and love we offer our thanks and ask God's blessing upon them.

Dennis G. Michno
Richard E. Mayberry

February 10, 1982
Feast of St. Scholastica

Church of St. Mary of the Harbor
Provincetown, Massachusetts

About the Author

DENNIS G. MICHNO, a priest of the Episcopal Church, formerly curate and director of music at All Saints Church in New York City, resides in Bayfield, Wisconsin. He served as a consultant to the Standing Liturgical Commission in the revision and production of *The Book of Common Prayer* (1979). Fr. Michno received his undergraduate degree from St. John's University, Collegeville, Minnesota, a Benedictine Abbey noted for liturgical studies. He did further graduate work in music at the Julliard School and later attended the General Theological Seminary where he received his Master of Divinity and Master of Sacred Theology. Father Michno is the author of *A Manual for Acolytes* (Morehouse-Barlow, 1981).

About the Illustrator

RICHARD E. MAYBERRY, a priest of the Episcopal Church, is rector of St. Francis' Church, Stamford, Connecticut. Previous to this position he was assistant to the rector at St. Mark's Church, Mt. Kisco, New York. Fr. Mayberry received his undergraduate degree in art from the University of Oregon and his Master of Divinity from the General Theological Seminary. He did the illustrations for *A Manual for Acolytes* (Morehouse-Barlow, 1981).

Index

Ablutions, 73

Absolution: on Ash Wednesday, 154; by a Bishop, 33, 45; of the Body, 274; after the Confession of Sin, 33, 45, 89, 248; at the Daily Office, 126, 136, 140; at the Good Friday Liturgy, 197; after the Prayers of the People (Form VI), 39, 43; at the Reconciliation of a Penitent, 232; at the Time of Death, 240

Academic Hood, 26

Acclamation: Easter, 34, 158, 210; Memorial, 270; music for, 269-70; Penitential, 155, 181, 248

Acclamation at the Entrance Rite, 32-34; Advent, 149; Baptism, 212-13; Confirmation, 219; Easter proclamation, 158, 209; Lent, 155; Good Friday, 192; Great Vigil of Easter, 209; Maundy Thursday, 187

Acolytes: at the Eucharist, 37; at the Good Friday Liturgy, 194-96; at the Palm Sunday Liturgy, 176-78; in a Solemn Procession, 168; at a Solemn Eucharist, 86-90; at Solemn Evensong, 142, 144; at a Solemn Te Deum, 145; at Stations of the Cross, 156-57; vestments for, 86

Acolytes, Commissioning of, 223

Act of Thanksgiving, for the Birth or Adoption of a Child, 218

Acts of the Apostles, lesson from, 111

Administration of Communion, 72

Adoption of a Child, Thanksgiving for, 218

Advent: Acclamation, 149; Collect at the Prayers of the People, 44; use of the Great Litany, 163; Lectionary, 111, 112, 118; Preface of, 55, 95, 99, 114; Saturday Evenings in, 149; Season of, 95; Weekday Eucharist during, 114, 149; Wreath, 133, 148-49; "O" Antiphons, 149

Aelred, 101

Affirmation of Vows, Blessing of a Civil Marriage, 229. See also Renewal of Vows

Affirmations: at Baptism, 214; at Confirmation, 220

Agapé, 77, 189

Agatha, 106

Agnes, 101

Agnus Dei, 71. See also Confractoria

Aidan, 104

Alb, 25; Blessing of, 263, 265

Alban, 103

Albert the Great, 108

Alcuin, 103

Alfred the Great, 105

All Faithful Departed, 105. See also All Souls' Day

All Hallow's Eve, 123

All Saints' Day, 98, 100, 113; Baptism on, 212; Collect at the Prayers of the People, 44; Eve, 123; Station in Procession, 253; Vigil, 123

All Saints' Day, Sunday after, 98; at Baptism, 212

All Saints, Preface of, 55, 98-100

All Souls' Day, 105; outline, 160-61; transferred, 160

Alleluia: at the Acclamation, 159; at the Bidding to a Solemn Procession, 168; at the Breaking of the Bread, 159; at the Burial of the Dead, 159, 162, 244; closure of, 96, 152; at the Daily Office, 126, 130, 136, 140-41, 142; at the Dismissal, 74, 159, 201, 209; at the Eucharist, 159, 272, during the Fifty Days of Easter, 158-59; at the Peace, 159; at Requiem Eucharists, 159, 162; at the Station in a Solemn Procession, 159, 250-54

Alleluia, when omitted, 140, 155, 161, 162, 181

Alleluia, Great, at the Vigil of Easter, 201, 210

Alleluia Verse, 36, 272; preparation of incense during, 80

Alms. See Gifts at the Offertory; Money Offering

Alpha and Omega, tracing in the Paschal Candle, 204

Alphege, 102

Altar, Blessing of, 267-68

Altar Book, The, (AB), 19

Altar Book, Blessing of, 267-68

Altar Candles, 27; on Good Friday, 191, 194-99; on Holy Saturday, 200; at the Great Vigil of Easter, 203, 209; at An Order of Worship for the Evening, 133

Altar Cloth, 31; on Good Friday, 191

Altar Cloths, Blessing of, 267-68

Altar Cross, censing of, 82-85

Altar Guild, Commissioning of Members, 223
Altar hangings, Blessings of, 263-64
Ambo, Blessing of, 263-64
Ambrose, 101
Amen: response at Communion, 72; at the conclusion of Eucharistic Prayer, 71, 267-68, at the conclusion of the Prayers of the People, 39, 40
Amen, Great. *See* Great Amen
Amice, 25
Andrew, St., 99; Eve, 122
Andrewes, Lancelot, 104
Angels, 100, 108
Anniversary of a Marriage, 230
Announcement of the Gospel, 37; on Holy Saturday, 200; of the Passion, 180
Announcement of Lessons, 36
Announcement of Reading, omission of at Noonday Service, 131
Announcement at Stations of the Cross, of station and title, 157
Announcements (Notices), 38, 75
Annunication, Feast of, 99; Eve of, 122
Anointing: at Baptism with the Oil of the Catechumens, 214; at Baptism with Chrism, 215-16; at Confirmation, 220; at the Time of Death, 240; reservation of, for the Sick, 239; of the Sick, 234, 236-38
Anselm, 102
Anskar, 101
Ante-Communion. *See* Liturgy of the Word; Word of God, The
Anthem: at the Anointing of the Sick, 234, 238; at Baptism, 213, 215, 216; at the Candlemas Procession, 151; at Devotions before the Sacrament, 261-62; at the Laying on of Hands, 234, 238; at Marriage, 225-26, 228; during the Rogation Procession, 167
Anthems at the Burial of the Dead: Burial Sentences, 242; Burial of a Priest, 272; at the Commendation, 162, 244; at the Committal, 245-46; at the conclusion of the Liturgy, 246
Anthems at the Daily Office: at Morning Prayer, 129; at An Order of Worship for the Evening, 133; at Evening Prayer, 139
Anthems at the Eucharist: at the Entrance, 32-34; before the Gospel, 36; at the Offertory, 47, 50; at the Breaking of the Bread, 71; during the Ministration of Communion, 72; music for, 272
Anthems during Holy Week: at the Entrance on Palm Sunday, 176; during the distribution of Palms, 177; during the Procession on Palm Sunday, 178; before the Passion Gospel, 179; before the Gospel on Maundy Thursday, 187; at the Washing of Feet on Maundy Thursday, 188, 255; after the Solemn Collects on Good Friday, 193; at the

Bringing in of the Cross, 194; at the Veneration of the Cross, 195, 256-57; while the Reserved Sacrament is brought to the Altar; 96; at the Commemoration of the Burial of Our Lord, 199; before the Gospel on Holy Saturday, 200; in place of the Prayers of the People on Holy Saturday, 200; after the Baptismal Liturgy at the Great Vigil of Easter, 209
Antiphons: at the Blessing of Church Furnishings and Ornaments, 263; on Candlemas, 151; at the Daily Offices, 127, 128, 141; at Devotions before the Sacrament, 263-64; at the Maundy Thursday Liturgy, 187; at the Stripping of the Altars on Good Friday, 189. *See also* Anthems
Antony, 101
Apostles' Creed: at the Burial of the Dead, 38, 242; at the Daily Office as the Luturgy of the Word, 91; at Evening Prayer, 138; at Marriage, 227; at Morning Prayer, 129; omitted at the Daily Office, 129, 138; at Solemn Evensong, 143
Apostles and Evangelists, Feasts of, Station in Procession, 253
Apostles, Preface of, 55, 99, 100-03
Aquinas, Thomas, 101
Archbishop of Canterbury, named in the Prayers of the People, 44
Ascension Day: Concluding Collect at the Prayers of the People, 44; days preceding, 166; Propers for, 97; Station in Procession, 252
Ascension, Preface of the, 55, 97, 115
Ashes: Blessing of, 154; Imposition of, 153-54; preparation of, 153
Ash Wednesday, 94, 96, 113; preparations for, 152-53; Proper Liturgy, 154
Aspergillum and bucket, 175-76, 203, 209, 225, 244
Asperging of the People, at the Great Vigil of Easter, 209
Assisting Ministers: at Baptism, 213-17; on Candlemas, 150; at the Eucharist, 35, 36, 45, 48, 50, 60, 63, 66, 70, 72, 73; at the Liturgies of Holy Week, 176-79, 187, 192, 195, 196-97, 200, 202, 204-10; at Marriage, 225-26; at Solemn Evensong, 142; in a Solemn Procession, 168; at a Solemn Te Deum, 154; vestments for, 25-26
Assisting Priest, at the First Eucharist of a Newly Ordained Priest, 271
Assumption of the Blessed Virgin Mary. *See* Mary the Virgin, St., Feast of
Athanasius, 102
Augustine of Canterbury, 103
Augustine of Hippo, 104
Aumbry, 73, 75, 261-62

Aumbry for the Sacrament, Blessing of, 263-64
Aumbry for Oils, Blessing of, 263-64

Banns, 225
Baptism, 212-17; days appropriate, 212; Emergency, 217; at the Great Vigil of Easter, 207-10; with Confirmation, Reception, and/or Reaffirmation, 222
Baptism of our Lord, Feast of, 95; Station in Procession, 251; Vigil, 122
Baptism, Preface of, 55, 98, 101-06, 217, 260
Baptismal Acclamation, 32-34, 213
Baptismal Candle, 216
Baptismal Covenant, 205, 214, 220, 222
Baptismal Font. *See* Font
Baptismal Garment. *See* Chrysom
Baptismal Litany. *See* Prayers for the Candidates
Baptismal Liturgy at the Great Vigil of Easter, 206-10
Baptismal Water, asperging of the people at the Great Vigil of Easter, 209
Barnabas, St., Feast of, 99; Eve of, 122
Bartholomew, St., Feast of, 99; Eve of, 123
Basil the Great, 103
Basin for the Washing of Feet, 186, 188
Becket, Thomas, 101
Bede the Venerable, 103
Bell, Blessing of, 263-64
Bells: at the Doxology and Great Amen, 56; at the Elevations, 56; at the Great Vigil of Easter, 209; omitted on Maundy Thursday, 186; at the *Sanctus,* 56; at a Solemn Te Deum, 145
Benches, Blessing of, 263-64
Benedict of Nursia, 18, 103
Benediction. *See* Devotions before the Sacrament
Benedictus (Song of Zechariah), 182, 246
Benedictus Dominus Deus, 128
Benedictus es, Domine, 182
Benedictus qui venit, 54, 268
Bernard, 104
Betrothal. *See* Presentation at Marriage
Bible, Blessing of, 263-64
Bidding: on Ash Wednesday, 154; at Baptism, 214; to the Baptismal Liturgy at the Great Vigil of Easter, 206; at Confirmation, Reception, Reaffirmation, 220, 222; at the Blessing of a Civil Marriage, 229; at the Kindling of the New Fire, 204; at the Liturgy of the Word at the Great Vigil of Easter, 206; at the Procession on Palm Sunday, 178; the people to kneel on Good Friday, 193; the people to kneel on Holy Saturday, 200; at the Solemn Collects on Good Friday, 192; at a Solemn Procession, 168; at the Thanksgiving for the Birth or Adoption of a Child, 218; at

the Washing of Feet on Maundy Thursday, 188
Binding of hands: at Marriage, 227; at the Blessing of a Civil Marriage, 229
Biography of a Saint, 155. *See also* Hagiography
Birth of a Child, Thanksgiving for, 218
Bishop: at the Absolution after the Confession of Sins, 45, 89; at Baptism, 216; Blessing of the Deacon before the Gospel, 88; Blessing of incense, 81; Blessings Reserved to, 263; Chrism, Consecration of, 206, 215, 221; Chrismation, 216, 219-22; at Confirmation, Reception, Reaffirmation, 219-22; at the Gospel, 37, 88; at Marriage, 225; at An Order of Worship for the Evening, 132; as the Principal Celebrant of the Eucharist, 78; at a Setting Apart for a Special Vocation, 224; at a Solemn Eucharist, 88; at Solemn Evensong, 143; in a Solemn Procession, 168
Bishops: named in the Great Litany, 165; named in the Prayers of the People, 39-43; of other Churches named in the Prayers of the People, 44
Bishop of Rome, named in the Prayers of the People, 44
Black Vestments, 105
Blessed Sacrament, Devotions before, 265-66
Blessed Virgin Mary: Conception of, 106; named in the Great Litany, 165; Nativity of, 107; Parents of, 104; named in the Prayers of the People, 39, 40, 42; Feasts of, Station in the Procession, 254. *See also* Mary the Virgin, St., Feast of
Blessing of the Family: at Baptism, 216; at the Thanksgiving for the Birth or Adoption of a Child, 218; at a service for a Child Baptized under Emergency Circumstances, 217
Blessings during Holy Week: of the Palms, 174-77; omitted on Maundy Thursday, 189; omitted on Good Friday, 197; of the New Fire, 202, 204; of the Paschal Candle, 202-04; of the Baptismal Water, 201, 207-08
Blessing of Light. *See* Lucernatium; Phos hilaron; Prayer for Light
Blessing of the People: on All Souls' Day, 161; on Ash Wednesday, 154; at the Burial of the Dead, 245; at Compline, 141; at the Eucharist, 74, 77, 79, 90, 92; at a Sung Eucharist, 74, 267-68; at the First Eucharist of a Newly Ordained Priest, 271; at Marriage, 228; at a public service of Ministration to the Sick, 238-39; at An Order of Worship for the Evening, 135; at a Public Service of Penitence, 248-49; after the Rogation Procession, 166; at a Solemn Te Deum, 145; following the Supplication, 165
Blessing, Nuptial: at an Anniversary of a Marriage, 230; at the Blessing of a Civil

Blessing, Nuptial *(continued)*

Marriage, 229; at the Celebration and Blessing of a Marriage, 227-28

Blessing of Objects: Ashes, 154; candles, 150-51; Creche, 265; food, 134; Holy Water, 270; incense, 80-81, 270; incense at the Offertory of the Eucharist, 266; Rings, 227, 229; Water, at Baptism, 215; Church Furnishings and Ornaments, 263-64. *See also* under title of Object

Blessing of Oil: Chrism, 206, 215, 221; of the Sick, 234, 238

Blessing Reserved to the Bishop, 263

Bloomer, Amelia Jenks, 103

Blue Vestments, 95

Boat (for incense), Blessing of, 263, 265

Book of Common Prayer, The, 1979, (BCP), 19

Book of Common Prayer, First, Commemoration of, 103

Book of Gospels, The, (BOG), 19

Book of Occasional Services, The, (BOS), 19

Books, Liturgical, 19

Bonaventure, 107

Boniface, 103

Borromeo, Charles, 108

Bow. *See* Simple Bow; Solemn Bow

Bow, at the Confession of Sin, 43

Bray, Thomas, 101

Bread, 31

Breaking of the Bread, 71; anthem, 267-68; at the Burial of the Dead, 244; at Concelebration, 79. *See also* Anthem; *Confractoria*

Brébeuf, Jean, 108

Breck, James Lloyd, 102

Brent, Charles Henry, 102

Bringing in of the Cross, on Good Friday, 190, 194

Bringing of the Sacrament to the Altar, on Good Friday, 196

Brooks, Phillips, 101

Burial Anthems, 242. *See also* Commemoration of the Faithful Departed; Requiem Eucharist

Burial of the Dead, 162, 241-46; without a Eucharist, 242; during Lent, 155, 162

Burial Office, 1928 Prayer Book, 246

Burial of One who does not Profess the Christian Faith, 246

Burial of Our Lord Jesus Christ, Commemoration of, 199

Burial of a Priest, 272

Burse, 31, 73

Butler, Joseph, 103

Calendar: of the Church Year, 94; Commemorations not in *The Book of Common Prayer* Calendar, 106-08; Holy Days and National Days, 99-100;

of Sundays and Principal Feasts, 95-98; of other Feasts and Fasts, not Holy Days, 101-05

Candlemas, 150, 152; Eve of, 122, 150; Station in Procession, 251. *See also* Presentation of Our Lord Jesus Christ in the Temple

Candidates: for Baptism, 206, 214-15; for Confirmation, 220; Prayers for, 214-15, 220-21; for Reception or Reaffirmation, 220-21; for a Special Vocation, 224

Candlelight Services, 27

Candles: at Baptism, 216-17; form for giving at Baptism, 216; on Candlemas, 150-52; at the Daily Office, 27; at the Eucharist, 27; on Good Friday, 190-91, 194-95, 197, 199; at the Gospel, 27, 37; at the Great Vigil of Easter, 202-04, 206, 209; on Holy Saturday, 200; at liturgical celebrations, 27; on Maundy Thursday, 186, 189; at An Order of Worship for the Evening, 27, 132-33; on Palm Sunday, 176, 178-79; at the Reading of the Passion, 179, 192; in processions, 27; before the Reserved Sacrament, 27, 75, 189; at a shrine, 27; as a sign of devotion, 27; at Stations of the Cross, 156. *See also* Paschal Candle; Torches

Candlesticks, Blessing of, 263-64

Canon. *See* Eucharistic Prayer

Canticles: at the Burial of the Dead, 242, 246; at the Daily Office, 128, 137, 141; at the Great Vigil of Easter, 202, 206, 209; during the Rogation Procession, 167; at Solemn Evensong, 143; at a service of Thanksgiving for the Birth or Adoption of a Child, 218. *See also* under title of Canticle

Canticles, table of: for use at Morning Prayer, 128; for use at Evening Prayer, 137

Cantor, 36, 144, 263

Canvassers, Parish, Commissioning of, 223

Cassock, 25-26

Cassock-alb, 25-26

Catechist, Commissioning of, 223

Catechumenate, 214

Catechumens, Oil of, (OC), at Baptism, 214

Catherine of Siena, 102

Cecilia, 108

Celebrant, vestments, 25

Celebrant's Chair. *See* Sedilia

Celebration and Blessing of a Marriage, 225-28

Censing, 22; of the Baptismal Font, 208; at the Commendation, 243; of the Altar Cross, 82, 83, 85; of the Gospel Book, 80, 88; during the Great Thanksgiving, 81; at marriage, 228; of the Ministers, 49, 80, 85, 89, 143; number of swings with the thurible, 84-85; of the Paschal Candle, 142, 205, 277; of the people, 49, 80, 85, 89, 143; of the Sacrament, 81, 189, 265; at the *Sanctus*, 81

Censing of the Altar: freestanding, 82, 85; fixed to a wall, 83, 85; at the Burial of the Dead, 243; at the Daily Office, 82, 83; at the Entrance, 80, 82, 83, 87, 152, 154, 169, 187, 209, 213, 226, 242; at the *Magnificat,* 143; at the Offeratory, 49, 83, 85; at An Order of Worship for the Evening, 134; at Solemn Evensong, 142-43; at a Solemn Te Deum, 145

Censing of the Gifts, at the Offertory, 49, 80, 84

Ceremonial and Manual Acts, 21-24

Ceremonies: at Baptism, 214-17; Baptismal Liturgy at the Great Vigil of Easter, 206-09; at the Burial of the Dead, 241-46; at the Burial of a Priest, 276; at Concelebration, 78; at Confirmation, 222; at Devotions before the Sacrament, 265-66; at the Entrance Rite, 34; at the First Eucharist of a Newly Ordained Priest, 275; at the Great Thanksgiving, Preface, 52; at the Great Thanksgiving, during the Eucharistic Prayer, 57-60, 61-63, 64-66, 67-70; at the Lighting of the New Fire, 204-05; at Morning or Evening Prayer as the Liturgy of the Word, 92; at the Ministration of the Sick, 238; at the Offeratory, 47-50; at the Passion Gospel, 179-80; at the Peace, 46; at the Prayers of the People, 43; at the Veneration of the Cross, 195-96; at the Washing of Feet, 188. *See also* under specific Liturgy, Office or Rite

Chad, 102

Chair, for the Bishop at Confirmation, 219

Chairs, Blessing of, 263-64

Chalice, 31, 47-49, 51, 71, 73

Chalice, Blessing of, 263-64

Chalice Bearers, Commissioning of, 223

Chantal, Jean Frances de, 107

Chapel, for Reservation of the Blessed Sacrament, 75, 189

Chanting: of the Collect of the Day, 36; of the Gospel, 36; of Lessons, 36; of the Prayers of the People, 88; of the Preface, 56; *also* parts of the Eucharist sung, 271

Charcoal, at the Blessing of the New Fire, 203-04

Charles, 106, 264

Chasuble: at the Burial of a Priest, 276; at Concelebration, 78; at the Eucharist, 25, 47; on Good Friday 191. *See also* under specific Liturgy

Choir, 36, 168, 270; Commissioning of members, 275

Chrism: at Baptism, 206, 215-17; at Confirmation, 220; Consecration of, by a Bishop, 206, 215, 221

Chrismation, at Baptism, 216, 217

Christ, in the reading of the Passion Gospel, 179, 192

Christ the King, 98; Collect at the Prayers of the People, 44; Station in Procession, 252

Christ our Passover, 71, 158, 161, 245, 271, 272; at Morning Prayer, 127. *See also* Anthem at the Breaking of the Bread; *Confractoria; Pascha Nostrum*

Christian Service, Form of Commissioning, 223

Christian Year, *See* Calendar of the Church Year

Christmas, 95, 113; Blessing of Creche, 265; Eve, 122; Season of, 95; Station at the Creche, 250; Weekday Eucharists during Christmas Season, 114

Christus factus est. See Anthem on Maundy Thursday; Tract for Palm Sunday

Chrysom, at Baptism, 216

Chrysostom, John, 101

Church Ornaments, Blessing of, 263-65

Church Year, Calendar of, 94

Ciborium, 73, 186

Cincture, 25

Civil Marriage, Blessing of a, 229

Clare, 104

Cleansing of Vessels. See Ablutions

Clement, 105

Clement of Alexandria, 101

Closing Hymns, 92

Closure of the Alleluia, 152

Coffin, 241, 244-45

Coffin, Sealing of, 272

Collect: at Devotions before the Sacrament, 266; in *Lesser Feasts and Fasts,* 121; at the Ministration to the Sick, 234, 237. *See also* under title of Day or Feast; Liturgy; Office

Collect, Concluding: on All Souls' Day, 161; at Baptism, Prayers for the Candidates, 206, 215; at the Burial of the Dead, 243; at Confirmation, Prayers for the Candidates, 220; at the Good Friday Liturgy, 197; at the Prayers of the People, 39, 41-44, 88, 117, 267-68; by the Bishop at Reception and/or Reaffirmation, 221; at Stations of the Cross, 156-57

Collect of the Day: at Baptism, 213; at Confirmation, 219; at the Daily Office, 120, 129, 132, 134, 135, 138, 144; at the Eucharist, 35; following the Great Litany, 163; at the Ministration to the Sick, 234, 237, music for, 239; omitted at the Daily Office preceding a Eucharist, 129, 138

Collect for Purity, 32, 87, 234, 237

Collects: on Eves of Feast Days, 120; at the Daily Office, 120, 135, 138, 141; at the Great Vigil of Easter, 205; appointed in the Lectionary, 110; at Morning or Evening Prayer as the Liturgy of the Word, 92; at a Station in Solemn Processions, 250-54; following the Supplication, 165

Colors, Liturgical. *See* under title of color

Columba, 103

Comfortable Words. *See* Sentence of Scripture

Commemoration of All Faithful Departed, 160, 161. *See also* All Souls' Day

Commemoration of the Burial of Our Lord Jesus Christ, 199

Commemoration of the Dead, Preface of, 55, 104, 105, 162

Commemorations in Eucharist Prayer D, 70

Commemorations: during Lent, 155; during the Fifty Days of Easter, 158; not listed in *BCP* Calendar, 106-08, 113; at the Daily Office, 121

Commendation, at the Burial of the Dead, 162, 240, 244-46

Commendatory Prayer for the Dying, *See* Ministration at the Time of Death

Commissioning of Lay Ministries. *See* under title of ministry

Committal, at the Burial of the Dead, 245-46

Commixture of wine and water at the Offertory, 47, 48, 49, 274

Common: of the Holy Angels, 108; of a Martyr, 106-08; of a Missionary, 106; of a Monastic, 106-08; of a Pastor, 106-08; of a Saint, 106-08; of a Teacher, 106-07; of a Theologian, 106, 108

Common meal. *See* Agapé

Communion: at the Ministration to the Sick, 235, 238; of the People, 72; Reservation, 75; Reservation for Good Friday, 188-89. *See also* Reserved Sacrament; Administration of Communion

Communion from the Reserved Sacrament, 76; on Good Friday, 196-97; at the Ministration to the Sick, 75, 235; under Special Circumstances, 76; not administered outside the Proper Liturgy of Good Friday, 199; not administered on Holy Saturday, 200

Compline, 140-41; with the Exhortation, 231; during Holy Week, 183

Concelebration, 78-79; at the First Eucharist of a Newly Ordained Priest, 271; at the Great Vigil of Easter, 203-10

Conception of the Blessed Virgin Mary, 106

Conclusion of the Eucharist, 74

Conclusion of the Eucharist Prayer. *See* Doxology; Great Doxology; Great Amen

Conclusion of the Liturgy on Good Friday: after the Solemn Collects, 193; after the Veneration of the Cross, 196; after Communion from the Reserved Sacrament, 197

Conclusion of a Requiem Eucharist *(Contakion for the Death)*, 162

Confession, Private, 232, 248, 249; heard by one who is not a priest, 232; secrecy of content absolute, 232; on Shrove Tuesday, 152. *See also* Reconciliation of a Penitent

Confession of St. Peter, 99; Eve of, 122

Confession of Sin, 45, 89, 91, 92, 188, 231, 237, 240, 248; at the Daily Office, 126, 136, 140; at the Entrance Rite, 33; at the Good Friday Liturgy, 196; in the Prayers of the People, 39-40, 43; omission of, 45, 126, 136, 163, 180; on Shrove Tuesday, 152

Confessor: bound by absolute moral secrecy, 232; vestments, 232

Confirmation, 219-22; at the Great Vigil of Easter, 206-07, 210

Confractoria, 71

Consecration of additional Elements, 74, 75

Consecration of a Grave, 246

Consecration of Samuel Seabury, 105

Consuming Consecrated Elements, 73

Constance and Companions, 104

Contakion for the Dead, 161, 244. *See also* Burial of the Dead; Requiem Eucharist

Conversion of St. Paul, Feast of, 99; Eve of, 122

Cope, 25, 26, 37, 188, 244; at the Good Friday Liturgy, 191; at the Litany in Procession, 164; at the Great Vigil of Easter, 202; at An Order of Worship for the Evening, 132; at the Palm Sunday Liturgy, 175; at a Solemn Eucharist, 86; at Solemn Evensong, 142; at a Solemn Te Deum, 145

Cornelius, 101

Corporal, 31, 73, 186, 196, 233, 235; at the Offertory, 47-49

Corpus Christi, Feast of, 97; Propers for the Eucharist, 260

Cotton, 202, 233

Cranmer, Thomas, 105

Creche: blessing of, 265; censing of, 85; Station at in Procession, 250

Credence, 31

Creed, 88. *See also* Apostles' Creed; Nicene Creed

Creed *(Credo)*, intonation, 267

Cross: at Baptism, signing with, 215; Blessing of, 267-68; censing of, 82, 83, 85; after the Good Friday Liturgy, 197-200; tracing of, in Paschal Candle, 204; for Veneration on Good Friday, 194-96

Cross, Processional: at the Burial of the Dead, 241; at the Committal, 245; during Lent, 155; at Marriage, 225; at the Palm Sunday Procession, 178; at a Solemn Eucharist, 86; at Solemn Evensong, 142; at a Solemn Procession, 168; at the Rogation Procession, 166

Cross, Sign of the. *See* Sign of the Cross

Crosses: removed for Good Friday, 189; veiled for Lent, 152; wooden, for Stations of the Cross, 156

Crowd, in the reading of the Passion Gospel, 179, 192

Crucifer, at Stations of the Cross, 156. *See also* Cross, Processional

Crucifix, for Veneration on Good Friday, 191, 194-95. *See also* Cross

Cruet, 31

Crummell, Alexander, 104

Cuthbert, 102

Cyprian, 104

Cyril, 102

Cyril and Methodius, 101

Daily Collects, list of: at Morning Prayer, 129; at Evening Prayer, 138

Daily Office, 126. *See also* under specific title of Office

Daily Office Lectionary, 91-92, 111, 118, 127

Dalmatic, 25, 86, 142, 189, 191

Date of Pentecost, relating to the Proper, 113

David, 102

Day of Pentecost, 97; Station in Procession, 252; Vigil of, 273-74

Days of Special Devotion, 94

Days of Special Thanksgiving, 145

Deacon: at Baptism, 214-15, 217; at the Burial of the Dead, 242; at the Celebration and Blessing of a Marriage, 226-29; at Concelebration, 78; censing of ministers and people, 80; at Confirmation, 219; as Officiant at the Daily Office, 126, 132, 136, 140; at the Eucharistic Liturgy in the absence of a Priest, 46; parts of the Liturgy sung by the Deacon, 267; concerning the Reconciliation of a Penitent, 232; administration of Communion from the Reserved Sacrament, 75-76; at the Ministration to the Sick, 234; at a Solemn Eucharist, 86-90; at Solemn Evensong, 142; at a Solemn Procession, 168; vestments, 25, 86. *See also* Assisting Minister

Deacon at the Eucharist: at the Entrance Rite, 32-34, 86; at the Gospel, 37, 88, 92; at the Prayers of the People, 39, 43, 88; at the Confession of Sin, 45, 89; at the Sentence of Scripture after the Confession of Sin, 45, 89; at the Offertory, 48-50; at the Great Thanksgiving, 60, 63, 66, 70, 89; at the Commemorations in Eucharistic Prayer D, 70; at the Invitation to Communion, 72, 90; at the administration of Communion, 72; at the Ablutions, 73; at the Dismissal, 74, 90

Deacon at the Liturgies of Holy Week: on Palm Sunday, 176-79; on Maundy Thursday, 188-89; on Good Friday, 192-97; on Holy Saturday, 200; at the Great Vigil of Easter, 202-10

Dead, Burial of. *See* Burial of the Dead

Dead, Preface of the. *See* Commemoration of the Dead, Preface of

Death, Ministration at the Time of, 240

Decalogue, 32-34, 152, 231, 248

Declaration of Consent, at Marriage, 226

Declaration of Forgiveness by a Deacon or Lay Person, 232

Declaration of the Marriage, at the Blessing of a Civil Marriage, 229

Dedication of a Church, Feast of the: Eve, 123; Station in Procession, 254

Dedication of a Church, Preface of, 55, 102-04

Dedication of Church Furnishings and Ornaments, 263. *See also* under title of object

Dedications. *See* Blessings under title of object

Delegates to Diocesan Convention, Commissioning of, 223

De Koven, James, 102

Denis, 108

Departed: named in the Great Litany, 165; named in the Prayers of the People, 39-43

Deputies to General Convention, Commissioning of, 223

Devotions: following An Order of Worship for the Evening, 134; following Stations of the Cross, 157

Devotions: before the Blessed Sacrament, 157, 261; before the Cross. *See* Veneration of the Cross; *Improperia;* Reproaches

Dies irae, 162

Director of Music, Commissioning of, 223

Dismissal, 77, 90, 268; at the Commital, 245-46; at Concelebration, 79; at the Eucharist, 74; at the Great Vigil of Easter, 209; at Marriage, 228; at the Ministration to the Sick, 235, 239; omitted on Good Friday, 197; omitted on Maundy Thursday, 189; at An Order of Worship for the Evening, 135; at the Reconciliation of a Penitent, 232; at the Rogation Procession, 166; at a Solemn Te Deum, 145; singing of, 267; following the Supplication, 165; at the Thanksgiving for the Birth or Adoption of a Child, 218

Distribution of Candles. *See* Candlemas; Great Vigil of Easter

Distribution of the Palms, 174-77

Dominic, 104

Donne, John, 102

Door of the Church, Station at, in Procession, 251-53

Dormition of the Blessed Virgin Mary. *See* Mary the Virgin, St., Feast of

Doxology, concluding the Prayers of the People, Form V, 42

Doxology, Great, 60, 64, 66, 70, 71; use of incense during, 81

DuBose, William Porcher, 104

Dunstan, 103

Easter: Acclamation, 158: Sundays of, 97

Easter Day, 97; Station in Procession, 252

Easter Dismissal, 158, 210

Easter, Fifty Days of, 158

Easter, Preface of, 55, 96, 97, 101, 115, 209, 244

Easter Proclamation, at the Great Vigil of Easter, 209. *See also* Easter, Acclamation

Easter Season, 96; Weekday Eucharists, 115

Easter Vigil. *See* Vigil of Easter

Easter Week, 97, 113, 158; Eucharists during, 115; at Morning Prayer, 127

Eastern Rites. *See* Liturgy of the Eastern Churches

Eastertide. *See* Fifty Days of Easter

Ecce, Deus, 182

Edmund, 105

Edward the Confessor, 108

Elevation: of the Bread, 57, 61, 65, 69; of the Chalice, 58, 62, 66, 69; of the Bread and Wine at the Memorial Acclamation, 62, 66, 69; of the Bread and Wine at the Great Doxology, 53, 60, 63, 66, 70; at the Invitation to Communion, 72; of the Elements at Concelebration, 79; use of incense, 81

Elizabeth of Hungary, 105

Ember Days, 94, 116

Emergency Baptism, 217; Service of Thanksgiving following, 217

Emma and Kamehameha, 105

Entrance Rite: on All Souls' Day, 160; on Ash Wednesday, 154; at Baptism, 213; at the Burial of the Dead, 241; on Candlemas, 150; at Confirmation, 219; at the Daily Office, 126, 130, 132, 136, 145; at the Eucharist, 32-34; before the Great Litany, 163-64; at the Liturgies of Holy Week, 176, 187, 192, 199, 200, 205, 209; at Marriage, 225; at a Solemn Eucharist, 86; at Solemn Evensong, 142; at a Solemn Procession, 168; at a Solemn Te Deum, 145

Ephrem of Edessa, 103

Epiclesis, 53, 59, 63, 65, 70, 79

Epiphany, 95; Concluding Collect at the Prayers of the People, 44; Season of, 95; Station in a Solemn Procession, 250; Weekday Eucharists, during the Season after Epiphany, 113-14

Epiphany, Preface of, 55, 96, 99, 102-05, 114, 152

Episcopal Chair. *See* Chair for the Bishop

Episcopal Service, 224

Epistle, 36; chanted or read by subdeacon, 87; lesson from 111; sung, 267. *See also* Lessons

Eucharist, 29-74; Bishop as Celebrant, 212, 219-22; First Eucharist of a Newly Ordained Priest, 271, following a Solemn Procession, 169; parts sung, 267-68; Weekday, 113-15, 181

Eucharistic Lectionary, 91, 92, 111

Eucharistic Prayer, I and II, 57-60; A and B, 61-63; C, 64-66; D, 67-70; conclusion of, sung, 267-68; on All Souls' Day, 161; at the Burial of the Dead, 244; on Maundy Thursday, 188; at an Order for Celebrating the Eucharist, 77

Eucharistic Propers: for Lent, 155; for Eastertide, 158

Eucharistic Vestments: Celebrant, Deacon, Assisting Priests, 25, 86; Concelebrants, 25, 78

Eve of the Day of Pentecost. *See* Vigil of Pentecost

Evening, An Order of Worship for the, 132-35

Evening Prayer, 136-39; with the Exhortation, 231; with the Great Litany, 163; during Holy Week, 181-83, 198-99; Lectionary, 118-23; as the Liturgy of the Word at the Eucharist, 91-92; Office of the Dead, 161; following An Order of Worship for the Evening, 134; as the Principal Service of the Day, 119; followed by a Solemn Te Deum, 145; on Shrove Tuesday, 152; with the Supplication, 165; with the Thanksgiving for the Birth or Adoption of a Child, 218. *See also* Solemn Evensong

Evening service, *See* Order of Worship for the Evening; *also,* Evening Prayer

Evensong. *See* Evening Prayer; Solemn Evensong

Eves of Major Feast Days, 119, 122, 123, 138; at Solemn Evensong, 142. *See also* under title of Feast

Examination of the Candidates: at Confirmation, Reception, Reaffirmation, 220; at Commitment to Christian Service, 223

Exhortation, An, 231, 248; on Shrove Tuesday, 152

Exhortation, Opening, at Marriage, 226

Exposition of the Sacrament. *See* Devotions before the Sacrament

Exsultet, at the Great Vigil of Easter, 202-03, 205

Extra-liturgical Devotion, 156, 261

Extreme Unction. *See* Ministration at the Time of Death

Fabian, 101

Fasts. *See* Lesser Feasts and Fasts; Days of Special Observance; Ash Wednesday; Fridays; Good Friday

Feast, transferring of a, 94

Feasts and Fasts in the Calendar, not Holy Days, 101-05

Feast Days, Solemn Evensong, 142. *See also* Eve; under title of Feast Day

Feasts of the Blessed Virgin Mary, Station in Processions, 254. *See also* Blessed Virgin Mary

Feasts of the Incarnation, Station in Procession, 253. *See also* under title of Feast

Feasts of Our Lord Jesus Christ. *See* under title of Feasts

Ferias. *See* Weekdays; Weekdays in Seasons

Ferrar, Nicholas, 101

Ferrer, Vincent, 107

Fifty Days of Easter, 94, 97, 148, 158; Concluding Collect at the Prayers of the People, 44; at the Daily Office, 127, 132, 139, 141, 143, 158; at the Dismissal, 74; Paschal Candle, 210

Fire, Blessing of. *See* Great Vigil of Easter

First Mass. *See* under Eucharist

First Sunday after Epiphany. *See* Baptism of Our Lord

First Sunday of Advent: Daily Office Lectionary, 118; Exhortation, 231; Great Litany, 163

First Sunday in Lent: Exhortation, 231; Great Litany, 163

Flagon, 31, 51, 71, 186, 189, 203

Flint, for the Kindling of the New Fire, 204

Flowers, on Maunday Thursday, 186

Font: Blessing of 263-64; Censing of, 85, 208; Station in Procession, 252-53

Forty Martyrs of Sebaste, 107

Francis of Assisi, 105

Francis de Sales, 106

Fraction. *See* Breaking of the Bread

Friday, Good. *See* Good Friday

Fridays, 94; in Lent, 155; Litany on, 163

Funerals. *See* Burial of the Dead

General Confession. *See* Confession of Sin

General Thanksgiving, 129, 130, 139, 249

Genuflecting, 22; at the Altar, 22; before the Blessed Sacrament, 22; at Concelebration, 79; at the Entrance Rite, 34; during the Eucharistic Prayer, 57-70; during the Passion Gospel, 180; during the Solemn Te Deum, 145; at Stations of the Cross, 157

George, 107

Gesture of Thanksgiving, during the Eucharistic Prayer, 52, 57-58, 61-62, 65, 68-69

Gifts, preparation of at the Offertory, 47-49

Giles, 107

Gloria in excelsis: appointed, 32; at Baptism, 213; on Candlemas, 151-52; censing of Altar, 80, 87; at Confirmation, 219; at the Great Vigil of Easter, 209; intonation of, 268; at Morning or Evening Prayer as the Liturgy of the Word, 92; at Marriage, 226; omitted in Lent, 155; omitted on Maundy Thursday, 186; sung, 272

Gloria Patri: at the Entrance Rite, 34, 150; at the Daily Office, 126, 128, 130, 131, 136, 137, 140; omitted after the Gradual Psalm, 36, 111; pointing of, 128; at Solemn Evensong, 142

Godparents, at Baptism, 214-16

Gold Vestments, 158

Good Friday: Proper Liturgy, 94, 96, 190-98; introduction, 190; outline, 190; preparations, 191; Evening, 199; Stations of the Cross, 156; Veneration of the Cross, 194-96, 256

Gospel: announcement of, 37; at Baptism, 212-13; at Confirmation, 219; Eucharistic Lectionary, 111; at Evening Prayer, 137; on Good Friday Evening, 199; on Holy Saturday, 200; in the language of the people, 37; in the Daily Office Lectionary, 118; at Morning or Evening Prayer as the Liturgy of the Word, 91-92; at Marriage, 226; at the Maundy Thursday Watch, 189; at the Ministration to the Sick, 234, 237; on Pentecost, proclaimed in several languages, 158, 273; prayer (by the Deacon) before the proclamation of, 37; proclamation of, 37; responses at, 37, 270; at a Requiem Eucharist, 162; Signs of the Cross, 37; sung, 267. *See also* Lessons at the Eucharist

Gospel Book: on Altar, 37; Blessing of, 267-68; censing of, 80, 88; at the Entrance Rite, 34; kissing of, 37

Gospel Canticles. *See* Sign of the Cross; under title of Canticle

Gospel Procession: at the Eucharist, 37; at Morning or Evening Prayer as the Liturgy of the Word, 226; at a Solemn Eucharist, 88

Grace, The: at the Commemoration of the Burial of Our Lord Jesus Christ, 199; at the Daily Office, 130, 139; at the Holy Saturday Liturgy, 200; following the Great Litany, 164; at Morning or Evening Prayer as the Liturgy of the Word, 92; at a Service of Penitence, 248

Gradual Psalm, 36. *See also* Psalm at the Eucharist

Grave, Consecration of a, 246

Great Alleluia, at the Great Vigil of Easter, 202, 209

Great Amen, 60, 64, 66, 70, 71, 267

Great Doxology, Elevation of the Elements: bells, 71; at Concelebration, 79; use of incense, 81

Great Fifty Days. *See* Fifty Days of Easter; Easter Season

Great Litany, The, 163-65; preceding the Eucharist, 33; at Evening Prayer, 139; at An Order of Worship for the Evening, 134; at the Great Vigil of Easter, 209; during Lent, 155; at Morning Prayer, 129; petitions inserted, 165, 167; sung in Rogation Procession, 166-67; at a Solemn Eucharist, 87

Great Thanksgiving, The, 54; Manual Acts, illustrated, 52-53; Manual Acts by the Celebrant, 57-66; at an Order for Celebrating

Great Thanksgiving, The *(continued)*

the Eucharist, 77-78; use of incense, 81; at a Solemn Eucharist, 89

Great Vigil of Easter, 96, 201-10; introduction, 201; outline, 202; preparations, 202-03; Baptismal Liturgy, 206-08; Concelebration, 78; *Te Deum*, 145

Green Vestments, 95, 98

Greeting. *See* Salutation

Gregory the Great, 102

Gregory the Illuminator, 102

Gregory of Nazianzus, 103

Gregory of Nyssa, 102

Grosseteste, Robert, 105

Hagiography, 121, 138, 155

Hallelujah. *See* Alleluia

Hands: on Altar, 53, 59; joined at breast, 70; clasped, 23; on corporal, 53; folded, 23; over the Gifts at the Epiclesis, 53, 59, 63, 65, 70; upon the head of a penitent, 232; over objects, 24

Hands extended: by the Bishop at Confirmation, 221; at the Ministration to the Sick, 238; for the Nuptial Blessing, 227; at the Blessing of Palms, 177; over a penitent, 232

Hangings, removed on Maundy Thursday, 189

Hannington, James, 105

Healing Service. *See* Public Ministration to the Sick

Helena, 107

Herbert, George, 101

High Mass. *See* Solemn Eucharist

Hilary, 101

Hilda of Whitby, 105

Hobart, John Henry, 104

Holy Communion, The, 73. *See also* Eucharist

Holy Cross Day, 99; Eve, 123; Station in Procession, 253

Holy Eucharist. *See* Eucharist

Holy Days and National Days, 92, 99; Calendar of, 99-100; Daily Office Lectionary, 111; Weekday Eucharists, 113

Holy Guardian Angels, 108

Holy Innocents, 99

Holy Name of Our Lord Jesus Christ, 95

Holy Saturday, Proper Liturgy, 96, 200

Holy Thursday. *See* Maundy Thursday

Holy Water, 266; at an Anniversary of a Marriage, 230; at the Blessing of Ashes, 154; at the Blessing of Candles, 151; at the Blessing of Church Furnishings and Ornaments, 263; at the Blessing of Palms, 175-77; at the Blessing of Rings, 227; at the Commendation, 244; at the Committal, 245; at the Consecration of a Grave, 246; at the lighting of the Advent Wreath, 149; at the Nuptial Blessing, 228; at Marriage, 225; at the Reception of the Body, 241

Holy Week, 96, 171-210; Daily Office, 130, 136, 181-83, 198-99; introduction, 172; omission of Alleluia, 126; Weekdays of, 94, 113, 115, 181-83. *See also* Days of Holy Week by title

Holy Week, Preface of, 55, 96, 99, 101, 103, 104, 105, 107, 115, 174, 180, 181, 188

Homily: at the Burial of the Dead, 242; at the Commemoration of the Burial of Our Lord Jesus Christ, 199; at the Daily Office, 130, 131, 134, 138; at Devotions before the Sacrament, 261; at the Great Vigil of Easter, 201, 210; at the Holy Saturday Liturgy, 200; at Marriage, 227; at the Maundy Thursday Liturgy, 185, 187; at the Ministration to the Sick (Public), 237; at a Public Service of Penitence, 248; at a Requiem Eucharist, 162. *See also* Sermon

Hooker, Richard, 105

Host, 31, 261. *See also* Bread

Hugh of Lincoln, 105

Human Rights, Proper for, 258

Humble Access, Prayer of, 72

Humeral Veil, 262

Huntington, James Otis Sargent, 105

Huntington, William Reed, 104

Hymnal 1940, The, 19

Hymnal 1982, The, 19

Hymns: use of Alleluia, 162; at Baptism, 212-13, 215-16; at the Burial of the Dead, 242, 245; at the Candlemas Procession, 151; at the Commemoration of the Burial of Our Lord Jesus Christ, 199; at the Daily Office, 129-30, 132, 134-35, 137-40, 183; at Devotions before the Sacrament, 261-62; at the Good Friday Liturgy, 190, 192-95, 197; at the Great Vigil of Easter, 206; at the lighting of the Advent Wreath, 149; at Marriage, 225-28; at the Maundy Thursday Liturgy, 255; on Palm Sunday, 178-79, 180; during the Rogation Procession, 166-67; at Stations of the Cross, 156-57; substituted for a canticle, 92; Hymn of Thanksgiving, 249. *See also* Hymns by title; *Te Deum*

Hymns at the Eucharist: at the Entrance, 32-34; before the Gospel (Sequence), 36; at the Offertory, 47-50; during the administration of Communion, 72; at the conclusion of the Liturgy, 74

Ignatius of Antioch, 105

Immersion, at Baptism, 215

Imposition of Ashes, 154

Improperia (Reproaches): at the Veneration of the Cross, 190, 195-96; at the Commemoration of the Burial of Our Lord Jesus Christ, 198; text of, 256-57

Incarnation, Feasts of, Station in Procession, 253. *See also* under title of Feast

Incarnation, Preface of, 55, 95, 99, 104, 106, 107, 114

Incense: on Ash Wednesday, 154; at Baptism, 213, 216; Bishop, preparation and Blessing of, 81, 86-90, 221; at the Blessing of Church Furnishings and Ornaments, 263; at the Burial of the Dead, 242-45; on Candlemas, 150, 151; at Devotions before the Sacrament, 261; forms for Blessing, 266; grains of incense inserted in the Paschal Candle, 202-03; at the Great Litany, 164; at the Great Vigil of Easter, 202-04, 207, 209; omitted on Good Friday, 192; omitted on Holy Saturday, 200; at Marriage, 225-26, 228; at An Order of Worship for the Evening, 132-34; on Maundy Thursday, 187-89; on Palm Sunday, 175-78; omitted at the reading of the Passion Gospel, 179; during the Rogation Procession, 166; at Solemn Evensong, 142-44; during Solemn Processions, 85, 168, 169; at a Station in a Solemn Procession, 85; during a Solemn Te Deum, 145. *See also* Censing; Thurifer

Incense at the Eucharist: at the Entrance Rite, 80, 86; at the Song of Praise, 80, 87; at the Gospel, 37, 80, 88; at the Offertory, 49, 80, 89; form for Blessing at the Offertory, 270; at the Great Thanksgiving, 80, 81, 89; at the *Sanctus,* 81, 89; at the Elevations, 81; at the Elevation during the Great Doxology, 81

Inclination. *See* Bow

Independence Day, 99

Inscription of the Paschal Candle, 202-04

Instrumental Music: at Marriage, 225-28; during a Solemn Procession, 168; when omitted, 180, 189, 192, 195, 197

Intercessions: at the Daily Office, 121, 129, 132, 139, 141, 183; added in the Great Litany, 165, 167; at Morning or Evening Prayer as the Liturgy of the Word, 92. *See also* Prayers of the People; Petitions

Intinction, 74, 233, 235

Introduction: to Holy Week, 172; to Palm Sunday, 173; to Maundy Thursday, 184; to Good Friday, 190; to the Great Vigil of Easter, 201

Introit. *See* Entrance; Anthem; Antiphon; Hymn; Psalm

Invitation to Communion, 71, 90; at the Good Friday Liturgy, 197; sung, 271

Invitation to Confession, 45, 248

Invitatory, 91; during Easter Week, 158; at Evening Prayer, 136-37; during the Fifty Days of Easter, 158; at Morning Prayer, 127; during Holy Week, 181

Irenaeus, 103

James, St., and St. Philip, Feast of, 99; Eve, 122

James of Jerusalem, St., Feast of, 100

Jerome, 105

Jogues, Isaac, 108

John, St., Feast of, 99; Eve, 122

John the Baptist, Nativity of, 99, Eve, 122

John of the Cross, 106

John of Damascus, 101

John, Gospel of, 111, 192, 199

Jones, Absalom, 101

Joseph, St., Feast of, 99

Joseph of Arimathaea, 104

Jubilate Deo, 91, 127

Jude, St., and St. Simon, Feast of, 100; Eve, 123

Julian of Norwich, Dame, 103

Justin, 103

Kamehameha and Emma, 105

Keble, John, 102

Kemper, Jackson, 103

Kempis, Thomas à, 103

Ken, Thomas, 102

Kindling of the New Fire, 201-03

King, Martin Luther, Jr., 102

Kiss of Peace. *See* Peace, The

Kissing of the Altar, 21, 47-49, 32-34

Kissing of the Cross at the Veneration, 195

Kissing of the Gospel Book, 21, 37, 88

Kneeling, 22; at the Altar, 22; on Ash Wednesday, 154; by the Candidates at Confirmation, 220; by the Candidates for Reception and/or Reaffirmation, 221; at the Commemoration of the Burial of Our Lord Jesus Christ, 199; for the Confession of Sin, 33, 45, 89, 232, 248; at the Daily Office, 129, 138; at Devotions before the Sacrament, 261-62; for the Eucharistic Prayer, 54; at the Good Friday Liturgy, 192-95; for the Great Litany, 163-64; at the Holy Saturday Liturgy, 200; during the Litany of Penitence, 154, 248; for the Nuptial Blessing, 227; during the Passion Gospel, 180, 193; at Solemn Evensong, 144. *See also* Genuflecting

Kyrie eleison: at the Eucharist, 32-33, 87, 160, 187, 234, 237, 242, 268; at the Daily Office, 132, 141, 183; in the Great Litany, 163; at the Great Vigil of Easter, 209. *See also* Song of Praise

Kyrie Pantokrator, 182

Lamps (candles), Blessing of, 267-68

Last Sunday after Epiphany, 96; Station in Procession, 251

Last Sunday after Pentecost, 98; Concluding Collect at the Prayers of the People, 44; Station in Procession, 252. *See also* Christ the King

Latimer, Hugh, 105

Laud, William, 101

Laurence, 104

Lavabo: bowl and towel, 31; after Communion on Good Friday, 197; at the Eucharist, 48; after the Imposition of Ashes, 154; prayer at the, 274. *See also* Washing of Hands

Law, William, 102

Lay Ministries, forms for Commissioning, 223

Lay Subdeacon. *See* Lay Reader; Subdeacon

Lay Person: administration of Communion at Concelebration, 79; officiating at Compline, 140; reading lessons at Confirmation, 219; reading lessons at the Daily Office, 128, 137; reading lessons at the Eucharist, 36; reading lessons at the Great Vigil of Easter, 206; at the Laying on of Hands, at a Public Service of Healing, 238; at the Ministration at the Time of Death, 240; at the Prayers of the People, 43; at the Reconciliation of a Penitent, 232; at Stations of the Cross, 156-57. *See also* Lay Reader

Lay Reader, 36; in the absence of a Priest or Deacon, 46; at the Liturgy of the Palms, 176; at the reading of the Passion Gospel, 179, 192; officiating at the Good Friday Liturgy, 196. *See also* Lay Person

Lay Readers, form of Commissioning, 223

Laying on of Hands: at Confirmation, 220; at the Ministration to the Sick, 234, 237-38; at the Reconciliation of a Penitent, 24, 232; at the anointing of the Sick, 238

Lectern, 36, 202

Lectern, Blessing of, 263-64

Lection. *See* Epistle; Lesson; Reading

Lectionary, Blessing of, 263-64

Lectionary, Daily Office, 110,118

Lectionary, Eucharistic, 110, 111

Lectionary Texts for Year A, (LTYA), 19, 110, 111

Lectionary Texts for Year B, (LTYB), 19, 110, 111

Lectionary Texts for Year C, (LTYC), 19, 110, 111

Lectionary Texts for Lesser Feasts and Fasts, (LTLFF), 19, 110, 112

Lectionary Texts for Various Occasions and Occasional Services; (LTVOOS), 19, 110, 112

Lectors, Commissioning of, 223

Lent, 94, 96, 148, 154-55; Acclamation at the Entrance Rite, 155; Concluding Collect at the Prayers of the People, 44; at the Daily Office, 126, 130, 136; Great Litany, 155, 163; omission of Alleluia, 155, 159; Stations of the Cross, 156-57; Weekdays of, 94; Weekday Eucharists, 114, 155

Lent, Preface of, 55, 96, 114, 154, 155

Lenten Antiphon, during Holy Week, 181

Lenten Array, 96, 148, 152, 155

Lenten Cross, for processions, 155, 156

Lenten Season, 96

Leo the Great, 105

Lesser Feasts and Fasts, (LFF), 19; at the Daily Office, 121, 138; at the Eucharist, 112, 113; Propers for the Fifty Days of Easter, 158; Propers for the Weekdays in Lent, 155

Lessons at the Daily Office: announcement of, 128, 137; conclusion of, 128, 137; Daily Office Lectionary, 118; Evening Prayer, 137; Morning Prayer, 128; An Order of Worship for the Evening, 133; Solemn Evensong, 143; on the Weekdays of Holy Week, 181-83. *See also* Daily Office

Lessons during Holy Week: Palm Sunday, 174, 176, 179; Weekdays, 181-83; Maundy Thursday, 185, 187, 189; Commemoration of the Burial of Our Lord Jesus Christ, 199; Holy Saturday, 200; The Great Vigil of Easter, 202, 206, 210

Lessons at the Eucharist: on Ash Wednesday, 154; on All Souls' Day, 160; announcement and conclusion of, 36; on Candlemas, 152; on Corpus Christi, 260; at Commemorations not listed in the Calendar, 106-08; during the Fifty Days of Easter, 97, 158; on Holy Days and National Days, 99-100, 111; during Lent, 96, 155; on Lesser Feasts and Fasts, 101-05, 112; at the Liturgy of the Word, 36; at Morning or Evening Prayer as the Liturgy of the Word, 91-92; at An Order for Celebrating the Eucharist, 77; on Principal Feasts, 95-98, 111; at a Solemn Eucharist, 87; on Sundays, 95-98, 111; singing of, 267; sung responses to, 268; on Various Occasions, 112. *See also* Epistle; Gospel

Lessons at Various Liturgies: at the lighting of the Advent Wreath, 149; at Baptism, 213; at the Burial of the Dead, 242; at the Blessing of a Civil Marriage, 229; at Confirmation, 219; at Devotions before the Sacrament, 261; at Marriage, 226; at the Ministration to the Sick, 234, 237; at a Public Service of Penitence, 248; at a Requiem Eucharist, 162; during the Rogation Procession, 166-167

Licensed Lay Persons, at the administration of the Chalice, 72

Light, Blessing of. *See* Lucernarium

Lighting of Candles. *See* Candles

Lighting of the Paschal Candle, 204

Lights, extinguished on Maundy Thursday, 189

Litany: at Devotions before the Sacrament, 261; at the Great Vigil of Easter, 207, 209; of Healing, 234, 237; of Penitence, 154, 248; in Procession, 164; at the Time of Death, 240, 272

Litany at the Eucharist. *See* Great Litany; Prayers of the People
Litany at the Daily Office. *See* under title of Office
Litany, Great. *See* Great Litany
Litany, Lesser. *See* under title of Litany
Liturgical Year. *See* Church Year
Liturgy of the Eastern Churches, 40, 42
Liturgy of Holy Communion, 92. *See also* Eucharist
Liturgies for Special Days, 148. *See also* under title of Day
Liturgy of the Word: at Concelebration, 78; on Holy Saturday, 200; at the Great Vigil of Easter, 206; at Morning or Evening Prayer as the Liturgy of the Word at the Eucharist, 91-92. *See also* Word of God
Lord's Day, Preface of the, 55, 95, 98
Lord's Prayer. *See* under title of Day, Liturgy, or Office
Lord's Prayer, at the Eucharist, 71
Lord's Supper. *See* Eucharist
Lord's Supper, Liturgy of the. *See* Maundy Thursday
Louis, 104
Lucernarium, 133, 149
Lucy, 106
Luke, St., Feast of, 100; Eve, 123
Luke, Gospel of, 111

Magnificat (Song of Mary): as an Act of Thanksgiving, 217-18; at the Daily Office, 128, 134, 137, 182; as the Song of Praise on the Feast of Annunciation, 155; at Solemn Evensong, 143
Major Feast Days, 91, 92, 113; in the Daily Office Lectionary, 118; at Evening Prayer, 118, 138; Eves of, 122-23; at Morning Prayer, 118. *See also* under title of the Feast or Day
Maniple, 25
Manual Acts, 23-24, 52-53; at Concelebration, 78-79; at the Great Thanksgiving, 52-54, 57-70; Eucharistic Prayer I and II, 57-60; Eucharistic Prayer A and B, 61-63; Eucharistic Prayer C, 64-66; Eucharistic Prayer D, 67-70; at the Salutation and Preface, 54
Margaret, 107
Margaret of Scotland, 105
Mark, St., Feast of, 99; Eve, 122
Mark, Gospel of, 111
Marriage: Anniversary of, 230; Celebration and Blessing of, 225-28; Civil, Blessing of, 229; intended to be celebrated with the Eucharist, 225; using the 1928 Prayer Book, 225; without a Eucharist, 228
Marriage, Preface of, 55, 228, 229
Martin of Tours, 105

Martyn, Henry, 105
Martyrs: of Japan, 101; of Lyons, 103; of Memphis, 104; of New Guinea, 104; of Uganda, 103
Martyrs, Feasts of. *See* under title of Saint
Martyrs, Preface of. *See* Preface of a Saint (3)
Martyrs. *See* Red Vestments
Mary the Virgin, St., Feast of, 99; Eve, 119, 123; Station in Procession, 254. *See also* Blessed Virgin Mary
Mary Magdalene, St., Feast of, 99; no Eve prescribed, 122
Mary and Martha of Bethany, 104
Mass. *See* Eucharist
Matins. *See* Morning Prayer
Matthew, St., Feast of, 100; Eve, 123
Matthew, Gospel of, 111
Matthias, St., Feast of, 99; Eve, 122
Maunday Thursday: Proper Liturgy, 96, 184-89; introduction, 184; outline, 185; preparations for, 186; color of vestments, 184-85; Song of Praise, 184, 187; Washing of Feet, 188, 255; Watch, 189
Maurice, Frederick Denison, 102
Meal, following An Order of Worship for the Evening, 134. *See also* Agapé
Meditation: at Devotions before the Sacrament, 261; at Evening Prayer, 138; at Noonday Service, 131; following Stations of the Cross, 157. *See also* Homily; Sermon
Memorial, 263
Memorial Acclamation. *See* Acclamation
Methodius, and Cyril, 101
Michael, St., and All Angels, Feast of, 100; Eve, 119, 123; Station in Procession, 254
Michaelmas. *See* Michael, St., Feast of
Ministration to the Sick, 76, 233-36
Ministration at the Time of Death, 240
Ministry of the Word, at Marriage, 226. *See also* Word of God; Liturgy of the Word
Missal. *See* Altar Book
Missal Stand. *See* Stand, for Altar Book
Mizeki, Bernard, 103
Moderators of Protestant Churches, named in the Prayers of the People, 44
Monday in Holy Week, 96, 181-83
Money Offering: at the Eucharist, 48-50; at the Daily Office, 130, 135, 139
Monnica, 103
Monstrance, 261-62
More, Thomas, 107
Morning Prayer, 126-30; with the Exhortation, 231; with the Great Litany, 163; during Holy Week, 181-83; Lectionary, 118-23; as the Liturgy of the Word at the Eucharist, 91-92; as the Principal Service of the Day, 119; followed by a Solemn Te Deum, 145; with Supplication, 129, 165; with the Thanksgiving for the Birth or Adoption of a Child, 218

Motet at the Offertory, 50
Mozarabic Tone, for Eucharistic Prayer D, 267
Music, 267-68; at the Eucharist, 38, 50, 72, 77; at Marriage, 225-29; on Palm Sunday, 180; during the Veneration of the Cross, 196, 257; at the Washing of Feet, 255. *See also* Anthem, Instrumental Music; Hymn; Psalm
Musical Instrument, Blessing of, 263, 265
Musicians, Commissioning of, 223
Muhlenberg, William Augustus, 102

Names: at Baptism 214-16; at Confirmation, 220; of the Departed on All Souls' Day, 160; at Marriage, 226; of those to be remembered in the Prayers of the People, 40, 41, 42, 43
Narrator, in the reading of the Passion Gospel, 179, 192
National Days, Calendar of, 99-100
National and Local Leaders, named in the Prayers of the People, 39, 42
Nativity of the Blessed Virgin Mary, 107
Nativity of John the Baptist, Feast of, 99; Eve, 122
Nativity of Our Lord Jesus Christ, Feast of, 95; Eve, 122. *See also* Christmas Day
Neale, John Mason, 104
New Fire, 202, 204
New Year's Day. *See* Holy Name of Our Lord Jesus Christ
New Year's Eve, Service for, 123
Newly Baptized, Reception of Holy Communion, 217
Nicene Creed, 38, 91, 180, 268. *See also* Creed
Nicholas, 101
Ninian, 104
Non-Scriptural Christian Literature, 77
Noonday, An Order of Service for, 130-32, 183
Nunc dimittis (Song of Simeon), 128, 137, 151, 246, 182. *See also* Candlemas
Nuptial Blessing, 225, 227, 228, 229
Nuptial Eucharist, 225-28
Nuptial Mass. *See* Nuptial Eucharist

OC. *See* Oil of Catechumens
OI. *See* Oil of the Sick
Oakerhater, David Pendleton, 104
Oblations. *See* Gifts at the Offertory
Offering of the Gifts, 47-51, 270
Offertory, at the Eucharist, 47-51; censing of the Gifts and Altar, 84-85; Prayers, 270. *See also* under title of specific Liturgy
Offertory, music at the, 50. *See also* Anthem; Hymn; Psalm
Offertory Procession, 49-50. *See also* under specific Liturgy
Offertory Sentences, 47-49
Office Hymns, *See* under title of Office; Hymn

Office: following An Order of Worship for the Evening, 134. *See also* Daily Office; title of specific Office
Office Lights, 27
Officers of Church Organizations, Commissioning of, 223
Officiant. *See* under specific Liturgy or Office; Vestments
Oil of Catechumens (OC), 214
Oil of Chrism, Consecration of: a Baptism, 215; at Confirmation, Reception, or Reaffirmation, 221; at the Great Vigil of Easter, 207
Oil Lamp, before the Reserved Sacrament, 75
Oil of the Sick (OI): anointing with, 233-34, 238, 240; Blessing of, 234, 238
Old Testament: in Daily Office Lectionary, 118; in Eucharistic Lectionary, 111. *See also* Lesson
Oppression, Proper for, 259
Orans Position, 23; at the Collect of the Day, 35; at the Collect Concluding the Prayers of the People, 44; at the Great Thanksgiving, 52, 57-69; at the Postcommunion Prayer, 73. *See also* Collects and Thanksgivings at specific Liturgies and Offices
Order for the Burial of the Dead. *See* Burial of the Dead
Order for Celebrating the Holy Eucharist, An, 77, 78
Order of Precedence, Sundays and Principle Feasts, 94
Order of Service for the Noonday, An, 130-32; with the Exhortation, 231; during Holy Week, 183
Order of Worship for the Evening, An, 132-35; at the lighting of the Advent Wreath, 149; use of candles, 27, 133; preceding the Eucharist, 134; with the Great Litany, 164; during Holy Week, 132, 183; use of incense, 134; preceding an Office, 134; preceding Solemn Evensong, 86; with a Solemn Te Deum, 145
Ordination, 271
Ordinations, Preface of, 55
Ordinations, Proper Postcommunion Prayer, 74
Organ: Blessing of, 263, 265; on Maundy Thursday, 189; at the Great Vigil of Easter, 209
Organist, Commissioning of, 223
Ornaments, Church: Blessing and Dedication of, 263-65; removed on Maundy Thursday, 189. *See also* under title of specific Church Ornament or Furnishing
O Salutaris Hostia, 261
Our Father. *See* Lord's Prayer
Outline of Holy Week Liturgies: Palm Sunday, 174; Maundy Thursday, 185; Good Friday, 190; Holy Saturday, 200; Great Vigil of Easter, 202. *See also* specific Liturgies and Offices

Pall, to cover chalice, 31
Pall, Funeral, Blessing of, 263, 265
Pall, at the Reception of the Body and the Burial of the Dead, 241
Palms: for Ashes, 153; Blessing of, 176; Distribution of, 176-77; Liturgy of the, 173-79; Procession with, 178-79; Station in Procession, 251
Palm Crosses, *See Note*, 177
Palm Gospel, Lesson at the Liturgy of the Palms, 173
Palm Sunday, Proper Liturgy, 96, 173-80; introduction, 173; outline, 174; preparations, 175; Station in Procession, 251; Solemn Reading of the Passion Gospel, 179-80
Pange Lingua, 189
Parents: at Baptism, 214; Blessing of the family, 216-18
Parents of the Blessed Virgin Mary, 104
Parish Visitors, Commissioning of, 223
Pascha Nostrum: at the Burial of the Dead, 245; during the Fifty Days of Easter, 158; at the Great Vigil of Easter, 209. *See also* Anthem at the Breaking of the Bread; Christ our Passover
Paschal Candle: at Baptism, 216; at the Burial of the Dead, 241-42, 245; on the Day of Pentecost, 158; during the Fifty Days of Easter, 97, 158; during Lent, 153; at An Order of Worship for the Evening, 132-33; at Requiem Eucharists, 162; at Solemn Evensong, 142; at the Vigil of Pentecost, 273-74
Paschal Candle at the Great Vigil of Easter: Inscription of, 204; Lighting of, 204; Procession with, 205-06; at the Blessing of Water, 208. *See also* Exsultet
Paschal Candle Stand, 203, 205
Passion Gospel, Solemn Reading of: on Palm Sunday, 179-80; on Good Friday, 192-93
Passion, Sunday of the. *See* Palm Sunday
Passion of our Lord, Symbols of the, 155. *See also* Sarum Lenten Array
Passiontide Red, 96; description of, 175; on Palm Sunday, 181; on Maundy Thursday, 184, 186; on Good Friday, 191; on Holy Saturday, 200
Passover, 184; Christian, 201
Pastoral Office, 219
Paten, 31
Paten, Blessing of, 263-64
Patriarchs of the Eastern Churches, named in the Prayers of the People, 44
Patrick, 102
Patronal Festival, 106; Eve of, 123; Station in Processing, 254
Patteson, John Coleridge, 104
Paul, St., and St. Peter, Feast of, 99; Eve, 122

Paul, St., Conversion of, 99; Eve, 122
Pavement Lights, 27
Peace, The, 45, 46; sung, 271-72. *See also* under specific Liturgies
Penance. *See* Confession of Sin; Reconciliation of a Penitent
Penitence, Public Service of, 248
Penitential Opening Acclamation, 34, 155, 181
Penitential Order, A: at the Entrance Rite, 33; with the Exhortation, 231; at a Healing Service, 237; on Maundy Thursday, 188; at the Public Service of Penitence, 248; on Shrove Tuesday, 152
Penitential Season: Concluding Collect at the Prayers of the People, 44; Opening Acclamation at the Entrance Rite, 155. *See also* Lent
Penitential Suffrage in the Prayers of the People, 39-45
Pentecost: Day of, 97, 158-59; Station in Procession, 252; Vigil of, 123, 277; Weekdays following, 113, 115
Pentecost, Last Sunday after. *See* Christ the King
Pentecost, Paschal Candle. *See* Paschal Candle
Pentecost, Preface of, 55, 97, 101, 102, 103, 104, 105, 106
Pentecost, Season after, 97, 98, 113, 115
Perpetua and her Companions, 102
Peter, St., and St. Paul, Feast of, 99; Eve, 122
Peter, St., Confession of, Feast of the, 99; Eve, 122
Petitions for the Departed. *See* Great Litany; Prayers of the People
Petitions for the Sick. *See* Great Litany; Litany of Healing; Prayers of the People
Petitions, in Eucharistic Prayer D, 70, 188
Philip, St., and St. James, Feast of, 99; Eve, 122
Phos hilaron: censing of the Altar during, 143; at Evening Prayer, 137; metrical version of, 137; omitted on Holy Saturday, 200; omitted during Holy Week, 181; at An Order of Worship for the Evening, 134; at Solemn Evensong, 142
Pictures, Blessing of, 263-64
Place of Reservation, 186; on Maundy Thursday, 189; darkened for the Good Friday Liturgy, 190
Pointing to the Gifts, 24, 53, 58, 62, 65
Polycarp, 101
Pontifical Blessing, 221
Pope, named in the Prayers of the People, 44
Position of Hands for Prayer, 23. *See also* Orans Position
Postcommunion Prayer, 73-74, 77, 90; for the Departed, 74, 161, 244; on Good Friday, 188; at Marriage, 74, 228-29; at Ordinations and Inductions, 74; for the Sick, 74, 235,

Postcommunion Prayer *(continued)*

239; at a Requiem Eucharist, 162; followed by a Solemn Te Deum, 145

Prayer Book, *See* Book of Common Prayer, 1979

Prayer Book Office, The (PBO), 19

Prayer Desks, Blessing of, 263-64

Prayer Groups, Commissioning of Members, 223

Prayer of Consecration. *See* Eucharistic Prayer; Great Thanksgiving

Prayer of St. Chrysostom, 130, 139

Prayer for the Whole State of Christ's Church (1928 Prayer Book), 39

Prayer over the People, 154, 155, 181

Prayers: after anointing, 238; for the Birth or Adoption of a Child, 218; at Emergency Baptism, 217; for Light, at the lighting of the Advent Wreath, 149; following the Great Litany, 164; following the Rogation Procession, 167; for the Sick, 234-36; for use by the Sick, 236

Prayers for the Candidates: at Baptism, 214-15; at the Baptismal Liturgy of the Great Vigil of Easter, 207; at Confirmation, Reception, Reaffirmation, 220, 222

Prayers for the Celebrant: before the Eucharist, 32, 273; after the Eucharist, 74, 269; at the Lavabo, 270; at the preparation of the Wine, 270; of preparation, at the First Eucharist of a Newly Ordained Priest, 271; at the Offering of the Alms, 270; at the Offering of the Bread, 270; at the Offering of the Cup, 270

Prayers at the Daily Office: Morning Prayer, 129; Noonday Service, 132; An Order of Worship for the Evening, 133, 135, 145; Evening Prayer, 138; at Solemn Evensong, 144; at Compline, 141. *See also* under specific Office

Prayers of the People, The: on All Souls' Day, 160; at Baptism, 214-16; at the Burial of the Dead, 242-43; Concluding Collect at, 44, 88; at Confirmation, 220-22; at the Eucharist, 39-43; Form I, 40; Form II, 41; Form III, 41; Form IV, 42; Form V, 42; Form VI, 43; at the Great Vigil of Easter, 210; on Holy Saturday, 200; during Lent, 155; at Marriage, 227, 229; at Morning or Evening Prayer as the Liturgy of the Word, 92; on Maundy Thursday, 188; on Palm Sunday, 180; provision for Petitions from the People, 41; omitted, 188, 163, 210; at a service of Public Ministration to the Sick, 234-37; at An Order for Celebrating the Holy Eucharist, 77; at a Requiem Eucharist, 162; at a Solemn Eucharist, 88; sung, 271-72; for the Whole State of Christ's Church and the World, 39-40

Prayers for Mission, at the Daily Office, 129, 139, 163, 183

Preaching, 38. *See also* Homily; Meditation; Sermon

Precedence, Order of, Sundays and Principal Feasts, 94, 111

Preface, Proper: at Baptism, 216; at Confirmation, Reception, and/or Reaffirmation, 221; at a Service of Public Ministration to the Sick, 238; sung, 267-68. *See also* under title of Day, Feast, Liturgy or Season

Prefaces, Proper, 54-56, 67, 110, 113

Prelude, inappropriate at An Order of Worship for the Evening, 132

Preparations: for the Eucharist, 31; of Ashes, 153; Holy Week, 175, 186, 190, 202-03; at the Offertory, 47-50

Presentation of Our Lord Jesus Christ in the Temple, Feast of the, 95; Eve, 122. *See also* Candlemas

Presentation of the Candidates: at Baptism, 214; at Confirmation, Reception, Reaffirmation, 220

Presentation of the Gifts at the Offertory, 47-50, 222; at Baptism, 216; at the Burial of the Dead, 243; at Confirmation, Reception, Reaffirmation, 221; at Marriage, 228; at the Anniversary of a Marriage, 230

Presentation, at Marriage, 226

Presentation of Symbols at the Commissioning for Lay Ministries, 223

President of the United States: named in the Great Litany, 165; named in the Prayers of the People, 39, 40, 42

Presiding Bishop: named in the Great Litany, 165; named in the Prayers of the People, 39-40, 42-43

Primate. *See* Presiding Bishop

Principal Celebrant, at Concelebration, 78

Principal Celebration of the Sunday, 92

Principal Feasts, Calendar of, 95-98

Principal Service of the Day, 119

Private Confession, 152, 232, 234, 240, 248

Procession: at Baptism, 214-16; on Candlemas, 150; at the Dedication and Blessing of Church Furnishings and Ornaments, 267; Great Litany, 163-64; at the Great Vigil of Easter, 205, 207-08; incense, use of, 85; on Palm Sunday, 178-79; Rogation, 166-67; at Stations of the Cross, 156-57; Solemn, 168-69. *See also* Entrance Rite

Processional Cross: for Lent, 155, 156; at Marriage, 225; omitted on Holy Saturday, 200; omitted on Good Friday, 192. *See also* Cross; Crucifer

Pronouncement of Marriage, 227

Proper. *See* under title of Day, Feast, Liturgy, Occasion, or Season

Proper Postcommunion Prayers, 74. *See also* under title of Occasion

Prostration, on Good Friday, 192
Psalms: Daily Office Lectionary, 118-23; Eucharistic Lectionary, 110-16
Psalms at the Daily Office: Morning Prayer, 127; Noonday Service, 131; An Order of Worship for the Evening, 133-34; Evening Prayer, 137; Solemn Evensong, 143; Compline, 140. See also under title of Office
Psalms at the Eucharist: Entrance, 32-34, 168, 268; Gradual, 36, 111, 268; Offertory, 47-51, 161, 272; Communion, 72, 161, 268; Solemn Eucharist, 87; sung, 268; at Morning or Evening Prayers as the Liturgy of the Word, 91
Psalms on Feast Days and other Occasions: All Souls' Day, 160; Ash Wednesday, 154; Baptism, 212-16; Burial of the Dead, 242; Burial of a Priest, 272; Candlemas, 150-52; Confirmation, 219; Devotions before the Sacrament, 261-62; Marriage, 225-28; Ministration to the Sick, 234, 237; Public Service of Penitence, 248-49; Requiem Eucharist, 162; Rogation Procession, 167; Thanksgiving for the Birth or Adoption of a Child, 217-18
Psalms during Holy Week: Palm Sunday, 174, 178-79; Weekdays, 181; Maundy Thursday, 185, 187, 189; Good Friday, 190, 192, 199; Holy Saturday, 200; Great Vigil of Easter, 202, 206, 210
Psalms, method of recitation, 128
Psalms, omission of verses, 127
Psalter, recitation in course, 127-28
Public Ministration to the Sick, 237-39
Pulpit, 92
Pulpit, Blessing of, 263-64
Purification of St. Mary the Virgin. See Candlemas; Presentation of Our Lord Jesus Christ in the Temple
Purificator, 31, 191, 202, 233, 235
Pusey, Edward Bouverie, 104
Pyx. See Ministration to the Sick

Questions: at Baptism, 214; at Confirmation, Reception, Reaffirmation, 220; at Marriage, 226; at the Reconciliation of a Penitent, Form Two, 232. See also Affirmations; Renunciations

Reader. See Lay Reader; Lesson
Reading: at Compline, 140; at Noonday Service, 131, 183. See also Lesson; Office
Reading from non-Scriptural Christian Literature, 129, 138
Reaffirmation of Baptismal Vows: at Baptism, 214; at Confirmation, Reception, Reaffirmation, 222-23; See also Baptismal Covenant; Great Vigil of Easter; Renewal of Baptismal Vows

Receiving of Gifts at the Offertory, 50
Reception, with Confirmation and/or Reaffirmation, 219-22
Reception of the Body, 241, 272. See also Burial of the Dead
Reception of Holy Communion: in both kinds, 72, 74; intinction, 74. See also Ministration to the Sick; Ministration at the Time of Death; Reserved Sacrament
Reconciliation of a Penitent, 232; Exhortation, 231; at the Ministration to the Sick, 234; at the Public Service of Penitence, 248; on Shrove Tuesday, 152; at the Time of Death, 240. See also Private Confession
Red Vestments, 97-108. See also Passiontide Red
Remigius, 105
Renewal of Vows: at Baptism, 214; at Confirmation, Reception, Reaffirmation, 220; at the Great Vigil of Easter, 207-10; at the Anniversary of a Marriage, 230
Renunciations: at Baptism, 214; at the Great Vigil of Easter, 206
Repository for Scriptures, Blessing of, 263-64
Reproaches at the Veneration of the Cross: at the Liturgy of Good Friday, 190, 195-96, 256-57; at the Commemoration of the Burial of Our Lord Jesus Christ, 199. See also Improperia
Requiem Eucharist, 162; use of the Alleluia, 159; at the Burial of the Dead, 241-44; during Lent, 155,162
Requiem Mass. See Requiem Eucharist
Reservation of the Blessed Sacrament, 51, 71, 75; on Maundy Thursday, 189; for the Good Friday Liturgy, 189; on Good Friday for emergencies, 197
Reserved Sacrament, 75; at Devotions before the Sacrament, 261-62; for the Good Friday Liturgy, 196-97; for the Ministration to the Sick, 233, 240; consumed on Wednesday of Holy Week, 184
Response, to a reading of Scripture: at Noonday Service, 131; at announcement and conclusion of the Passion Gospel, 180, 193; on Holy Saturday, 200
Responsive Reading of the Psalms, 36
Resurrection Proclamation, 245-46. See also Acclamation
Reverence: of the Altar, 21; of the Reserved Sacrament, 21. See also Bow; Genuflecting; Kissing of the Altar
Richard, 102
Ridley, Nicholas, 105
Rings: at Marriage, 227; at the Blessing of a Civil Marriage, 229
Rite III Eucharist. See Order for Celebrating the Holy Eucharist

Rogation Days, 94, 117
Rogation Procession, 158, 166-67
Rogation Sunday, 166
Rood, Station at the, 253

Sacrament. *See* under title and Liturgy of specific Sacrament
Sacrament, Blessed, administered in one kind, 236; devotions before, 261-62
Sacrament Lamp, 27, 186
Sacrament, Reserved. *See* Reserved Sacrament
Sacristan, Commissioning of a, 223
Saints: named in the Daily Office suffrages, 121; named in the Great Litany, 165; named in the Prayers of the People, 39-44. *See also* under name of Saint
Saints' Days: at the Daily Office, 120-21; Eves of, 122-23; during the Fifty Days of Easter, 158; during Lent, 155; Lesser, 101-05, 112; Major, 95-100, 111; not listed in Calendar, 106-08, 112; Station in Procession, 253; transferring of, 94, 112; Weekday Eucharists, 113. *See also* under name of Saint
Saint, Preface of a, 55, 101-08. *See also* under name of Saint
Salt, at the Blessing of Water, 266
Salutation: before the Collect of the Day, 35; at the Great Thanksgiving, 54; following the Great Litany, 164; at An Order of Worship for the Evening, 132; sung, 267-68
Salvator Mundi. See Tract for Maundy Thursday
Sanctuary Lamp. *See* Sacrament Lamp
Sanctus, 54; bells at, 56; incense at, 81; sung, 268
Sarum Lenten Array, 148. *See also* Lenten Array
Saturday Evenings: during Lent, 149; at Compline, 141; at Evening Prayer, 138; at Solemn Evensong, 142
Scarf, 26. *See also* Tippet
Schereschewsky, Samuel Isaac Joseph, 105
Scholastica, 106
Scripture: ordering of, 110. *See also* Calendar; Lectionary; Lessons; under specific Liturgies and Offices
Seal of Baptism. *See* Chrismation; Sign of the Cross
Sealing of the Coffin, 272
Secrecy of Confession. *See* Reconciliation of a Penitent
Seder, 184
Sedilia, 35-36, 38, 86-88, 92
Selwyn, George Augustus, 102
Sentence of Administration, Holy Communion, 72
Sentence of Scripture: after the Absolution, 45; after the Confession of Sin, 89; at the Entrance Rite, 33; omission of, 45

Sequence Hymn, 36, 268; preparation of incense, 80. *See also* under specific Liturgies
Sergius, 104
Sermon: Baptism, 213; at Confirmation, 219; at the Daily Office, 130, 134, 139; at the Eucharist, 38, 88, 91, 92; on Good Friday, 192, 197; during Holy Week, 180, 187, 192, 197, 210; at Public Ministration to the Sick, 237; following Stations of the Cross, 157. *See also* Homily; Meditation; under title of Liturgies and Offices
Server: at the Eucharist, 47, 49, 73; form of Commissioning, 223. *See also* Acolyte; Assisting Minister; Crucifer; Thurifer
Service Book, Blessing of, 263-64
Service of Light: Great Vigil of Easter, 204-05. *See also* Advent Wreath; Candlemas; An Order of Worship for the Evening
Seton, Elizabeth Ann, 106
Short Lesson. *See* Reading
Showing of the Gifts: Bread, 57, 61, 65, 69; Wine, 58, 62, 66, 69; illustrations, 52
Shrove Tuesday, 152, 231
Sick: Ministration to the, 233-36; named in the Great Litany, 165; named in the Prayers of the People, 39-43
Sign of the Cross, 24; at Baptism, 215, 216; with the Blessed Sacrament, 262; at Blessings of objects, 263; at the Burial of the Dead, 245, 246; at the Daily Office, 128, 130, 136, 137, 139, 140, 141; at the Eucharist, 33, 34, 38, 43, 45, 54, 59, 63, 65, 66, 70, 84; at the Gospel Canticles, 128, 137; at the Nuptial Blessing, 228; with Oil of the Sick, 234, 238; over the Palm Branches, 177; by the Bishop at Reception or Reaffirmation, 221; at the Reconciliation of a Penitent, 232
Signation, at Baptism, 216, 217
Silence at the Daily Office: at Morning Prayer, 128, 129; at Noonday Service, 131; at An Order of Worship for the Evening, 134; at Evening Prayer, 137; at Compline, 140, 141
Silence at the Eucharist, 27; at the Entrance, 32, 33; before the Collect of the Day, 27; at the Prayers of the People, 40, 41, 42; before the Confession of Sin, 32, 33, 45; during the Great Thanksgiving, 57-58, 61-63, 66, 69, 71, 77; before the Postcommunion Prayer, 73
Silence during the Holy Week Liturgies: Palm Sunday, 180; Maundy Thursday, 184, 189; Good Friday, 192, 193, 194, 196, 197, 198; Holy Saturday, 200; Great Vigil of Easter, 202, 207
Silent Concelebration, 78
Silent Devotion, 261-262
Silent Thanksgiving, 77
Simeon, Charles, 105
Simeon, Song of. *See* Nunc dimittis

Simon, St. and St. Jude, Feast of, 100; Eve, 123
Simple Bow, 21
Singer, form of Commissioning, 223
Sitting, 22, 36, 127, 128, 137, 205, 229
Sixth Sunday of Easter, Rogation Procession, 166
Solemn Bow, 21; reverence to the Altar, 34; at the Altar, 53; before the Blessed Sacrament, 21; at the Confession of Sin, 43, 45; at the Entrance on Good Friday, 192; during the Eucharistic Prayer, 57-70; during the Nicene Creed, 38; during the Passion Gospel, 180; during the *Sanctus*, 54; at Stations of the Cross, 157; during a Solemn Te Deum, 145
Solemn Collects on Good Friday, 193
Solemn Eucharist, 85-90
Solemn Evensong, 142-44
Solemn Liturgy of the Passion and Death of Our Lord Jesus Christ, 190-97
Solemn Mass. *See* Solemn Eucharist
Solemn Procession: order of, 168; route of, 169; preceding the Eucharist, 33, 87; use of incense, 85; Station in, 250-54
Solemn Te Deum, 145
Song of Mary. *See* Magnificat
Song of Simeon. *See* Nunc dimittis
Song of Praise, 32, 80, 87, 92, 185, 187, 209, 213, 219, 226, 267-68. *See also* under title of canticle or hymn
Special Vocation, Setting Apart for a, 224
Sponsors, at Baptism, 206, 214-16
Sprinkling. *See* Asperging
Stabat Mater, 156, 157
Stand, for Altar Book, 31
Standing, 22; at the Daily Office, 127, 128, 129, 137, 140, 141, 144; at the Eucharist, 39, 43, 45, 54, 92; for the Great Litany, 163-64; at the Great Vigil of Easter, 206; at Stations of the Cross, 157
Stanton, Elizabeth Cady, 103
Station in Solemn Processions, 169, 250-54; use of incense, 85; during the Palm Sunday Procession, 178, 251
Stations: at the Bringing in of the Cross on Good Friday, 194; in Procession with the Paschal Candle, 205; in the Rogation Procession, 165
Stations of the Cross, 156-57; during Lent, 155; on Good Friday, 198
Statues, Blessing of, 263, 265
Stephen, St., 99
Stephen of Hungary, 107
Stole, 25, 26, 86; at Concelebration, 78; at Marriage, 225, 227; at the Reconciliation of a Penitent, 232
Stripping of Altars, on Maundy Thursday, 189
Stylus, for the Inscription of the Paschal Candle, 203-04

Subdeacon, at a Solemn Eucharist, 37, 86-90; at the Liturgies of Holy Week, 176-79, 203-09; during a Solemn Procession, 168. *See also* Lay Reader
Suffrages: at Evening Prayer, 138; during Holy Week, 183; at Morning Prayer, 129; at Solemn Evensong, 144; at a Solemn Te Deum, 145
Summary of the Law, 32, 34, 87, 234, 237
Sunday after All Saints' Day, 98; Vigil, 123. *See also* Baptism
Sunday before Holy Cross Day, 231
Sunday of the Passion, Palm Sunday, 173-80; Station in Procession, 251. *See also* Palm Sunday
Sundays: at the Daily Office, 119; Eucharistic Lectionary, 111, 119; Evening Prayer, 119; Eve of a Major Feast Day, 120; Morning Prayer, 119; Solemn Evensong, 142
Sundays, Preface. *See* Lord's Day, Preface of the
Sundays of Easter, 97
Sundays after Pentecost, 98
Sundays and Principal Feasts, Calendar of, 94-98
Sung Eucharist (Sung Mass), 267-68
Supplication, The, 163, 164, 165; at the Daily Office, 129, 134, 139
Surplice, 25, 26; Blessing of, 263, 265
Sursum Corda, 54, 267-68
Sylvester, 106
Symbols, at the Commissioning of Lay Ministries, 223
Symbols of the Passion of Our Lord, 155
Swithun, 107

Tabernacle, 73, 75, 261-62; Blessing of, 263-64. *See also* Aumbry; Reservation of the Sacrament
Table, for gifts for the Offertory Procession, 31
Table, Holy. *See* Altar
Tantum ergo, Sacramentum, 261
Taylor, Jeremy, 104
Te Deum: on the Feast of St. Joseph, 155; at the First Eucharist of a Newly Ordained Priest, 270; at the Great Vigil of Easter, 209; intonation of, 145; at Morning Prayer, 129; Solemn, 145
Teacher, Commissioning of a, 223
Tenebrae, 183
Teresa of Avila, 105
Thanksgiving: Anniversary of a Marriage, 230; for the Birth or Adoption of a Child, 217, 218; over the Water, at Baptism, 215; at the Great Vigil of Easter, 207-09; for an Infant Baptized under Emergency Circumstances, 217
Thanksgiving Day, 100; Eve, 123
Thanksgiving, Service of. *See* Solemn Te Deum
Thanksgivings: at the Daily Office, 129, 139,

141; in the Prayers of the People, 41, 43
Theodore of Tarsus, 104
Thomas St., Feast of, 99; Eve, 122
Thomas à Kempis, 103
Three Hours, Good Friday, 198
Three Year Cycle, Eucharistic Lectionary, 111
Thurible. *See* Incense; Thurifer
Thurible, Blessing of, 263, 265
Thurifer: on Ash Wednesday, 154; at the Burial
of the Dead, 241-46; on Candlemas, 150-51;
at Devotions before the Sacrament, 261-62;
at the Eucharist, 80-85; at the Gospel, 37, 80;
at the Great Thanksgiving, 81; during Holy
Week, 173-80, 184-89, 200-09; at Marriage,
225-28; at the Offertory, 49, 80, 82-83; at An
Order of Worship for the Evening, 132; at the
Rogation Procession, 166; at a Solemn
Eucharist, 86-90; at Solemn Evensong, 142-
43; in a Solemn Procession, 85, 168-69; at a
Solemn Te Deum, 145
Timothy and Titus, 101
Tippet, 126, 130, 136, 140. *See also* Scarf
Torches, 132, 144, 145, 150, 179, 192, 194-95,
199, 241, 245. *See also* Acolyte; Candles
Towel, 154, 186, 188
Tract, 268; on Ash Wednesday, 154; on Palm
Sunday, 174, 179; on Maundy Thursday, 187;
on Good Friday, 192; on Holy Saturday, 200
Transferring a Feast, 94
Transfiguration, Feast of, 98; Eve, 122; Station
in Procession, 253
Trinitarian Supplication, in The Great Litany,
166
Trinity Sunday, 97; Station in Procession, 252
Trinity Sunday, Preface of, 55, 97, 99, 100-03,
108
Trisagion, 32-33, 156-57, 160, 187, 196, 232,
234, 237, 242, 256-57, 268. *See also*
Reproaches; Song of Praise; Stations of the
Cross
Truth, Sojourner, 103
Tubman, Harriet Ross, 103
Tuesday before Ash Wednesday. *See* Shrove
Tuesday
Tuesday in Holy Week, 96, 181-83
Tunicle, 86, 142, 191
Tyndale, William, 105

Ubi caritas, 188, 255
Unction. *See* Anointing
Unveiling of the Chalice, 47-49
Urn, at the Burial of the Dead, 241, 244-45

Various Occasions, Propers for, 94, 113, 258-59
Various Occasions, Proper Preface for, 115
Veil, 73; for chalice, 31; for urn at the Burial of
the Dead, 241
Veiling of Crosses, 189

Veils, Passiontide. *See* Shrove Tuesday;
Maundy Thursday
Veneration of the Cross, 190, 194-96, 198, 256-
57. *See also* Improperia; Reproaches
Veni Creator Spiritus, 271
Venite, 91, 127
Versicle and Response: at the Bringing in of the
Cross on Good Friday, 194; at the Daily
Office, 126, 132, 136, 140-42; at Devotions
before the Sacrament, 262; at the Palm
Sunday Procession, 178; in the Prayers of the
People, 40; at a Station in a Solemn
Procession, 250-54; at a Solemn Te Deum,
145; at Stations of the Cross, 156-57; fol-
lowing the Supplication, 165
Vespers. *See* An Order of Worship for the
Evening; Evening Prayer; Solemn Evensong
Vessel for Incense (boat), Blessing of, 263, 265
Vesting of the Body, Burial of a Priest, 272
Vestments, 25, 26, 78, 86
Vestments, Blessing of, 263, 265
Vestry, Commissioning of members, 223
Vianney, Jean-Baptiste, 107
Vidi Aquam, 209, 270
Vigil: on the Eve of Baptism, 123; before the
Burial of the Dead, 241; before the Burial of
a Priest, 276; of Easter, 200-09; of Feast
Days, 122-23; of Pentecost, 97, 123, 158, 273
Vincent, 101
Vincent de Paul, 108
Violet Vestments, 95, 96, 105, 155
Visitation, Feast of the, 99; Eve, 122
Visitation, Propers used on Feasts of the
Blessed Virgin Mary, 106, 107
Votive Masses. *See* Various Occasions
Vows, at Marriage, 227, 229. *See also*
Baptismal Vows; Renewal of Baptismal
Vows; Confirmation; Reaffirmation; Reception

Walking, 22; Stations of the Cross, 156-57
Wardens, Commissioning of, 223
Washing of Feet, 184, 188
Washing of Hands, 220; after the Imposition of
Ashes, 154. *See also* Lavabo
Watch at Funerals. *See* Vigil, Burial of the Dead
Watch, on Maundy Thursday, 184-85, 189
Water: at the Ablutions, 73; at Baptism, 215; for
the Washing of Feet, 186, 188
Water, Holy. *See* Holy Water
Way of the Cross. *See* Stations of the Cross
Weddings. *See* Marriage, Celebration and
Blessing of
Wednesdays: during Lent, 155, 163; of Holy
Week, 96, 181-83, 231
Weekdays: after Ascension Day, 115; during the
Easter Season, 115; of Holy Week, 181-83;
during Lent, 155; between Pentecost and
Trinity Sunday, 113; during the Season after

Pentecost, 115; between Holy Innocents' Day and the First Sunday after Christmas, 114; between the First Sunday after Christmas and Epiphany, 114

Weekday Eucharists, 113; during the Fifty Days of Easter, 158; during Lent, 155

Welcome: at Baptism, 216; for an Infant Baptized under Emergency Circumstances, 217

Wesley, John and Charles, 102

White, William, 103

White cloth, on Altar, 31

White Garment *(Chrysom)* at Baptism, 216

White Robe. *See* Chrysom

White Vestments, 95-108, 158, 186, 201

Whitsunday. *See* Pentecost

Wilberforce, William, 104

Wilfred, 108

Williams, Channing Moore, 101

Willibrord, 105

Window, Blessing of, 263-64

Wine. *See* Ablutions; Chalice; Gifts at the Offertory

Witness. *See* Marriage: Sponsors

Words of Institution at Concelebration, 79

Word of God, The, 36. *See also* under title of specific Liturgy

World Hunger, Proper for, 261

Wulfstan, 101

Xavier, Francis, 106

Year, tracing in the Paschal Candle, 204

Year A, Lessons, 111; at the Liturgy of the Palms, 174, 176; Passion Narrative, 179

Year B, Lessons, 111; at the Liturgy of the Palms, 174, 176; Passion Narrative, 179

Year C, Lessons, 111; at the Liturgy of the Palms, 174, 176; Passion Narrative, 179

Year One: Daily Office Lectionary, 118; Holy Week, 182

Year Two: Daily Office Lectionary, 118; Holy Week, 182

Zechariah, Song of. *See* Benedictus